FALCON®

HELENA, MONTANA

_A_FALCON GUIDE®

Falcon® is continually expanding its list of recreational guidebooks. All books include detailed descriptions, accurate maps, and all the information necessary for enjoyable trips. You can order extra copies of this book and get information and prices for other Falcon® guidebooks by writing Falcon, P.O. Box 1718, Helena, MT 59624 or calling toll-free 1-800-582-2665. Please ask for a free copy of our current catalog. Visit our website at www.falcon.com or contact us via e-mail at falcon@falcon.com.

© 2000 Falcon® Publishing, Inc., Helena, Montana.
Printed in the United States of America.

1 2 3 4 5 6 7 8 9 0 MG 04 03 02 01 00

Falcon and FalconGuide are registered trademarks of Falcon® Publishing, Inc.

All inside black and white photos by William Kappele.

Cataloging-in-Publication Data is on file at the Library of Congress.

CAUTION

Outdoor recreational activities are by their very nature potentially hazardous. All participants in such activities must assume the responsibility for their own actions and safety. The information contained in this guidebook cannot replace sound judgment and good decision-making skills, which help reduce risk exposure; nor does the scope of this book allow for disclosure of all the potential hazards and risks involved in such activities.

Learn as much as possible about the outdoor recreational activities in which you participate, prepare for the unexpected, and be cautious. The reward will be a safer and more enjoyable experience.

♻ Text pages printed on recycled paper.

Contents

Acknowledgments

The acknowledgment page is always the toughest one to write in a book like this. There are so many people who contributed in so many ways that it is a real task to remember them all. Service station attendants gave tips on places to visit or sights to see that we hadn't heard about. Waitresses in restaurants gave directions to places we had heard of, but couldn't find. Friends of friends of friends knew someone whose family had lived in the area for generations and asked if we had seen such and such. In short, in the months we spent in this beautiful and friendly state, and throughout the nearly 10,000 miles we put in researching these drives, we talked to a whole lot of people, and most of them had some kind of information for us. We wish that we could acknowledge every name here, but we can't. We can, though, say thank you to everyone we talked to, and we hope you read and enjoy the book.

There were, of course, some major players in our research efforts. At the top of the list has to be Dan Kidd of the Kentucky Department of Travel. Not only did he take us on a fantastic tour of the Bluegrass Country, but he provided us with newspaper clippings, copies of articles from magazines, and even a whole list of recipes for Kentucky Hot Browns. He also arranged for us to pick through the department's slide files and to borrow any that we wished. Thanks again, Dan, and we hope we've done justice to your beautiful state.

Dan also introduced us to Toss Chandler of Versailles, whose family has lived in the area for more than 200 years. She took time out of her very busy schedule to show us around the beautiful Pisgah Historic Area. Thanks again, Toss, and we hope that you, too, enjoy the book.

Thanks to the Kentucky Department of Transportation for supplying maps and descriptions of all of the Kentucky Scenic Byways.

Thanks also to all of the city and county tourism offices who sent us so much material about Kentucky that we almost had to build an addition on the house to hold it.

Roger Dales and his wife of Bowling Green interrupted their lunch to help us find our way out of town and on to Rough River Lake. Thanks, folks.

Sandra Young, a ranger at Paintsville Lake, told us about the beauty of Kentucky 32, and this information led to Drive 4—Louisa to Morehead. Thanks Sandra.

Last, but by no means least, we want to thank Beth Cooke of the Kentucky Department of Travel and all of those who work with her for providing the best travel site on the Internet—The Official Kentucky Vacation Guide. The information available on this site goes on forever. If you can't find what you are looking for here, you just don't need to know it.

Locator Map

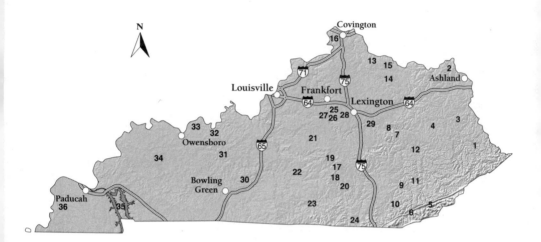

Map Legend

Scenic Drive - paved		Interstate		
Scenic Drive - gravel		U. S. Highway		
Scenic Side Trip - paved		State and County Roads		
Scenic Side Trip - gravel		Forest Service Roads		
Interstate		Wilderness Area National/State Park		
Other Roads (paved)		National Forest Boundary		
Other Roads (gravel)		State Boundary		
Bridge		Map Orientation		
Building		Scale of Miles		
Point of Interest		Scenic Drive Location		
Campground				
Hiking Trail				
River/Creek				
Lakes				

Introduction

Prior to the middle of the 18th century, only American Indians lived on the land that would one day become Kentucky. These Indians had been preceded by several cultures that included the Paleo-Indians, the Archaic Indians, the Woodland Indians, and the Adena Indians. All of these were probably descendants of the Asians who had crossed the arctic land bridge some 30,000 years ago and spread out across the continent.

Kentucky was first a territory, then just a very large and almost inaccessible county in Virginia locked away from the rest of the country by a combination of the Ohio and Mississippi rivers, the unbroken eastern mountains, and dense forests. These formidable barriers held back westward expansion for a time; but while the desire of the human being to push back the frontiers may be slowed down, in the end it is unstoppable.

Among the first stirrings in what would one day become a great commonwealth took place in 1729 when Captain Charles Lemoyne de Longueil, a French-Canadian soldier/explorer came down the Ohio River from the Great Lakes region and discovered the Big Bone Lick. At the time, he was acting as a part of the military escort for a French engineer who was charting the course of the Ohio. It may well be that these were the first white men to enter Kentucky.

The great tide of humanity that poured into Kentucky and tamed the wilderness did not begin until a little more than 20 years later, and it did not pour through Big Bone Lick, but through the Cumberland Gap down on the Tennessee/Virginia Border. By the middle 1700s, a lot of surveying and granting of land in the west was being done by the government of Virginia. In 1749, Dr. Thomas Walker was hired by the Loyal Land Company to lead an expedition into what is now Kentucky to survey and explore its land grant of 800,000 acres. In 1750, Walker and his party followed the old Indian road through the Cumberland Gap and continued north. At a point that he judged to be about 50 miles from the Virginia and North Carolina dividing line, he decided to stop and build a cabin in order to establish a claim. This cabin is believed to be the first such house built in Kentucky. While some of the party was engaged in building the cabin, Walker and the rest continued on in their explorations. After returning to the cabin, he and the rest of the party packed up and headed north to continue their explorations. Eventually, they headed east and returned over some very rugged country to Virginia. It is an interesting footnote that while Daniel Boone usually gets all of the credit for opening Kentucky to settlement, it was Dr. Thomas Walker who discovered the major entrance to the area: The Cumberland Gap. Hundreds of thousands of hunters, explorers, and settlers would pour through the now-famous opening into the frontier. He also explored much of Kentucky 17 years before Daniel Boone ever saw it. It is interesting

Ringo's Mill Bridge (Drive 14).

to note that because Walker had not found the lush Bluegrass country, but bogged down in the trackless, rugged forests of the eastern mountains, he issued a negative report to the Loyal Land Company, which caused them not to take up the land grant.

Daniel Boone may not have been the first into Kentucky, and he may not have been the only "long rifle" to explore the territory and establish settlements, but he is, without question, the most well known. The name Daniel Boone evokes images of the "frontiersman" with his long rifle and tomahawk fending off Indian attacks and angry bears with one hand while hacking settlements out of the danger-filled forests with the other.

This pulp fiction view may be overblown, but there is no denying that Daniel Boone was a true hero of the frontier and a man whose name is synonymous with Kentucky. This restless wanderer was born in a log farmhouse in Berks County, Pennsylvania, on November 2, 1734. Daniel was the sixth child of the eleven born to Squire and Sarah Boone. In 1750, Squire packed up his family and made a long journey to North Carolina where they settled in the Yadkin Valley. After an excursion with Braddock's expedition to try to drive the French from what is now Pittsburgh, Daniel returned home and married Rebecca Bryan, with whom he eventually had 10 children.

In 1775, after years of exploring in Kentucky, Boone was hired to take 30 men and cut a trail 300 miles long from Virginia through the Cumberland Gap and on into Kentucky. They hacked their way to a spot on the

Kentucky River just below what is now Winchester where they stopped and formed Boonesborough, the second permanent settlement in Kentucky.

Boone continued to hunt, explore, and lead settlers into Kentucky. He tried his hand at a number of businesses, but the urge to wander always overtook him. It was Rebecca who held the family together while he roamed the wilderness. His inattention to details caused him to be pursued by legal difficulties over land filings, and inaccurate surveying and unpaid taxes left him disillusioned and poor. He received a tract of land and moved to the Louisiana Territory, but when the United States bought the Territory in 1803, he was once again without any land. He made his final move, this time to Missouri, where he lived out his life, dying on September 26, 1820. He was buried on a hillside overlooking the Missouri River, but was later moved back to Kentucky to the cemetery at Frankfort.

Physiographic Regions

The face of Kentucky has certainly changed from the trackless wilderness that Boone first saw, but the general physiographic regions remain the same today. Most authorities list six of these areas.

The first is the eastern mountains, that formidable wall of rock and dense forest that for so long kept settlements out of the state. The mountain region is more than 10,000 square miles, and runs from the West Virginia, Virginia, and Tennessee borders northeast to an area east of Vanceburg, Kentucky. Some of the prettiest scenery in the state is in this region, and today you can drive through it on modern paved highways while still enjoying some of the beauty that the "long hunters" treasured. Anyone looking at the density of some of those forests cannot help but wonder at both the desire and the incredible physical effort it must have taken to wrest homes, farms, and roads from the unrelenting grip of nature.

The second physiographic region is known as The Knobs. These heavily wooded cone-shaped hills are eroded remnants left from the actions of the retreating ice and its ensuing melt water as the last great Ice Age came to an end. The Knobs form a semi-circle around the Bluegrass, beginning at the Ohio River near Louisville and ending at the western edge of the eastern mountains.

The third region is the lush area known as the Bluegrass. This is the spot where the early settlers headed and which houses most of Kentucky's population today. It is bordered on the west, south, and east by The Knobs and on the north by the Ohio River. Virtually all of the original forests have been cleared, and the land is used almost exclusively for agriculture and the raising of cattle and horses. This is the area that most people who have never been to Kentucky think of when the name of the state comes up. There is no doubt that the green rolling fields with scattered woodlands, winding rivers and streams, and the amazing horse farms makes the area one of the most beautiful anywhere. But there is a lot more to Kentucky, and the fact that the Bluegrass gets so much attention is sometimes a sore point to those who live in other parts of the state.

Fourth on the physiographic list is the area known as the Pennyrile. The name is really Pennyroyal and was named for a small flower of the mint family common to the area. If you say Pennyroyal there, though, people may ask: "You ain't from around here are you?" The Pennyrile is the southern part of the central plain, of which the Bluegrass is the northern part. It stretches from the western edge of the Bluegrass down to the Tennessee border, across to the Land Between the Lakes and up and over to the Ohio River. The scenery of the Pennyrile is varied, and includes lakes, rivers and streams, rolling farmland, forested hills, and an area known as the Barrens. The Barrens is an area with fewer trees than most other areas in the state, due probably to the fact that Indians used to burn it regularly to aid their hunting by providing grasslands where the buffalo could feed. The word "barren" has nothing to do with the fertility of the soil in this really beautiful area. In fact, we laugh as we drive through it and think of all of the miles we have driven in the deserts of the west—Craters of the Moon in Idaho is barren. The Barrens in Kentucky is a rain forest in comparison.

The Western Coalfields make up the fifth area. They are bordered on the north and west by the Ohio River and on the south by the semi-circle of the Pennyrile. This area of Kentucky gained notoriety in the early 20th century because of the strip mining of coal. Today, it will take some searching to find evidence of this activity. The scenery in the Western Coalfields is outstanding, as many of the mining areas have been reclaimed.

The final physiographic region is known as The Purchase. The name comes from a transaction between the United States and the Chickasaw Indians wherein all of the Chickasaw lands east of the Mississippi River and north of the Mississippi state line were purchased by the United States for $300,000. Most of the land was in Tennessee and was referred to as West Tennessee. The balance, approximately 2,000 square miles, was added to Kentucky and became known as the Jackson Purchase after General Andrew Jackson, who had been one of the negotiators in the treaty.

The Purchase consists mostly of low hills, bottomland, and the Mississippi River floodplain. It is bounded on the south by the Tennessee border, on the east by the Land Between the Lakes region, and on the north and east by the Ohio and Mississippi rivers.

A Few Facts and Figures
A large chunk of wilderness territory became Kentucky County, Virginia, in 1776. In 1780, the county was divided into Fayette, Jefferson, and Lincoln counties. Twelve years later, in 1792, Kentucky became the fifteenth state in the nation.

Cave Run Lake from Zilpo Road (Drive 8).

Creating counties must have become a state pastime. By 1886 there were 119. Today, there are 120. As we drove around the state, we joked that one could go out for a quart of milk and cross four county lines. Actually, Kentuckians have always been fiercely devoted to their home counties. Even today, many relate more to their county than to their city or town. One of the reasons for so many counties stems from the rule that no county seat could be more than one day's ride from a person's home. In the early days, one couldn't get far on horseback through the rugged country.

- The capital of Kentucky is Frankfort.
- The state flower is the goldenrod.
- The state bird is the redbird, which is commonly known as the Kentucky cardinal.
- The state fossil is the brachiopod.
- The state mineral is the freshwater pearl.
- The state song is "My Old Kentucky Home, Good Night."
- The state tree is the tulip poplar. (Until 1994, it was the Kentucky coffee tree.)
- The state fish is the Kentucky Bass.
- The state wild animal is the gray squirrel.
- The highest point in Kentucky is Black Mountain in Harlan County. It is 4,145 feet above sea level.
- The lowest point in the state is the Mississippi River at Fulton County. It is 257 feet above sea level.
- Kentucky has more miles of running water than any state with the exception of Alaska.

In this book, we have assembled 36 drives totaling a bit less than 2,500 miles. We drove nearly 10,000 miles in searching them out. All are on paved roads, although some of the roads are very narrow. We concentrated mainly on secondary, uncrowded roads, but some are on parkways and more heavily traveled roads. We didn't exclude parkways and interstates because they are without scenery, though. Most of Kentucky's parkways and interstates have magnificent scenery along their routes. If you are just passing through the state, you can get to your appointments and have a beautiful drive along the way. You can't get closer to having your cake and eating it too than that.

We have tried to point out whenever possible such things as narrow roads, dangerous curves, or potential weather problems. Of course, people will differ on just what a narrow road is, so take our descriptions as a guide. We have also given mileage to the 10th of a mile, but as we all know, odometers rarely agree, so use these as a guide also.

Finally, please use our drives as a beginning and not as an end. There is so much beauty in this state to see that it would take years to see it all. If you see a side road that looks promising, just take it. Be Daniel Boone with wheels and air conditioning. After all, the best may be just over that next hill or around the next bend.

So pack up the car, make sure the iron is unplugged, and head for Kentucky. We hope you will have as much fun on your drives as we did on ours.

Cumberland Falls—Kentucky has more running water than any state except Alaska.

1

The Country Music Highway
From the Tennessee Border to the Ohio River

General description: The 158-mile-long Kentucky portion of U.S. Highway 23 runs from the Virginia border to just northwest of Ashland. Called The Country Music Highway, this stretch of road honors Kentucky-native country music stars Billy Ray Cyrus, Naomi and Wynona Judd, Tom T. Hall, Keith Whitley, Ricky Skaggs, Crystal Gayle, Loretta Lynn, Hylo Brown, Dwight Yoakam, and Patty Loveless. Along the route, you will see signs with the highway designation and the names of these entertainers. Of course, you will also see some spectacular mountain scenery from a beautiful four-lane divided highway.

Special attractions: Country music stars' signs, a bit of Kentucky's industrial area along the Ohio River, rolling hills, and coal seams in the massive limestone walls along the road.

Location: From south to north along the eastern border of the state.

Drive route numbers: U.S. 23.

Travel season: All year, but spring with flowers and trees in bloom and fall with the beautiful foliage may be best. U.S. 23 is a major route, and will be clear in all but the worst weather. If you like your trees with snow, you might want to try a winter trip.

Camping: Camping areas within 15 miles of the drive include Greenbo Lake State Resort Park, Carter Caves State Resort Park, Grayson Lake State Park, Jenny Wiley State Resort Park, and Breaks Interstate Park.

Services: Motels in Ashland, Louisa, Paintsville, Prestonsburg, and Pikeville. Bed and Breakfast in Louisa. Restaurants and/or fast food establishments at South Shore; Greenup, Catlettsburg, Louisa, Paintsville, Prestonsburg and Pikeville.

Nearby attractions: Jesse Stuart State Nature Preserve, Wayne National Forest, Greenbo Lake State Resort Park, Jenny Wiley State Resort Park, the Kentucky Highlands Museum, Yatesville Lake State Park, Paintsville Lake State Park, Butcher Hollow, the birthplace of Loretta Lynn, Mountain HomePlace, a living history village, and Breaks Interstate Park. In May, near Prestonsburg, you can watch the reenactment of the Civil War Battle of Middle Creek. In October, Paintsville has the Kentucky Apple Festival.

The drive

In 1994, the Kentucky General Assembly designated the portion of U.S. 23 from the Virginia state line to the Ohio River at South Shore just northwest of Ashland as "The Country Music Highway." This came after many years of work by Billie Jean Osborne, a former music teacher in the Floyd County schools who discovered that the hometowns of 11 country music stars were only a short distance from the highway. As you travel the length of the road, you will see large, brown signs with the names of Patty Loveless (Elkhorn City in Pike County), Dwight Yoakam (Betsy Layne in Floyd County), Hylo Brown (Paintsville in Johnson County), Crystal Gayle (Van Lear in Johnson County), Loretta Lynn (Butcher Hollow and Van Lear in Johnson County), Keith Whitley (Sandy Hook in Elliott County), Ricky Skaggs (Blaine in Lawrence County), Tom T. Hall (Olive Hill in Carter County), The Judds (Ashland in Boyd County), and Billy Ray Cyrus (Flatwoods in Greenup County).

There is a lot more to U.S. 23 than country music stars' hometowns and signs, though. To take advantage of the entire length of the road, set your odometer at zero and begin the drive at the Virginia state line just south of Jenkins. At the time of this writing, a great road cut was being carved out of the mountain to widen and relocate the highway. At 4 miles, you will enter Jenkins, an old coal-mining town with houses so close to the road that you almost feel you are driving on their front porches. Jenkins was started by the Consolidation Coal Company in 1911 and named for George C. Jenkins, the financier who funded the operation. In the late 1940s, Jenkins, Burdine, and a number of small coal camps were incorporated into one 7.5-mile-long city.

At 5.8 miles, there is a limestone cut on the right side of the road and the Burdine Elementary School on the left. The old town of Burdine can be seen about 20 feet down to the left below the road. At 8.1 miles is the Patty Loveless sign on the right. For the next mile or so, the road curves back and forth and passes under several railroad bridges carrying what appears to be the same track. All along the way are limestone walls and lots of trees. It is a pretty drive along a generally good two-lane blacktop highway with a center stripe, but no shoulders.

At 13.3 miles, you pass through Dorton, where the road becomes a four-lane divided highway. At 15.0 miles, U.S. 23 starts a climb up into the green wooded mountains and passes through the first of many huge limestone road cuts. The views are beautiful from the wide highway and the trees are abundant. At 19.6 miles, there is a little brick church with a white spire on the right-hand side of the road. You did remember the camera didn't you? Between Dorton and Pikeville, houses can be seen now and then back

Drive 1: The Country Music Highway
From the Tennessee Border to the Ohio River

In 1994, the Kentucky General Assembly designated a portion of U.S. Highway 23 as "The Country Music Highway."

in the trees on the hillsides, some barely visible through the foliage.

U.S. 23, with its 4 lanes and wide-green median feels like an interstate, but this can be a problem if you are not used to it. People tend to get their speed up higher than the limit and, suddenly, a traffic light will appear. Be sure to watch your speed. After all, it is easier to enjoy the scenery when it's not a blur.

At 28.4 miles, U.S. 460 and KY 80 go right toward Elkhorn City and Breaks Interstate Park. If you have the time, or if you are looking for a place to stay, Breaks may be the place for you. There are cottages, a motor lodge, and a campground with 122 sites at this unique park , which is one of only 2 state parks in the United States created jointly by 2 states. There are also about 12 miles of hiking trails that range from easy to difficult. If you would just like to stop for lunch, there are both a fine restaurant and numerous picnicking spots throughout the park. Often called "the Grand Canyon of the South," it boasts a 1,000-foot deep, 5-mile-long gorge that is the largest canyon east of the Mississippi.

Back on U.S. 23, at 32.7 miles, you will be in Pikeville, the county seat of Pike County. Pikeville was laid out in the early spring of 1824 on Peach Orchard Bottom. Originally named Liberty, it was renamed Pikeville after the county which, in turn, had been named for the famed explorer Zebulon

Pike, the discoverer of Pike's Peak. Pikeville and Pike County grew to prominence because of the huge stands of forest to be harvested as timber and the vast fields of coal to be mined. The timber was shipped downstream to the Big Sandy River, then to the Ohio River and the markets at Catlettsburg and Cincinnati. Overzealous cutting of the timber depleted the forests, which are just now making a comeback. Since 1910, Pike County has been one of the major coal-producing areas in the United States, and coal production continues to this day to be the largest employer in the area.

Pike County was also the home of the infamous feud between the Hatfields and the McCoys. The McCoys lived here; the Hatfields lived just across the line in West Virginia. The story has been muddled through the years, and the truth may never be known, but the whole thing seems to have begun in the mid-1800s with a lot of real and imagined wrongs done by each of the clans. The patriarch of the McCoy clan was Ole Ran'l McCoy, who married his cousin Sarah and with her had 16 children. On the Hatfield side, was Devil Anse Hatfield who, with his wife Levicy, fathered 13 children. There appears to have been a good deal of marrying and intermarrying between the clans over the years, and the feuding took place off and on. The big event seems to have been when Roseanna McCoy chose Johnse Hatfield as her intended husband, though why that particular match started trouble remains a mystery. All kinds of mayhem ensued for years, and when the feud finally ended about 1891, 13 were dead. The irony is that after creating the whole mess, Ole Ran'l McCoy and Devil Anse Hatfield, two of the original feuders, lived well into their 80s.

As you leave Pikeville, watch your speed, as you will encounter 4 traffic lights in about 10 miles. At 42.7 miles is the Dwight Yoakam country music sign. From here on to Prestonsburg, U.S. 23 travels through great mountain scenery on both sides of the road. At 55.1 miles, KY 80 goes south to Hazard. In 2 more miles, you will see the city limits sign for Prestonsburg.

In 1791, John Spurlock built a house on the site that would, one day, become Prestonsburg. This qualifies the town as the oldest settlement in the Big Sandy Valley. The town was later named for John Preston, a surveyor from Virginia, who camped at the site in 1791. Three miles west of town is the site of the Battle of Middle Creek, one of the important battles of the Civil War.

A few miles north of Prestonsburg, you will see the junction with KY 3 and the turnoff to Jenny Wiley State Resort Park. This beautiful park in the heart of the Appalachians is on 1,100-acre Dewey Lake. The park offers a lodge, cottages, a 117-site campground with utility hookups, a grocery store, and a 224-seat dining room. There are also more than 10 miles of hiking trails of varying lengths and difficulty levels. If you are a really serious hiker, the park is the southern terminus of the Jenny Wiley Trail that runs 185

Along U.S. 23 north of Louisa.

miles from the park to South Shore on the Ohio River. The park is named for a true heroine of the Kentucky frontier who was captured by Indians, but eventually escaped and made her way home through the wilderness.

As we drive along the wide, smooth highway in modern comfort, looking at the amazing mountain scenery, it is hard to imagine how truly tough our ancestors really were.

Back to the reality of the present, at 60.1 miles there is a traffic light at the junction of KY 1428. The Loretta Lynn, Crystal Gayle, and Hylo Brown Country Music Highway sign shows up at 64.3 miles. The turnoff to Paintsville to the right and Salyersville to the left are at 70.7 miles. For the next 11 miles, the mountain scenery continues on both sides of the road. At 80.8 miles is the sign for Ricky Skaggs. The first of two turnoffs to the right going to Louisa is at 95.1 miles. Four miles more brings you to the second Louisa turnoff and a complex with a service station, restaurant, and gift shop. The gift shop area has a lot of country-music memorabilia.

At 103.5 miles there is a big power plant on the right. It may be stretching it a bit to call it scenic, but when steam is coming off the cooling towers, it is impressive. Beyond the second Louisa turnoff, the view broadens out. The trees are now more on a level with the highway rather than up the hillsides. A limestone road cut appears 4.5 miles from the power plant on the left. It is not as massive as those farther south and it has a lot of grass and foliage growing out of it, giving it a much softer look. Beyond the power plant, at 109.1 miles, you will come upon the sign for the Judds. About a mile beyond the sign is a pretty white church and two red barns sitting in green fields with the wooded hills behind them.

After 20 miles or so of more nice scenery, at 121 miles, you will have encountered three traffic lights and will be in Catlettsburg. This historic town is located at the confluence of the Big Sandy River and the Ohio River. This strategic location has made it a major center for commerce and travelers on the rivers since Alexander Catlett and his son Horatio first founded it in around 1798. In the mid-nineteenth century it was an important steamboat landing and was called "Mouth of the Sandy" or "Big Sandy Landing."

The title of this book is Scenic Driving Kentucky, but scenery is sometimes in the eye of the beholder. The beauty of the forests and rolling hills ends at Catlettsburg, and for a while, the view amounts to city streets, a coke plant, blast furnaces, and other monuments to the industrial age. We happen to be fascinated with such stuff, but if you are not, take heart. In about 6 miles, you will enter the old city of Ashland. For history buffs, there is much to do and see here. See the section of the appendix on where to write for more information. Beyond Ashland, the mountains return on the left and the Ohio River appears on the right. At 14 miles beyond Ashland, at Greenup, KY 1 goes left to the Jesse Stuart State Nature Preserve. This 733-acre preserve is named for the internationally known Kentucky writer. Here you can hike more than 3 miles of trails that wind through the country made famous in his writing.

If you continue along KY 1 for about 8 more miles, you will come to Greenbo Lake State Resort Park. Here hikers can explore 25 miles of easy-to-difficult self-guided trails through some beautiful forest country. For the fisherman, the 225-acre lake offers a chance to catch bass, bluegill, catfish, and trout. The campground includes 63 sites with utility hookups, dump stations, service buildings with showers, and a grocery store.

Back on U.S. 23, beyond Ashland, there is some very nice scenery all the way to the bridge that carries U.S. 23 from Kentucky to Portsmouth, Ohio. If you decide to go all the way, you will reach the bridge at 158.0 miles. If you want still more adventure, why not cross the bridge, get some great views of the Ohio River, and have lunch in Portsmouth?

2

Vanceburg to Grayson

Mountain Scenery and a Covered Bridge

General description: This 94.3- or 101.8-mile drive begins near the old Ohio River town of Vanceburg and ends in Grayson on I-64 west of Catlettsburg. There are two options for the first part of the drive. The first option begins on KY 9/10 at the turnoff to Vanceburg and runs northeast along KY 8 through many small towns along the Ohio River to South Shore. Here, it turns south on KY 7 and goes 1.4 miles to the junction with KY 784. The second option continues on KY 9/10 past the Vanceburg turnoff to KY 784 where it goes left to the junction of KY 7. The second part of the drive runs from the junction of KY 784 and KY 7 south on KY 7 to Grayson. There is an option at the end of the drive to go over to the Oldtown covered bridge. Bridge lovers should not miss this one.

Special attractions: Spectacular scenery, two covered bridges, Greenbo Lake State Resort Park and Carter Caves.

Location: Northeast corner.

Drive route numbers: KY10, 9, 8, 7, 784, 1; U.S. 23.

Travel season: Spring and fall are best, but summer would be fine. Winter could be beautiful, but could be dangerous if there were snow and ice.

Camping: Greenbo Lake State Resort Park, Grayson Lake State Park, and Carter Caves State Resort Park.

Services: Motels in Grayson and a lodge at Greenbo Lake State Resort Park. Carter Caves State Resort Park has both a lodge and cottages. Restaurants and/or fast food in Vanceburg, South Shore, and Grayson.

Nearby attractions: Grayson Lake State Park, Carter Caves State Resort Park.

 The drive

We chose to begin this drive at the junction of KY 10 and KY 3037 just southwest of Vanceburg, but if you are coming from the Maysville area, you can add more than 25 miles of some very pretty driving through some of Kentucky's finest scenery. From its intersection with U.S. 62/68 just west of Maysville, KY 9 passes through some beautiful rolling bluegrass hills for about 20 miles or so. After that, the hills begin to get higher, and by the time you approach the beginning of the drive, they will have turned into beautifully wooded mountains. At 16.9 miles from Maysville, KY 10 joins KY 9.

Drive 2: Vanceburg to Grayson
Mountain Scenery and a Covered Bridge

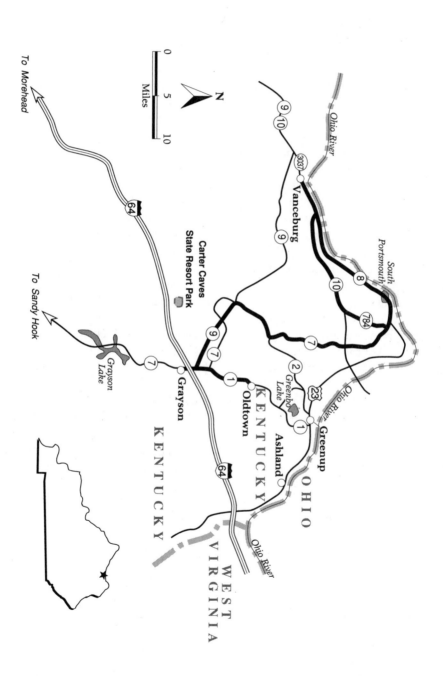

This is of interest not only because KY 10 is part of one of our drive options, but because it is designated as the Mary Ingles Trail after a pioneer woman who was captured by Indians, escaped, and made her way home much the same way as Jenny Wiley (see Drive 1).

In 1750, Mary Draper and William Ingles were wed near what is now Blacksburg, Virginia. There's was the first marriage of English colonists west of the Alleghenies. In July of 1755, their farm was prospering. Mary had given birth to two sons and was pregnant with their third child. Although there was trouble brewing farther north in Pennsylvania, where the French and the Indians had banded together to keep the English colonists from spreading westward, no one really expected any trouble this far south along the old Indian road. But on July 8, a band of Shawnee attacked Draper's Meadows, massacred nearly all of the residents, stole what they wanted, and burned the rest. Mary Ingles and her two sons were taken captive and forced to accompany the Indian marauders into what is now Kentucky. Three days after the massacre, Mary gave birth to a baby girl. She knew that she would be killed if she could not go on, so, she and the baby rode on horseback. They eventually arrived at Big Bone Lick, where her 2 sons were taken from her and sent away, and she was put to work making salt with an old Dutch woman captive from Pennsylvania.

The two women talked often about escaping, and one day, with the warriors away, their chance finally came. There was one horrible decision to make, however. Mary's baby was only three months old and there were several hundred miles of wilderness between Big Bone Lick and home in Virginia. We can only imagine her grief as she wrapped the baby in a blanket, placed her in a bark cradle, kissed her good-bye, and headed off on her unbelievable journey.

They had no idea of a direct route to Virginia, so they took the much longer, but surer route along the Ohio River. Mary knew that if she could find the mouth of the Kanawha River, she could follow it to the valley near her home at Draper's Meadows. For weeks, they fought their way through brush and cane fields, slogged through marshes and across streams, and struggled over the mountains. They rarely had any shelter at night, and had only nuts, berries, roots and such to eat. At one point, they found an old horse grazing in a field and took turns riding it. The terrain was so rough, though, that much of the time they both had to walk anyway.

At long last, they came to the Big Sandy River not far from what is now Catlettsburg, Kentucky. After struggling to get across, and losing the horse in the process, the two women headed downstream to the Ohio River, not trusting their ability to navigate overland. After finally finding the Kanawha and heading south, the trip got even worse. Day after day, they struggled on. The nights were bitter cold and they had very little to eat. Many days and nights like this were too much for the old Dutch woman. She began to

The Oldtown Bridge.

blame Mary for their plight and eventually fought with her and threatened to kill her. Mary stumbled off on her own and kept on. She found a canoe on the river bank and, with the help of a broken branch managed to pole herself upstream. Finally coming out of the mountain gorge, she found herself at the cabin of Adam Harmon, just 15 miles from her home. She had been battling the wilderness for forty three days.

Mary Ingles went on to have three more daughters and a son with her husband William. She died in 1815 at the age of 83. There is much more to the Mary Ingles story, so if you are interested, you might want to read the historical novel *Follow the River* by James Alexander Thoms.

Option 1

At the junction of KY 9/10 and KY 3037, go left toward Vanceburg. In a couple of miles, you will enter Vanceburg, an old river town that was founded by Moses Baird and Joseph Calvin Vance in 1797. The land was purchased from Alexander Keith Marshall, brother of Supreme Court Justice John Marshall. The post office was established in 1815, the town was chartered in 1827 and, in 1863, became the county seat of Lewis County. Old-timers still call Vanceburg "Alum City" after deposits of alum on a nearby hillside.

In Vanceburg, take KY 8 east. This road generally follows the Ohio River to South Portsmouth. There are nice views of the river along the way, but very few places to pull over to take pictures. (So don't worry about forgetting that extra film. You had better get some before you start down KY 7, though.) At about 9 miles, you will come to Garrison, which was originally called Stone City for the many stone quarries from which stone was shipped down the Ohio from the local landing. About 9 miles more will bring you to Firebrick. This little town whose post office was established in 1892 was named for a firebrick plant that is no longer in operation. In a couple of miles, you will pass the bridge over the Ohio to West Portsmouth, Ohio, and in another mile KY 8 becomes U.S. 23 at the bridge to Portsmouth, Ohio. In another mile or so, you reach the junction of U.S. 23 and KY 7 in South Shore. Turn south on KY 7. As soon as you are out of town, the scenery begins. There are lots of beautiful, wooded mountain hillsides "up close and personal." In about a mile and a half, you will come to the junction with KY 784.

Option 2
At the junction of KY 9 and KY 3037, set your odometer to zero and head east on KY 10. Along this route for nearly 20 miles, you will be treated to some increasingly beautiful mountain views along with limestone road cuts. At 19.6 miles, you will see a sign for KY 784 going left. Do not take this turn, though if you forget and do take it, no great harm will be done, since it just winds up the hill and comes back down and back out to KY 10, but it is an unnecessary and not particularly pretty detour. At 22.9 miles, the correct junction of KY 784 goes left. The road immediately dives into the trees and passes through the tiny community of Letitia. For approximately 10 miles, you will see a few homes, another small community, and lots of pretty rolling farmland and wooded mountainsides. KY 784 is a fairly narrow road, so the scenery is up close and personal, unlike that on KY 10. At 32.3 miles you will come to a stop sign at the junction of KY 7.

At the junction, head south on KY 7. The entrance to the Lakes Golf Club is on the left at 3.9 miles. The course is not visible from the road, and without the sign, there would be no reason to suspect that a golf course would be anywhere to be found in all of this rural mountain country. At 7.1 miles, one of the treats of the drive appears suddenly on the left: Bennett's Mill covered bridge. This is one of the very few covered bridges in Kentucky that is still open to traffic. It was built in 1855 over Tygart's Creek and, for bridge lovers, it is a 150-foot Wheeler truss design, the only such construction still remaining. After you have enjoyed the bridge and taken all the pictures you want (We told you to get film. Remember?), continue south on KY 7. At 7.9 miles, you will come to a stop sign at the intersection of KY 7 and KY 10. Cross the intersection and continue south on KY 7. At 14.5 miles you will be in Load. All of KY 7 is a beautiful drive, but we think that the part from KY 10 to Grayson is particularly spectacular. You will see wooded mountainsides, rolling mountain meadows, and small farms, and pass through canopies of oaks and along forests of tulip poplar, black and white oak, white and yellow pine, and elm. This drive should be a riot of color in the fall. At 17.8 miles, KY 2 goes left to Greenbo Lake. If you are so inclined, you can take a loop around the lake by going across KY 2 to KY 1459, to KY 1. This will bring you back to KY 7 about a mile from Grayson. It has the advantage of taking you through Oldtown, so you won't have to make the side trip to the Oldtown covered bridge. The scenery on the loop is comparable to that on KY 7.

If you choose to stay on KY 7, you will pass through the tiny community of Warnock, see a high limestone wall next to the road on your left, and go by a few small businesses before reaching the stop sign at the intersection of KY 7 and KY 9. Although you can stay on KY 7 and wind through more mountains, cross KY 9 again and end up joining KY 9 just outside of Grayson; we liked the wide-open scenery from KY 9. It is the same as that on KY 7, but not quite so close. No matter which route you choose, highways KY 7, 9, and 1 all come together near Interstate 64 less than a mile from Grayson. If you haven't seen the Oldtown Bridge, and would like to, this is where you start the side trip.

At the junction, go left on KY 7/1 for 0.8 mile. At this point, KY 7 goes left. Keep straight ahead on KY 1. At 7.2 miles from the junction, there is a road going right. It is a little hard to see, so keep your eyes peeled. If you come to the old post office on the left, you missed the road. Turn around and go back 0.5 mile to a fork going left. The bridge is just 0.1 mile from KY 1. You will see it as soon as you turn onto the road. The 187-foot-long bridge was built around 1880 and is of double post and brace construction.

Get all of those pictures taken? Now retrace your route to Grayson and get a couple of cholesterol burgers for lunch.

3

Grayson to Paintsville
A Lake-to-Lake Tour

General description: The drive of 54.2 miles heads south from Grayson on KY 7 and winds past some rocky limestone road cuts past the entrance to Grayson Lake. From here, as it continues southwest, it twists and turns through lush woods. Much of the trip is down in the hollows, with the trees towering above. Among the woods, homes, and farms lie both corn and tobacco fields. We feel that KY 706 is one of the best rural drives in the book. With few buildings, overhead wires, or other signs of civilization, it is about as close to pristine as a road in Kentucky gets.

Special attractions: Grayson Lake State Park, Paintsville Lake State Park, boating, camping, fishing, hiking, and picnicking.

Location: East-central.

Drive route numbers: KY 7, 40, 706, 172, 2275; U.S. 40.

Travel season: Spring through fall would be best. Winter could be beautiful, but some roads might be hazardous.

Camping: Campgrounds at Carter Caves State Resort Park and Grayson Lake State Park.

Services: Motels in Grayson and Paintsville. Restaurants and/or fast food establishments in Grayson and Paintsville.

Nearby attractions: Carter Caves State Resort Park, Jenny Wiley State Resort Park.

 The drive

Grayson is the county seat of Carter County and lies just south of Interstate 64, a little more than 20 miles from the Ohio and West Virginia borders near Catlettsburg. Although it is somewhat unclear, the town was probably named after William Grayson, an aide to General George Washington. Grayson is located on the 70,000 acres of land that was issued to the Grayson family by Governor Shelby in 1795.

Carter Caves State Resort Park is a real jewel in the state park system. Within its boundaries are 20 miles of nature trails through the woods. These are graded from easy to difficult, so there is a hike for everyone. There are also tours, both lighted and unlighted, through several of the more than 20 caves. Cascade Cave boasts a 30-foot-high underground waterfall, X Cave is named for its shape and contains many unique formations; and the largest

Drive 3: Grayson to Paintsville
A Lake-to-Lake Tour

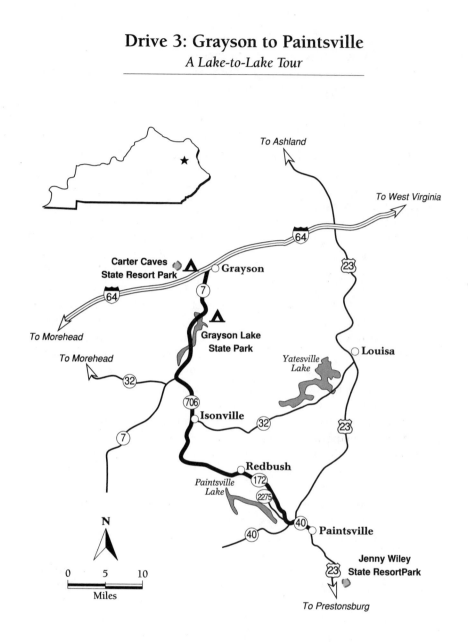

To Ashland

To West Virginia

Carter Caves
State Resort Park

Grayson

Grayson Lake
State Park

To Morehead

To Morehead

Yatesville
Lake

Louisa

Isonville

Redbush

Paintsville
Lake

Paintsville

N

Jenny Wiley
State ResortPark

0   5   10

Miles

To Prestonsburg

of the caves, Bat Cave, is the winter home to thousands of rare bats, including the Indiana bat. It has been estimated that up to 28,000 of this federally listed endangered species spend the winter in Bat Cave. Because of this, the cave is open to tours only in the summer.

If bats are not your thing, you can play a few rounds on the 9-hole regulation golf course complete with a pro shop and rentals of clubs, pull carts, and riding carts. There is also tennis, a guided trail ride, a community pool, and a pool for lodge and cottage guests. There are boats for rent on Carter Caves Lake, Kentucky's only trophy bass lake. A 28-room lodge and 15 cottages that range from efficiencies to two-bedroom models are also available. If you brought your tent along, you can try one of the 89 camp-sites with utilities, rest rooms, and showers. Traditional Kentucky dishes are offered in the 115-seat dining room for breakfast, lunch, and dinner.

All right, if you weren't lured away to Carter Caves, then let's get back to the intersection of U.S. 60 and KY 7 in Grayson and head south. At 3.7 miles from the junction, the road climbs up through a limestone road cut with lots of trees growing out of the limestone. At 6.3 miles the road crosses the dam at Grayson Lake. There is a place to pull out at the far end of the dam that gives a nice view down the lake. In the next mile, you will be presented with the first of the beautiful tree-covered mountains that will be seen throughout this drive. Most common are oak, white and yellow pine, elm, and tulip poplar. At 9.0 miles the road crosses the Grayson Lake/Clifty Creek Embayment. Embayment? Mr. Webster tells me that this is a bay or similar-appearing formation.

At 10.2 miles the entrance to Grayson Lake State Park is on the left. Grayson Lake covers 1,512 acres and has 74.2 miles of shoreline. The shore-line varies from sandy beach to steep sandstone bluffs. Unlike Carter Caves, Grayson State Park has no lodgings, but there is a 71-site campground with utilities, restrooms, showers, and laundry facilities. There is also a marina with boat and pontoon boat rentals. If you are pinched for time, but want to get the flavor of the park, you can take the 0.8-mile Beech-Hemlock Forest Trail, where you will see ferns, lichen, rhododendrons, and the unusual beech-hemlock trees.

Back on KY 7, you will cross a bridge over an arm of Grayson Lake at 10.7 miles. From here on until you come to the little town of Bruin at 12.5 miles, the road climbs and drops and swings back and forth as it winds through green walls of trees. At 15.4 miles, there is an old abandoned shack that has all but disappeared under the tangle of vines growing over and through it. Less than a mile further at 16.2 miles, you will come upon a silver-colored steel bridge. Just before the bridge, KY 706 goes left. Turn left onto 706 and prepare yourself for 15 miles of Kentucky mountain beauty. The first thing you will notice is that the road is very narrow and has no center stripe or shoulders. It is perfectly safe if you drive slowly. Neither of us can imagine why anyone would want to rush through this gorgeous place.

At 20.3 miles, KY 706 comes to a T intersection. Go right to stay on KY 706, but watch for this turn. When we were there, the sign was missing. If you go left and pass the post office and school, you went the wrong way. You will soon know, since the road turns from blacktop to gravel. Guess how we found that out? The scenery on KY 706 after the right turn is beautiful

The view from the visitor center at Paintsville Lake State Park.

and close. At 2.0 miles from the T the road makes a real hairpin turn going down and to the left. At 0.7 mile farther, there is another sharp left. At 4.0 miles, there is a stop sign at the junction of KY 32 at Isonville. Go right at the stop and in 0.1 mile, go left. There was no sign here either, so watch carefully for the turn. By 6 miles, there is a little meadow on the left and you will begin to see a few more houses and farms. At 9.4 miles you will enter Crockett, and at 10.9 you will be at the junction of KY 172. The Crockett post office is on the right at the junction. The post office was established in 1900. First called Wheeler Town because of the many Wheeler families who lived there, the name was changed to Crockett after David Crockett Fannin, the son of the first postmaster, Peter Fannin, who was undoubtedly named for the pioneer legend.

Turn left on KY 172 at the junction by the post office and head for Paintsville. The first thing you will notice here is that the road is considerably wider, there are both a double yellow centerline and white shoulder lines. At 14.1 miles, you are in Moon. All sorts of possibilities come to mind as to how this town was named, but the story is that the first postmaster, James F. Wallin, submitted the name to postal authorities, claiming to have been inspired by a moonlit night in 1905. Moon is a string of homes and small farms stretched along the highway and framed with meadows and wooded mountainsides.

At 20.5 miles you will be in downtown Redbush. The post office here was established in 1890 with William A. Williams as postmaster. The town was named for the great numbers of small pin oak trees whose leaves turn red in the fall. At 22.7 miles, the road goes downhill through the trees past homes and small farms. There is more evidence of civilization along here than there was on KY 706, but the scenery beyond is just as nice. At 28.5 miles, there is a rugged limestone road cut on the left. It is made of big chunks and is not as tailored looking as many in the state. At 31.1 miles, KY 172 ends at the junction with KY 40.

KY 40 goes left to Paintsville, but at this junction, you are only 2.4 miles from the visitor center at Paintsville Lake State Park, so you might as well run up and take a look at a truly pretty lake. The visitor center has a fantastic view of the lake. Paintsville Lake was constructed pursuant to the Flood Control Act of 1965 in order to help keep down the flood levels on the Big Sandy and Ohio Rivers. Some additional benefits are recreational use, water quality control, and fish and wildlife management. The lake is approximately 18 miles long and fills a number of gorges and winding canyons. With an average depth of 38 feet and with some spots as deep as 105 feet, Paintsville Lake is deep enough and cold enough to support a permanent trout population. Fishermen can look forward to hooking some bluegill, bass, walleye, carp, and crappie.

The park consists of 242 acres of mostly undeveloped land. There are no camping or lodging facilities, but there is a day use picnic area with shelters, a boat launch ramp, and rest rooms. There is also a privately owned marina within the park boundaries with 166 slips. You can rent fishing gear, buy bait, and rent a boat at the marina. Doesn't fresh-caught trout sound better for lunch than another pizza?

After finishing off the trout, you should retrace your route to the junction of KY 2275 and KY 40. Go left on KY 40 toward the city with the interesting name of Paintsville. The name was taken from nearby Paint Creek, which, in turn, got its name from some strangely painted trees found along its banks by early settlers. The trees were stripped of their bark, sometimes as high up as 30 feet, and painted with figures of animals and birds in red and black. The town was laid out on the site of the old Paint Lick Station trading post around 1812, but was not officially recognized by the Kentucky State Legislature until 1834. In that same year, Paintsville became the county seat of the new Johnson County. In addition to the painted trees, the creek had salty springs that attracted game. Early hunters called the creek Paint Lick Creek and this name can still be found on some very old maps.

Continue on KY 40 as it passes under U.S. 23 and winds down into downtown Paintsville. There is much to be seen in town for history buffs, but our favorite was the Mayo Memorial Church and the old three-story, 40-room Mayo mansion that is now the Our Lady of the Mountains school.

4

Louisa to Morehead
Through the Eastern Mountains

General description: The 61.7-mile-long section of KY 32 from Louisa to Morehead winds and twists its way through some of the prettiest mountain scenery in Kentucky. As it leaves U.S. 23 near Louisa, it climbs immediately into mountains covered with stands of oak, walnut, hickory, tulip poplar, and redbud. All along the drive, the road will twist and turn through the mountain scenery. Canopies of oak, occasional farms, and some long views of Yatesville Lake are just some of the sights that await you.

Special attractions: Yatesville Lake State Park, Daniel Boone National Forest.

Location: East-central to East.

Drive route number: KY32.

Travel season: Spring through fall, with winter a possibility if the roads are clear.

Camping: Campgrounds at Cave Run Lake, and The Falls Campground at Yatesville Lake.

Services: Motels in Morehead and Louisa. Bed and Breakfasts can be found in Morehead, Sandy Hook, Blaine, and Louisa. Restaurants and/or fast food establishments in Morehead, Sandy Hook, and Louisa.

Nearby attractions: Grayson Lake State Park, Cave Run Lake, Yatesville Lake Wildlife Viewing Area.

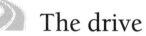 # The drive

We were at the visitor center at Paintsville Lake State Park talking to one of the rangers about scenic places to drive in the area. She asked if we had been along KY 32 up through Blaine. We had not, so we got directions and headed out. What we found has become one of our favorite drives, and we bet it will be one of yours, too. The road is good, wide enough, and very safe. However, you will get lots of steering wheel practice as it snakes through the mountains. Be sure your coffee cup is only half full.

The drive begins just outside of Louisa, an old river town on the Big Sandy River that dates back to the flatboat era. During the time of the Napoleonic wars, bearskins were taken in the area surrounding the town and sent to Europe by way of the Big Sandy, the Ohio, and the Mississippi Rivers. The Europeans made the bearskins into headgear for Napoleon's grenadiers.

Drive 4: Louisa to Morehead
Through the Eastern Mountains

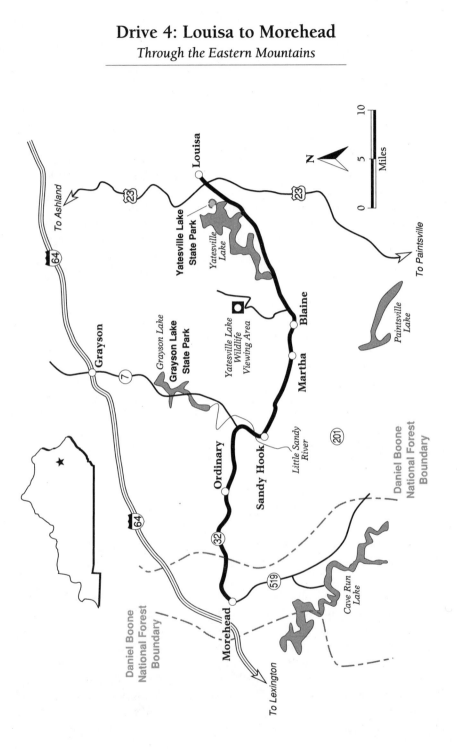

The flatboats gave way to packets and barges, and the cargo changed from bearskins to logs. Millions of logs from the upper valley forests were funneled through Louisa to the sawmills along the Ohio River.

As with most areas in the eastern mountains, stories of the early days abound. One is that George Washington once owned more than 2,000 acres of land on both sides of the Big Sandy, including the present site of Louisa. The story was given a little credibility by the presence of a survey marker with the initials "GW." Of course a skeptic might conclude that the mark simply stood for "Gee Whiz."

Another story is perhaps the most famous in Kentucky. It is told that in 1760 a man by the name of John Swift and a party of men came through the mountains from Alexandria, Virginia, to a place in Kentucky where they knew of a silver mine. The story goes on that they worked the mine in the summers for nine years. There is a manuscript of their adventures that details the dates of their trips and the names of the party's members. It also gives an account of coins and treasure hidden either because of Indians or because they were caught in weather that made it impossible to get it out. Many would-be treasure hunters feel that the journal points to the area around Paint Creek, and, in fact, the Mine Fork of Paint Creek was named for the mine in the journal. Of course, the details were vague and almost every county in eastern Kentucky has a story about how the mine and the treasure are in their area. Treasure hunting for the "lost mine" has been a hobby for many not only in Kentucky, but also in Virginia, North Carolina, and Tennessee. If you should happen to find the treasure or the mine, we feel that a modest 10 percent would be a reasonable token of your appreciation for our setting you on the trail to such riches.

Well, now that you know more about Louisa than you cared to, set your odometer at zero at the junction of KY 32 and U.S. 23. As you start west on KY 32, you immediately begin to climb into the forested mountains. You will be on a good two-lane blacktop road with a double yellow center stripe and white shoulder markers. At 3.2 miles there is a small group of houses. This may be Busseyville, but like so many towns in Kentucky, it is not marked. At 3.4 miles, you will be going downhill through a canopy of trees with houses on both sides of the road. The Busseyville Variety Store pops up at 3.6 miles. By 4.3 miles, you are out in the open and passing through a rust-colored limestone road cut. At 5.4 miles you will pass an arm of Yatesville Lake, a reservoir, one of Kentucky's newest and the largest in the far-eastern region of the state.

This fine fishing hole was a long time in coming, though. Way back in 1954, The U.S. Army Corps of Engineers began a study of the Big Sandy Basin. The study eventually recommended the construction of four major reservoirs in the area. In 1964, the study was supplemented by a report that recommended several other lakes. Yatesville was one of the recommenda-

Along KY 32 east of Sandy Hook.

tions. The Flood Control Act of 1965 authorized the projects, so Yatesville Lake became a part of the system of flood control, water quality improvements, recreation, and fish and wildlife conservation. The environmental impact report was filed in 1972, land acquisition began in 1973, and the construction contract was awarded in 1977. However, President Carter's review of projects stopped the funding and the contract was put on hold. Funding was restored in 1983 and construction finally began in 1984. In August of 1991, the gates were closed at the dam and the lake began filling.

For the next few miles, the road snakes back and forth, climbs up and drops down as it makes its way through the wooded mountainsides. At 9.3 miles the road passes another arm of Yatesville Lake. At 10.3 miles there is an old shack on the right that is slowly being devoured by the undergrowth. At 10.5 and 11.7 miles, you will have more nice views of Yatesville Lake. At 13.0 miles, the road swings left and on the right up in the trees is a house almost hidden by the foliage. At 16.1 miles the beginnings of Blaine can be seen down in the hollow to the left. At 16.5 miles you will cross a bridge over Hood Creek and enter Blaine.

At Blaine you can take KY 201 north to the Yatesville Lake Wildlife Viewing Area. Here in the hilly woodlands, you can visit the observation area above reconstructed wetlands. You will have a chance to see deer, squirrel, raccoon, grouse, wild turkey, various migratory waterfowl, and even bald eagles. The U.S Army Corps of Engineers manages the area and there is no camping at the site. Don't forget the camera.

Between Blaine and Martha, which you reach at 19.9 miles, you will pass a number of small farms. At 21.7 miles, you will come to Billy Boy's Grocery Store on the right. At 23.9 miles, you will enter Mazie, and pass an old building on the right that calls itself the "Mazie Mall." The origin of the town's name is in dispute. Some say it was a misreading of the last name of Britt Maxie, who had submitted his name to become postmaster. Others say that the town was named after the mother or grandmother of a local preacher.

At 26.5 miles the road is following a little hollow with just enough room for the houses between the road and the mountains. Small tilled fields are located between the houses. At 30.2 miles, the city limits sign for Isonville appears. At 30.6 miles you will see the Isonville Elementary School on the left and an old collapsing barn on the right. At 31.0 miles, KY 706 goes right. At 31.1 miles, KY 706 goes left (see Drive 3). At 33.7 you will be at the junction with KY 719 at Fannin. At 36.4 miles, KY 7 joins KY 32 in Sandy Hook, the county seat of Elliott County. Sandy Hook was settled in the 1820s and was named for the bend in the Little Sandy River.

At 40.1 miles, you will be in Newfoundland. KY 7 goes right and KY 32 goes straight ahead at 40.5 miles. At 42.5 miles, the road crosses a ridge. It is short, but there are great views in both directions. At 47 miles there is a beautiful weathered-gray barn to the right with nothing but sky for a back-

Yatesville Lake west of Louisa.

ground. At 52 miles you enter Ordinary. The post office was established in 1884 by George W. Carter. The story goes that while trying to think of a name for the new post office, someone said that it was such an ordinary place that it was hard to come up with a name. We don't know if the story is accurate, but we like it anyway. At 53.9 miles, KY 504 goes right and just past the junction, you will enter Elliottville. At 61.7 miles, you will be at the Morehead city limits.

5

Hazard to Pineville

Coal Country to the Cumberland Gap

General description: This beautiful 107-mile drive begins near the old coal-mining town of Hazard and works its way past a town with the head-turning name of Sassafras, ambles by the entrance to Carr Creek State Park and Carr Fork Lake, and continues on to Whitesburg. From Whitesburg, the drive climbs up into the mountains and along a Kentucky designated scenic byway. For 10 miles or so the road climbs through the heavily wooded mountains with many views through the trees across the valley to distant ridges. Beyond the scenic byway portion of the drive, a turnoff to the old coal towns of Benham and Lynch appear. All along this route, trees and power line poles can be seen covered with kudzu vines.

Special attractions: Pine Mountain State Scenic Byway, coal museums, Lilley Cornett Woods, kudzu.

Location: Southeastern corner along the Virginia border.

Drive route numbers: KY 15; U.S. 119, 25E.

Travel season: Any time of the year should be fine, but winter, especially on the scenic byway section, could be dangerous if the weather is bad.

Camping: Campgrounds at Buckhorn Lake State Resort Park, Carr Fork Lake, Kingdom Come State Park, Pine Mountain State Resort Park, and Cumberland Gap National Historical Park.

Services: Motels in Hazard, Whitesburg, Harlan, and Pineville. There is a bed and breakfast in Whitesburg. Restaurants and/or fast food in Hazard, Whitesburg, Baxter, Harlan, and Pineville.

Nearby attractions: Pine Mountain State Resort Park, Cumberland Gap National Historical Park, Carr Creek State Park, Lilley Cornett Woods, Kingdom Come State Park, Kentucky Coal Mining Museum, Big Black Mountain, Bad Branch State Nature Preserve.

The drive

We begin this drive at the junction of KY 80 and KY 15 just north of Hazard. In a coal-mining area like this, it is easy to think of the town being named for the dangers associated with mining, but such was not the case. The events leading up to the War of 1812 caused grave concern among Kentuckians, since they felt that their security was threatened. Records show that at least 4,000 Kentucky men fought in the Battle of Lake Erie with Oliver Hazard Perry. Thus, it is thought that General Elijah Combs, Sr., the

Drive 5: Hazard to Pineville

Coal Country to the Cumberland Gap

founder of Perry County, named the county after the hero of that famous naval battle. The first post office was established in 1824 with Elijah Combs, Jr. as postmaster and was named Perry Court House. In 1854, the name was changed to Hazard.

Strange stories abound in the Kentucky mountains, and in an area that has seen habitation by European settlers since, at least, the 1700s, the stories can get very strange, indeed. Such is the one about the blue people of Troublesome Creek. Now you may think that living in the isolation of the

Kentucky mountains in the 1800s would make anyone blue, but we are not talking about clinical depression, we are talking about people who were blue. This strange skin coloration began more than 100 years ago when Martin Fugate, a French orphan, emigrated to the mountains north of what is now Hazard in 1820 and claimed a land grant on the banks of Troublesome Creek. He probably had no idea just how prophetic the name of the creek would become. Martin and his wife, Elizabeth, a red-haired, pale-skinned woman, had seven children. Four of these were blue. As the clan multiplied in its isolation, Fugates married Fugates, often their first cousins. When they didn't intermarry, they married the neighbors closest to them. This was a common practice in the mountains, since the families lived far from the rest of the world deep in the hollows.

So it was in this natural "biosphere," that Martin and Elizabeth's blue children multiplied and passed on the blue skin color to their descendants. When their son Zachariah married his mother's sister, they began a line of succession that would lead to the birth of Benjy Stacy in a modern hospital in Hazard more than 100 years later. When Benjy was born, he was so dark blue that he was nearly purple. His parents were evidently not concerned, but the doctors surely were. Benjy was taken immediately to a clinic in Lexington where two days of tests revealed nothing to account for his color. Gradually, relatives began to come forth with stories about the "blue Fugates of Troublesome Creek." There had been stories in the area for years about the blue people, but they kept to themselves so well that very few people had ever seen them. One could suppose that since their condition was not threatening to anyone, but just a curiosity, no great attention was paid to it. As the story began to unfold, one relative described Benjy's great grandmother, Luna Fugate, as being the bluest woman she had ever seen. Luna's father, Levy Fugate, was one of the sons of Zachariah Fugate. He had married and settled on Ball Creek, not far from Troublesome Creek. They had eight children, one of whom was Luna. Luna married John Stacy who remembers that all of Luna's family was blue. Luna Fugate Stacy bore at least 13 children and died at age 84. The clinic had seen her only a few times in all of those years, and never for a serious illness. All of the blue people were known for longevity. Most lived into their 80s and 90s and seemed never to have any illness associated with the blueness.

Benjy was even more fortunate. Within a few weeks of his birth, he lost the blue tint. His birth got the medical researchers going, though, and the mystery was finally solved. Dr. Madison Cawein, a hematologist at the University of Kentucky Medical Center found the descendants of Martin Fugate in the hills near Hazard and drew blood from them. Eventually, he demonstrated that the blue skin coloration was the result of a deficiency in an enzyme, and that it was genetically transmitted. The absolutely amazing thing is that Martin Fugate and his wife—two people in the remote hills of

Kudzu in Whitesburg.

Kentucky—could possibly have the same rare recessive gene. The blue people were generally not very happy about their affliction, so when Dr. Cawein discovered a way to remove the blue color, they were extremely happy. He discovered that injections of methylene blue would remove the color in minutes. Unfortunately, it was temporary, so he supplied them with methylene blue pills to be taken every day. It worked. In the process, however, some of the methylene blue was excreted in the urine, and one old gentleman told the doctor that he could see the blue running right out of his skin.

Set your odometer at zero at the junction of KY 80 and KY 15, and head south on KY 15 toward Hazard. At 1.9 miles, KY 15 splits, with the left fork being the business route through town and the right fork going toward Whitesburg. At the fork, there is a huge hillside on the right that is covered with kudzu. In the next 2 miles along the road, you will see Hazard off to the left. At 4 miles, the business route joins the bypass. At 6.6 miles the road is winding through the mountains. Off to the left, there are houses hidden in the trees about halfway up the mountain. At 9.1 miles, you will see a sign to Lilley Cornett Woods on the right.

At 9.9 miles, there is kudzu all over the trees on the right. At 10.9 miles, there is massive kudzu on both sides of the road. At 14.4 miles, there is a huge limestone road cut on the left. Along here KY 15 is a nice, wide two-lane road with a double yellow center stripe and white shoulder lines, wide shoulders, and passing lanes on the uphill stretches. At 17.1 miles there is a big limestone road cut with coal seams in it, and there is also a beautiful mountain view ahead. At 18.5 miles, KY 15 goes over a high bridge across an arm of Carr Fork Lake. At 18.8 miles, you pass a high limestone road cut on the right and more views of Carr Fork Lake on the left. Another bridge over an arm of Carr Fork Lake shows up at 20.3 miles. At 21.7 miles the road enters the city limits of Red Fox. At 24.6 miles, the road curves downhill to the right and provides some great long mountain views ahead. At 25.8 miles, you will enter Isom.

Lilley Cornett Woods is a national natural landmark and state wildlife refuge located on KY 1103 at Skyline. The total area is 554 acres, with 252 acres dedicated to old-growth forest consisting primarily of beech, white oak, chestnut oak, and hemlock. The concept of protection for this area began shortly after World War I, when Lilley Cornett bought a tract of land here. He realized that many of Kentucky's forests were being cut down for timber and for land clearing, and, while the forests did come back, there were differences between the old and new growth. It used to be said in the old days that the forests of Kentucky were so dense that a squirrel could cross the state from east to west and never touch the ground. Lilley Cornett wanted to protect this squirrel interstate. Of course, the land cleared for farms and towns never became forest again. Public access to the woods is by guided tours only. There is a visitor center and a small technical library at the site.

At 27.5 miles, you will be on a nice wide road looking at beautiful, wide, wooded mountain views, and at 33.4 miles you will be in Whitesburg.

At the junction of KY 15 and U.S. 119 at the north end of Whitesburg go right on KY 119. At 0.9 mile, you will come to a traffic light. Keep going straight ahead. At 2.3 miles, KY 119 goes right. This is the beginning of one of the Kentucky Scenic Byways known as the Pine Mountain State Scenic Byway. The road immediately jumps into the trees and starts to climb the mountain. For the next 9 miles or so, the road is a little narrow and contains a lot of sharp turns. Keep an eye out for oncoming traffic. At 4.8 miles, there is a turnout on the right on a curve. There is a great view across the mountains. The foliage can be a little thick in spring and summer, but good pictures are usually possible. At 7.0 miles, there are the remains of an old stone structure on the left. At 7.5 miles, there is a parking area for the Little Shepherd Hiking Trail. At about 8 miles, KY 932 goes left to the Bad Branch State Nature Preserve. Within the more than 2,000 acres of the preserve, you can hike on 7.4 miles of strenuous trail or just relax and engage in a little bird watching or nature photography.

At 10.3 miles, the Kentucky Scenic Byway ends. At 10.6 miles, you enter Oven Fork. The Oven Fork Mercantile is on the right. After the end of the scenic byway, the terrain widens out quite a bit, the views are broader, and the mountains are farther from the road. At 20 miles, there is a high,

Cora Kappele, one of the authors, at Cumberland Gap National Park.

stepped limestone road cut. Unlike most others, this one is cut back like stair steps. At 22.4 miles you will see the city limits sign for Cumberland. At 22.6 miles, KY 1264 goes right to Kingdom Come State Park. This park has some of the best rock formations in the state, as well as beautiful views of Black Mountain and the surrounding valley. There are primitive campsites, hiking trails, fishing in a 3.5-acre lake, pedal boating, picnicking and, of course, a gift shop. Within the park, there is also a 225-acre nature preserve. This is a wilderness area that protects the endangered Indiana bat. Hiking in the preserve is permitted, but be aware that there are no formal trails, the terrain is rugged, and there are steep cliffs and poisonous snakes.

Back on KY 119, at 23.4 miles, KY 160 goes to the old company coal towns of Lynch and Benham. Lynch was built by the U.S. Coal and Coke Company, a division of U.S. Steel, in 1917 and named for its first president, Thomas Lynch. At its peak, the population of Lynch was 10,000, which made it the largest coal camp in the world. Today, you can take a walking tour of Mine Portal 31 and see the original powerhouse, railroad depot, commissary, lamp house, bathhouse, firehouse, water plant, coal tipple, and mine portal.

Benham was built by International Harvester to provide coke for the South Chicago Steel Works. The town was built in a circle and contained the mine offices, company store, hospital, theater, clubhouse, school, church, and bandstand. If you want to get an idea of how life was in the heyday of coal mining, stop at the Kentucky Coal Mining Museum on Main Street and visit the Coal Miners' Park next door.

A mile beyond the KY 160 junction, there is a traffic light at the junction of KY 179. This section of KY 119 feels almost like an interstate, but traffic lights do pop up every now and then. You will go under a bridge and enter a long limestone road cut. At 30.2 miles the road goes under a coal conveyor. At 31.7 miles, there is a coal-loading operation and another overhead conveyor. At 44.8 miles, KY 119 goes right to Pineville. If you are hungry, need gas or film, go straight ahead on KY 421 into Harlan. You can always come back and continue on to Pineville. It is 28.5 more miles to Pineville, and along the way you will see some great mountain scenery. You will also see a lot more kudzu.

Pueraria lobata is the official scientific name for this unique vine that now covers about 7 million acres of the Deep South. It was introduced into the United States by the Japanese at the Centennial Exposition in Philadelphia in 1876. American gardeners thought this vine with its large leaves and sweet-smelling blooms would be great for ornamental purposes. In Florida, Charles and Lillie Pleas promoted the vine as forage for animals. They sold kudzu plants through the mail from their nursery. During the Great Depression of the 1930s, the government promoted the use of kudzu for erosion control. The Civilian Conservation Corps was enlisted to plant the vines. In the 1940s, as much as eight dollars an acre was paid to farmers to plant their fields with kudzu. So far, it sounds great. The problem is that these things are mega-growing machines. They just love the climate of the southeastern United States and can grow as much as a foot a day during the summer months. They will climb anything they touch. As you will see along this drive, kudzu vines will turn power poles, telephone poles, and trees into a kind of weird sculpture. They do help in erosion control, but they can also kill whole forests, not by choking the trees, but by preventing the needed sunlight from getting to the leaves. Most herbicides have very little, if any, effect on kudzu. In fact, at least one herbicide increases the growth. Killing them, even with the best herbicides, can take up to ten years or repeated applications. Some researchers have had success in raising Angora goats in fields of kudzu. Their aggressive grazing does actually kill the vines. Of course, it is hard to train an Angora goat to climb a telephone pole for his lunch. We have all heard the admonition that if life gives you lemons, make lemonade. Well, how about if life gives you kudzu, make kudzu blossom jelly? One lady in Georgia does just that, along with syrup, baskets, and books of recipes and basket-making instructions. An entrepreneur in North Carolina cuts and bales kudzu hay for cattle. His wife makes deep-fried kudzu leaves and kudzu quiche. So don't despair. If you awaken some morning to find your car engulfed in kudzu, just make a few baskets, bale some hay for your cow, and whip up a nice quiche for lunch.

6

Pineville to Harlan
Where Coal was King

General description: This is another mountain drive through 90 miles of beautiful wooded hollows and along ridges. There are a number of abandoned as well as operating coal mines to be seen along the way. At one point, there is a large sawmill in operation. Between Hyden and Harlan, the road criss crosses a stream and passes a mixture of old and new houses. Just before Harlan, the road crosses a ridge and runs through a large limestone crushing operation.

Special attractions: Daniel Boone National Forest, coal mines, limestone crusher.

Location: Southeast corner along the Virginia border.

Drive route numbers: KY 66; U.S. 421.

Travel season: All year should be fine, but spring and fall would be best. Winter would be nice if the roads were clear.

Camping: Campgrounds at Pine Mountain State Resort Park and Cumberland Gap National Historical Park.

Services: Motels in Pineville, Harlan, and Middlesboro. Restaurants and fast food in Pineville, Hyden, Baxter, Harlan, and Middlesboro

Nearby attractions: Pine Mountain State Resort Park, Cumberland Gap National Historical Park, Buckhorn Lake State Resort Park, Rock Hotel, Chained Rock, Wilderness Road Tours, and The Henderson Settlement at Frakes.

 The drive

While you are in Pineville, you would be remiss if you pass up a chance to visit the Cumberland Gap area just a few miles to the south. The Cumberland Gap, which is really just a break in the long mountain wall of the Appalachians, probably played a greater role in the westward movement than any geographical and/or geological feature with the possible exception of the Rocky Mountains. It has been called the Gateway to the West, the Gibraltar of America, and the Keystone of the Confederacy. Long before humans discovered the Gap, animals used it as an easier access to the fertile valleys and wooded mountains of Kentucky and Tennessee. American Indians used the Gap to push their "Warriors' Path" through the Appalachians as they moved from North Carolina and Virginia into Kentucky and on to

Drive 6: Pineville to Harlan

Where Coal was King

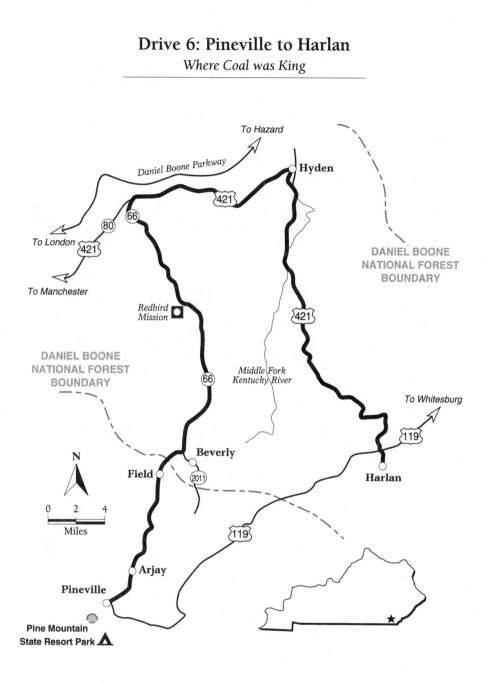

To Hazard

Daniel Boone Parkway

Hyden

421

66

80

To London

421

To Manchester

Redbird
Mission

DANIEL BOONE
NATIONAL FOREST
BOUNDARY

421

DANIEL BOONE
NATIONAL FOREST
BOUNDARY

Middle Fork
Kentucky River

To Whitesburg

66

119

N

Beverly

Field

2011

Harlan

0   2   4
Miles

119

Arjay

Pineville

Pine Mountain
State Resort Park

Ohio. In 1750, Dr. Thomas Walker and his small party were the first white men to go through the Gap. Walker marked the location and opened the floodgates to the west. Hunting parties used the Gap to get to the plentiful game in Kentucky, and early explorers filed through on their persistent push to the west. Close on their heels were the settlers looking for freedom and fertile land.

It is estimated that prior to the Revolutionary War, 12,000 had passed through the Gap on their way to the new frontier. From 1775 to 1796, between 100,000 and 200,000 people used the road through Cumberland Gap. As you sail along on U.S. 25E, try and picture a trail so rough and difficult that in all of those years no wagon ever passed over it. The trail, which was called the Wilderness Road, was a hazardous path through canebrakes and marshes. It crossed rivers and streams, crawled over wooded mountains, and penetrated deep forests.

Stories of the heroes of the Cumberland Gap and of the Wilderness Road abound, but without doubt the most famous of these incredibly tough and resilient people was Daniel Boone. He was probably the major force in opening up the old Warriors' Path from the Gap to the Ohio River. This became the Wilderness Road. Motorists today can follow the general path that began at the Gap and ran through the Cumberland River Gorge at what is now Pineville. From there, it twisted a tortuous path through the mountains of eastern Kentucky. At Hazel Patch, the road forked. The right fork went north to Big Hill and on to Boonesborough on the Kentucky River. The left fork went through Crab Orchard, Danville, Harrodsburg and on to Falls of the Ohio, which is now Louisville. The closest a motorist today can come to the original route is to start at the Gap on U.S. 25E and take this road to Corbin. From Corbin, U.S. 25 goes through Richmond and on to Lexington. The left fork is U.S. 150 from Mount Vernon through Crab Orchard, Danville, and Bardstown and on to Louisville.

Before you leave the Gap area, you might want to visit the Cumberland Gap National Historical Park. There is a visitor center, museum, and a bookstore with some excellent books on the area. There are more than 50 miles of hiking trails in the 20,000 acres of forest within the park. You can also visit the Pinnacle Overlook for some fantastic views of the mountains, Iron Furnace, Fort McCook, and the Hensley Settlement.

If you have the time, or if you plan to stay in the Pineville area for a while, try Pine Mountain State Resort Park. In addition to a fine lodge and nine log cabins, there is a 36-site campground. There are no utility hookups, but there is a central services building with showers and rest rooms. Grills and picnic tables are also available. You might want to try some of the 8.5 miles of hiking trails with such enticing names as Honeymoon Falls, Rock Hotel, Living Stairway, and Chained Rock. Chained Rock is the big sight to see in the park. It is a huge boulder that hangs over the town of

An old coal mine along KY 66 north of Pineville.

Pineville, high up on the mountain. There are several stories about how it came to be chained, but our favorite is one about children in town who couldn't sleep at night for fear that the rocks would come tumbling down on them. To calm them, the parents told them that the rocks were chained to the mountain and couldn't fall. As the story got around, people from other communities came to Pineville and asked how to get to the chained rocks. As a publicity stunt, a chain was obtained from an old steam shovel and mounted on a rock high on the mountain.

Maybe chained rocks don't interest you. In this case, if you don't mind hiking more than three strenuous miles of uneven trail, you can visit the Pine Mountain State Park Nature Preserve. This protected area of more than 1,600 acres lies within the Pine Mountain State Resort Park and contains an old-growth forest of hemlock, tulip poplar, and white oak. Many of the trees are 200 to 300 years old. There is also a significant archaeological site known as Rock Hotel that was inhabited by prehistoric Native Americans .

Now let's get on with the drive. Set your odometer at zero at the junction of U.S. 25E and KY 66 in Pineville. Go north on KY 66 and within a mile, you will be out of town and into the trees. By 2.0 miles you will be in a wall of green. The trees here do not form a full canopy, but they come close at times. At 4.1 miles you will be in Arjay. The strange name of the town was derived from the initials of R. J. Asher, a coal operator in the area. The first 15 miles or so of this drive winds and climbs through some very beautiful mountain scenery. Unfortunately, it also shows what man can do to this beauty. We included it in the book for two reasons. First, there truly is some outstanding mountain scenery, and, second, we think that all of us need to be reminded from time to time what can happen when we don't pay attention to our planet. Don't despair, though. The next 15 or 17 miles are just as pretty and the ugliness of shacks and coal mines is gone.

At 7.8 miles, there is a large coal operation on the left. The road through here is two-lane blacktop with a double yellow center stripe. There are no white shoulder marks and no shoulders. The road is good, and there are no blind curves, but keep an eye out for coal trucks. In our more than 9,000 miles of these roads in researching this book, we never encountered a coal truck that was being driven recklessly. However, when a vehicle goes by with tires taller than your car, it can give you pause. At 9.3 miles, there is a coal tipple on the left. There is an old crumbling coal mine on the left at 10.4 miles. Several structures at the mine could make very interesting photos. Within another mile, there are nice modern brick homes on the left, right next to some dilapidated old shacks. At 12 miles, the road goes under a coal conveyor, and at 12.2 miles, it goes under a second conveyor and passes a big mine on the right. At 15 miles the road is winding back and forth downhill. There are beautiful views across the mountains.

From 15.8 through 17.0 miles the road passes through Field, a small community of well-kept houses. At 17.6 miles, there is a stop sign at the junction with KY 2011. On the left at the junction, there is a big, old structure that looks as though it might once have been a boarding house. Go left at the junction, staying on KY 66. You will wind along through walls of trees, lots of limestone road cuts, and lots more kudzu. At 19.7 miles, the road hops over a little hill and offers a view of a big coal mine off to the left. At 20.6 miles, you will be in a nice canopy of trees as the road twists downhill. At 23.8 miles, there is the unexpected sight of the big Red Bird Mission on the left.

The Red Bird Mission was founded in 1921 in this remote corner of Kentucky by the Evangelical Church to provide education and Christian evangelism to the isolated residents of the area. The school operated from 1921 to 1988 as a settlement school, although the present building was not dedicated until 1983. The story of the Appalachian Settlement Schools is another of those tales of dedicated people going to extraordinary lengths to help others. Most were modeled after the progressive schools of the urban areas of the northeast in the 1920s. One such school was at Jane Addams's Hull House in Chicago. Grades were de-emphasized in favor of character development (sound familiar?). They were largely staffed and run by idealistic young women from central Kentucky and New England, as women's colleges were turning out well-trained graduates who wanted to use their college educations, but were up against the stigma of "proper" jobs for women. Fortunately for Appalachia, many of them decided to respond to the desperate need for teachers in that area. Scores of settlement schools sprang up throughout Appalachia. They taught the crafts of the mountains and shared ideas. The crafts and the music of Appalachia brought collectors and entrepreneurs into the mountains and, in turn, gave a glimpse of the outside world to this formerly isolated part of the country. It must have worked, since we now see banjos and dulcimers in New York and Los Angeles and microwaves and satellite dishes in Appalachia.

Beyond the Red Bird Mission, at 25.3 miles, there is a small group of homes nearly hidden in the trees to the left. At 30.3 miles, the road enters Creekville. At 32.8 miles, there is a high limestone road cut on the left. At 33.3 miles, there are some more old weathered barns on a hillside to the left. At 37.2 miles , you will come upon the Red Bird Ranger Station sitting in the middle of a huge lawn on the left.

At 37.9 miles, you enter Peabody, and in another mile, you will be at the junction of KY 66/KY 80/U.S. 421. Go right on U.S. 421. At 39.7 miles, KY 66 goes left. Stay on U.S. 421. At 40.0 miles, you enter Big Creek. At 40.2 miles, you will see the Big Creek post office on the left. At 41.6 miles, a small brick building on the right houses the Bear Branch post office. From the junction to Hyden, which shows up at 54.6 miles, there are many homes and businesses as well as a lot of great mountain scenery. In Hyden, U.S. 421

loops to the right and heads south. At 54.0 miles, there is a stop sign. KY 80 goes left. Keep straight ahead on U.S. 421 through Hyden.

Hyden's claim to fame is that it is the place where the Frontier Nursing Service (FNS), the first organized midwifery service in America, was founded in 1925 by Mary Breckenridge. She had had experience with midwifery services in France, England, Scotland, New Zealand, and Australia and came to Appalachia to offer her services. Mary soon realized that providing nursing care and midwifery services in this isolated area was of prime importance. Until that time, such services had been provided by the older women—the grannies—of the families. Unfortunately, their well-meaning attempts were based mostly on superstition rather than medicine. The old ways predominated in this roadless, isolated area and some of those ways included marrying young and having lots of children. Appalachia had one of the highest birthrates in the nation. In order to traverse the mountain country, the nurses of the FNS rode on horses or mules, often in darkness, rain, and snow to tend to their patients. Of course, all of this effort took money, so Mary became a fund raiser and publicist for the service. In addition, each family subscribing to the service was charged a small annual fee, much like our modern HMOs. A birth was extra, but it was a very small fee. Ten years after the founding of the service, a 12-bed hospital was built near Hyden. The hospital is now named the Mary Breckenridge Hospital and has a new Women's Health Care Center. Mary Breckenridge died in 1965.

After leaving Hyden, U.S. 421 goes through the small towns of Muncey Creek, Stinnett, and Mozelle. All along the way, there are great mountain views. At 69.6 miles, there are big patches of kudzu up on the left, and at 70.5 miles, the hillsides are covered with it. At 71.3 miles, there is a very big coal mine on the right. If you don't see anyone around, they are probably off eating deep-fried kudzu leaves. At 80.7 miles you will come to a Y. The right fork is KY 221, which goes back to Pineville. Take the left fork. This is U.S. 421 going to Harlan. Just before the junction you may see a large patch on the mountain to the left where it appears some kind of mining is taking place. Just after the Y, you will see that it is a very big limestone crushing operation. In fact, you will drive right through the middle of it. At 82 miles, there is a very steep and narrow road cut. There are lots of coal trucks on this stretch, so be careful on the curves. At 85.9 miles, there is a stop sign at the intersection with U.S. 119. Keep straight ahead on U.S. 421 for 4.1 miles to Harlan.

7

The Red River Gorge Loop
A Unique Geologic Area

General description: This 27-mile drive starts at Slade at the junction of KY 15 and KY 11 just off the Mountain Parkway southeast of Lexington. From there it follows KY 15 as it winds back and forth across the parkway to the small town of Pine Ridge. At Pine Ridge, it turns left onto KY 715 and climbs and twists through the Red River Gorge Geological Area past some of the most spectacular scenery in Kentucky.
Special attractions: Rock formations, Daniel Boone National Forest.
Location: East-central.
Drive route numbers: Kentucky Highways 77, 15, 715 .
Travel season: Spring through fall.
Camping: Campgrounds at Natural Bridge State Resort Park.
Services: Lodging is available at Natural Bridge State Resort Park. Cabins and bed and breakfasts are available at several locations in the Natural Bridge area. Restaurant at Natural Bridge State Resort Park.
Nearby attractions: Natural Bridge State Resort Park.

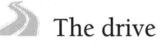 The drive

Most of this drive is in the Red River Gorge Geological Area, a land of natural arches, unusual vegetation and animal life, rock shelters, wooded mountains, and miles and miles of hiking trails. Fortunately for those who do not relish seeing their scenery on foot with a pack full of goodies on their backs, there is a good road through the area from which much of the beauty may be enjoyed.

Since most of the scenic beauty of the Red River Gorge is rock, it may be helpful to give a brief explanation as to what kind it is, how it got there, and how it got into the shapes it is in. First, all of the rock layers in the Gorge are sedimentary rock. Sedimentary rock, for those who have been out of school as long as we have, is simply rock that was formed by the deposition of mud, sand, organic material, etc., usually at the bottom of a lake or sea. The three types of sedimentary rock are shale, limestone, and sandstone. All three types are found in the Gorge, and all were deposited during either the Pennsylvanian or Mississippian periods. Both of these periods are a part of the longer Carboniferous period. The Pennsylvanian period occurred about 320 million years ago, and the Mississippian period at about

Drive 7: The Red River Gorge Loop

A Unique Geologic Area

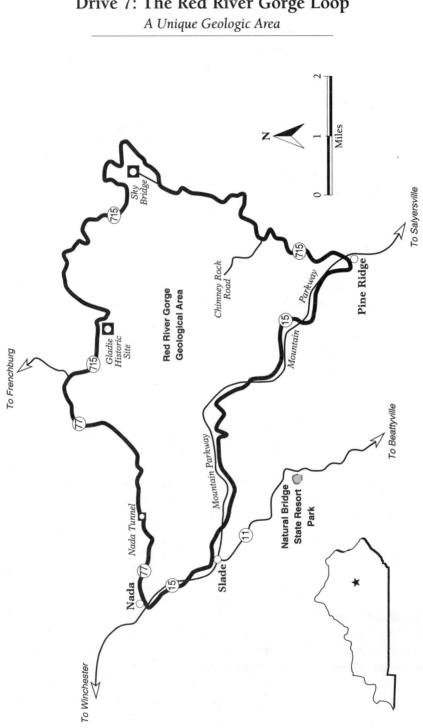

360 million years, give or take a month. At least several times during these periods, shallow seas, rivers, and swamps covered the area. When they dried up, deposits in the water settled to the bottom. After many such wet and dry cycles, the layers became very thick, and the weight of the whole mass compressed the bottom layers into rock. The materials in the deposits, of course, determined the type of rock. The shales, which are formed by clay-rich mud, are soft and erode very easily. Consequently, none of the arches is formed in the shale layers. Limestone is also formed in mud, but this mud, which is known as calcareous mud, contains a fairly high percentage of seashells. The limestone is much harder than the shale, but it is rather easily eroded by constant exposure to running water. Arches do form in limestone, and there are some in the Gorge. Finally, there is sandstone. The basic ingredient is, of course, sand. Sandstone in the Gorge contains, in addition to the sand, a number of pebbles. This is sometimes called pebble stone, and was laid down mostly in large river deltas, rather than in shallow seas. The cementing agent in this sandstone is limonite, which makes this stone particularly erosion resistant, and is the reason why many of the formations have taken shape. The softer layers below the sandstone erode away due to the action of rain, wind, and freezing, and leave the tough sandstone cap more or less intact. The Gorge is a geological wonder.

The first white men to come close to the Gorge showed up around 1750. One of them was Dr. Thomas Walker, the man who marked the

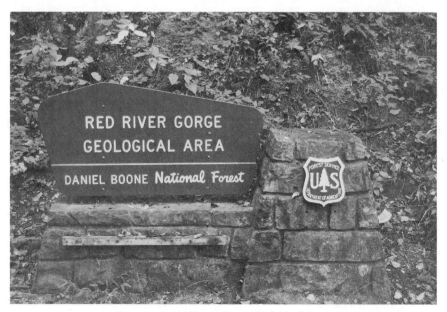

Entrance to Red River Gorge Geological Area.

Old log home at the Gladie Historic Site.

Cumberland Gap. Another was Daniel Boone. It is not known whether Boone ever entered the Gorge , but he and the others who came along made possible the eventual settling of the area. The rugged character of the Gorge did not lend itself to farming, but over the years a little mining took place and some serious logging pretty well removed the forests. Some of the trees were up to 8 feet in diameter and were more than 400 years old. Virtually all were cut down and either hauled or floated away.

Set your odometer at zero at the junction of KY 15 and KY 11 at Slade. Go east on KY 15 for 0.6 mile where the road passes over the Mountain Parkway. At 2.0 miles, you will be on a pretty stretch where the road winds uphill through the trees. At 2.7 miles you pass the junction with Tunnel Ridge Road. At 3.3 miles, you cross over the Mountain Parkway again. At 5.1 miles you pass over the Mountain Parkway once more. At 6.4 miles you will enter Pine Ridge. At 6.6 miles, KY 715 (the Sky Bridge Road) goes left. It is a little hard to see the junction coming up, so keep a sharp eye out. Go left on KY 715 and at 6.9 miles—you guessed it—cross over the Mountain Parkway one more time. At 7.1 miles you will see the sign for the Red River Gorge Geological Area. From here on, the road is narrow and without a center stripe or shoulders. It is good blacktop, though, and completely safe if you exercise reasonable caution.

At 7.3 miles, the road enters the Daniel Boone National Forest, and you will be in a canopy of trees. At 9.8 miles you will come to the junction with Chimney Rock Road. Chimney Rock Road is a narrow gravel road that runs about 4 miles to an overlook. There is a very nice view of the Gorge, but we felt that it was not really any better than the ones that can be seen from the blacktop road. If you don't mind 8 miles of gravel, you will also pass some trailheads and primitive campsites on the way to the overlook. The gravel is easily driven in a car. It is by no means a four-wheel-drive road.

When you are back at the junction of Chimney Rock Road and KY 715, go left on KY 715 and in 0.7 mile you will come to the parking area for the Wildcat Trailhead. Wildcat Trail runs for 1.3 miles to the Swift Camp Creek Trail. It is rated as a moderate hike, but there is an elevation loss of about 200 feet. Remember it is uphill on the way back. At 1.7 miles you will come to the parking area for the Angel Windows Trailhead and the Parched Corn Overlook. Angel Windows consists of two small arches, the larger of the two being about 5 feet high and 7 feet long. The hike is just a little more than 0.5 mile round trip. The overlook provides a view of the wooded valley below. It is not the most spectacular view in the Gorge, but it is right next to the road. On down the road, at 2.0 miles past the junction with Chimney Rock Road, is the trailhead for Swift Camp Creek Trail and Rough Trail. Swift Camp Creek Trail is rated as very strenuous. It is 7.6 miles long, and has an elevation loss of 300 feet. The section of Rough Trail that runs from

The Nada Tunnel, only 12 feet high and 13 feet wide, was built in 1911 as a railroad tunnel back in the logging days.

here to the Chimney Rock Road is rated as moderate to strenuous. It is only 1.8 miles long, but there is an area where you must drop down about 300 feet and then climb back up the road. At 2.5 miles, the parking area for the trailhead to Whistling Arch will appear. This arch is not spectacular, but it has one thing in its favor: it is only a 0.2-mile round trip from the parking area. The arch is about 11 feet long and 4 feet high, and it is actually an arch in formation. Come back after lunch to see if it has grown. At 2.6 miles, KY 715 makes a hairpin turn to the right and plunges downhill. Just before the turn, you will see a big sign pointing to Sky Bridge.

Go straight ahead on the Sky Bridge Road and you will see the turnout for Devil's Canyon Overlook. It is a short walk to the viewing area. In another 0.4 mile from Devil's Canyon Overlook is the parking area for the Swift Creek Overlook. At 3.4 miles, there is a turnoff to the right to the Sky Bridge Viewing Area. If you go straight ahead, you will enter the parking area for the Sky Bridge Hiking Trail. Just before entering the parking area, there are rest rooms on the left. If the area is crowded, you might want to park in the hiking trail area and walk to the viewpoints. If it isn't crowded, go right for 0.1 mile to the loop at the beginning of the walk to the viewpoint. The loop here is small. There is room for only two or three cars on the side of the road. You can walk the short distance and get some great, although distant, views of the big Sky Bridge Arch.

When you finish at the Sky Bridge area, retrace your route to the hairpin curve on KY 715. Go left on KY 715. At 4.7 miles from the Sky Bridge turnoff, you will see the turnoff to the Gladie Historic Site on the left. At the site, you can see a renovated cabin of the original owner of this land. In the stones used for the foundation of the cabin you can see seashell fossils. There is a barn with a good collection of early tools and machinery related to early farm life and the timber industry. Just beyond the meadow along Gladie Creek, there is a small buffalo herd. You will reach the junction of KY 715 and KY 77. Turn left on KY 77 and in 0.7 mile, the road makes a sharp left turn, crosses a silver-colored steel bridge, makes a sharp right turn, and climbs uphill through the trees. At 10.4 miles, there is a hairpin turn to the left and a steep climb uphill. At 10.8 miles, you will pass under a large overhanging rock and come to the entrance of the Nada Tunnel.

This interesting tunnel, only 12 feet high and 13 feet wide, was built in 1911 as a railroad tunnel back in the logging days. For those not expecting it, the tunnel comes as quite a surprise. Granted the road has been narrow, but not this narrow. After the tunnel, you will wind down through the trees to the little community of Nada at 12.8 miles. Sixty plus years ago, this was a thriving lumber town, but the lumber industry left and nothing took its place. It is about 0.3 mile to the junction of KY 77 and KY 11/15. Turn left on KY 11/15 and return to Slade. From here, you may want to go a few miles down KY 11 to Natural Bridge State Resort Park.

Looking up at Natural Bridge.

8

Cave Run Lake Loop
40-inch Muskies and Fall Color

General description: This 67.7-mile drive makes a long loop around 8,270-acre Cave Run Lake.
Special attractions: Fall color, National Scenic Byway, Pioneer Weapons Wildlife Management Area, Tater Knob Fire Tower, Hiking.
Location: East-central.
Drive route numbers: KY 211, 1274, 801; U.S. 60; Clear Creek Road.
Travel season: Fall is best, but spring and summer are also fine.
Camping: Campgrounds at many areas around Cave Run Lake and at the end of Zilpo Road.
Services: Motels and bed and breakfasts in Morehead. Restaurants and fast food in Salt Lick and Morehead.
Nearby attractions: Cave Run Lake and the northern part of the Daniel Boone National Forest are on or near the drive.

The drive

Cave Run Lake was authorized by the Flood Control Act of 1936 with the primary purpose of controlling the downstream flooding along the Licking River. Secondary uses were to help maintain water quality during low flow times on the lower Licking, to act as a water supply, and to provide recreational activities. It is now one of the best muskie fishing lakes around. Construction was begun in 1965 by the Louisville District of the Army Corps of Engineers, who designed, built, and still operate the dam. The lake became operational in February 1974, and since that time has been credited with preventing more than $68 million worth of flood-related damages.

Set your odometer at zero at the intersection of KY 801 and U.S. 60 west of Morehead. The maps call this area Farmers. Drive west on U.S. 60 for 3.6 miles to the junction of KY 211 and U.S. 60 in Salt Lick. Turn left on KY 211 toward Frenchburg. In just half a block, the road turns sharply back to the right. At 3.8 miles, the road again turns left and passes the Salt Lick post office. Within a block, it goes right again. At 4.5 miles, just outside of town, the road curves left and heads toward the hills. At 5.9 miles, the road is in the middle of a "bowl" of farmland surrounded by hills. The two-lane blacktop road has a double yellow centerline but with no shoulders. At 7.2

Cave Run Lake Loop
40-inch Muskies and Fall Color

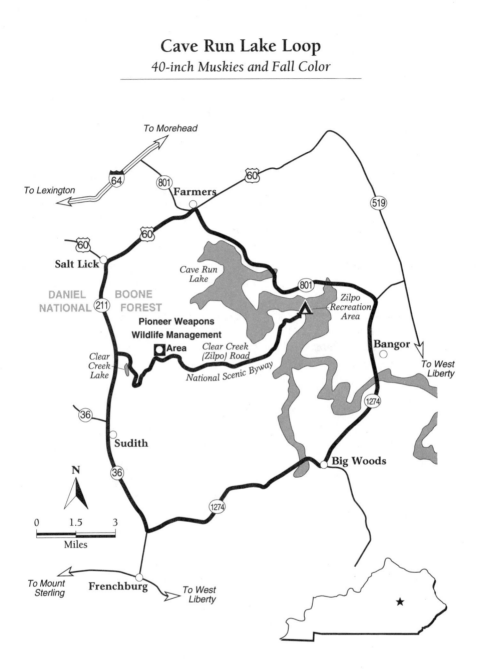

miles, Clear Creek Road goes left. Although the sign says Clear Creek Road, it is more popularly known as Zilpo Road, a National Scenic Byway. Some of the maps also list it as Forest Road 129. Whatever the name, you will be glad you drove it.

At 0.8 mile from the junction, you will pass the Clear Creek Store on the right. At 1.4 miles, the road enters the Daniel Boone National Forest. There is a nice view of Clear Creek Lake on the right at 1.5 miles. For the next few miles, the road wanders back and forth through walls of trees. There are not full canopies here, but just dense green walls. At 3.9 miles go left following the sign to the Pioneer Weapons Area and the Tater Knob Fire Tower. At 4.3 miles, there is a limestone wall on the right with trees growing out of it. The trunks are completely covered with vines. At 5.9 miles, you will be in the Pioneer Weapons Area. This unique area was created on 7,610 acres through a cooperative effort of the Kentucky Department of Fish and Wildlife Resources and the United States Department of Agriculture Forest Service. Although the land is developed and managed for multiple use, a major emphasis is placed on wildlife management. To encourage wildlife, meadows have been created and water holes have been developed. The white-tailed deer and the wild turkey have been brought back to the area, and are hunted here, as are squirrels, ruffed grouse, and woodcock. Hunting with modern breech-loading firearms is prohibited. Hunters must use muzzle-loading firearms, including shotguns and pistols, or bows or crossbows.

Muzzle-loaders include the flintlock, which was used by the pioneers in the time of Daniel Boone, and the percussion cap rifle, which was used in the Civil War. Use of these weapons requires a number of steps that are slow and cumbersome by today's standards. First, a measured amount of black powder is poured down the barrel. Then a lead bullet wrapped in a lubricated cloth patch is rammed down the barrel against the powder charge. When the trigger is pulled, a small amount of burning powder enters the barrel through a vent and ignites the rammed charge. In the flintlock rifle, this small charge is ignited by a flint striking steel, much like a cigarette lighter. In the percussion cap rifle, a small cap much like the primer in a modern shell does the igniting. Of course, bow hunters may use the area also. They use long bows, recurved bows, compound bows, and crossbows. The hunting area boundary is clearly marked with yellow signs and yellow marks on the trees.

Past the Pioneer Weapons Area at 8.5 miles is the turnoff to the Tater Knob Fire Tower. There is a blacktop road to a parking loop at the start of the trail to the tower, but every time we have been there it has been chained off. It is a very short walk, though, and it is in a beautiful setting. The trail from the parking loop to the tower is a little steep in spots, but we think it is worth it. You will have to decide whether to walk to the tower or not. After all, you can always turn around and go back. On the other hand, if you don't

Cave Run Lake from Zilpo Road.

go all the way, you'll never see a most beautiful view across the forested mountains, and you won't get a great photograph of this really interesting old tower.

The Tater Knob tower was built in 1934, three years before the Daniel Boone National Forest was established. The rugged terrain and poor roads made the job very difficult, but using mule teams, dynamite, and hand labor, the Civilian Conservation Corps built a 1.25-mile long road to the base of the cliff below the tower site. Until 1959, the 35-foot tower was home to the lookouts. A 14-by-14-foot cabin atop the tower housed a wood stove, two cots, a cabinet, storage box, small table and stool, an alidade, and the all-important telephone. When a fire was spotted, the lookout used the alidade, a plate with a protractor engraved with compass degrees to find the direction from his tower. He then called another tower, where the lookout would do the same thing. Where the directional lines crossed on the map was the location of the fire. By today's standards with airplanes, helicopters, and a global positioning system, this seems pretty primitive, but it worked and saved a lot of forestland.

In 1959, the old wooden tower was torn down and replaced with a metal one. The lookouts no longer lived at the tower, but walked to work up the trail each day. If you take the trail to the tower, you will appreciate this "walk to work." In 1993, the tower was restored and opened for public access. Tater Knob is the last remaining fire tower in the Daniel Boone

National Forest, and is listed in the National Historic Lookout Register.

Back on Zilpo Road, you will continue to twist and turn through the trees with occasional glimpses of Cave Run Lake. At 12.0 miles you enter the Zilpo Recreation Area, and at 12.4 miles you arrive at the entrance to the Zilpo Campground.

Retrace your route to the junction with KY 211. Turn left on KY 211 toward Frenchburg. At 1.2 miles from the junction, there are old, weathered barns and buildings on both sides of the road. You will pass through small communities and by some small farms until you come to a stop sign at the junction with KY 36 at 3.2 miles. Turn left on KY 36. This is a good two-lane, blacktop road with a double yellow centerline and white shoulder lines. There are no shoulders, but it is a good wide road. At 4.3 miles, you will pass Granny Byrd's Grocery on the right. We couldn't find a sign, but we believe that this is Sudith, a town first established as Carrington in 1890. In 1904, it was renamed Sudith after a state legislator from the area.

At 8.2 miles, go left on KY 1274. At 10.1 miles, there is another old collapsing barn on the right. At 11.1 miles, you will pass Hog Branch Road on the right. At 12.2 miles, you will enter the Daniel Boone National Forest. For the next 4 miles or so, you will run alongside a high limestone road cut on your left. In places there is a tall, heavy-duty steel fence to protect the road (and passing motorists) from falling rock. In one stretch, the road is moved a lane or two away from the cut for the same reason. Just as we were through the area, thinking that all of this must be overkill, we spotted a big pile of limestone partially on the road on the left. Let's have more overkill.

Just beyond this point, at 16 miles, the road curves to the right away from the cut and crosses an arm of Cave Run Lake. At 16.8 miles, there is a road cut through a limestone ridge. The cut is straight up on both sides and is right next to the road. It feels like being in a well. By 17.3 miles, the road has come out on top and is running along a ridge with houses on both sides of the road. This is the community of Big Woods. At 20.3 miles, the road drops down again through another steep-sided road cut. There is a great view through the notch of the mountains ahead. At 21.3 miles, you will cross a high bridge over another arm of Cave Run Lake. At 22.8 miles, a small store, a gas station, and a road down to the Bangor boat dock appear. At 23.9 miles, there is a beautiful view across the valley to the wooded mountains on the right. At 25.2 miles, you will come to the junction of KY 1274 and KY 801. Go straight ahead on KY 801.

This is a new, wide two-lane, blacktop road with a double yellow centerline, white shoulder lines, and wide shoulders. It immediately begins to curve downhill through the trees and through another of the many limestone road cuts. At 27.2 miles, there is a long view down the lake. At 29.1 miles, there are views of the lake in both directions. From here, for about 10 miles to the road across the dam, there are many boat ramps, fishing areas, picnic grounds, and campgrounds. At 29.5 miles, there is a pullout and parking for lake viewing at Longview Vista. At 30.4 miles, you will see the entrance to the Twin Knobs Recreation Area, where there are 216 campsites that accommodate everything from a tent to large RVs. The campground has modern rest rooms with showers, foot trails, boat ramps, a 2,000-foot beach, volleyball courts, and horseshoe pits. At 32.5 miles, there is a good view of the dam. In the next 2 miles you will come to the road to the visitor center, the Corps of Engineers Office, and the Minor E. Clark Fish Hatchery, one of the largest state-owned warmwater fish hatcheries in the United States. Largemouth bass, smallmouth bass, muskellunge, striped bass, and walleye are all grown here. The hatchery produces between three and four million fingerlings each year for stocking Kentucky's lakes, rivers, and streams. In just a little over a mile from the hatchery, you will be back at the starting point at the junction of KY 801 and U.S. 60.

9

Manchester to Berea
Along U.S. 421

General description: This 53-mile drive starts at Manchester which sits on U.S. 421 just off the Daniel Boone Parkway east of London. From Manchester, the road curves to the northwest through towns with such interesting names as Burning Springs, Egypt, Gray Hawk, and Clover Bottom until it reaches Berea.

Special attractions: Berea College, John B. Stephenson Memorial Forest State Nature Preserve, Daniel Boone National Forest.

Location: East-central.

Drive route numbers: U.S. 421, KY 21.

Travel season: Spring through fall is fine. Winter can be pretty if the roads are clear.

Camping: Campgrounds at Berea and McKee.

Services: Motels and bed and breakfasts in Berea, Manchester, and McKee. Restaurants and/or fast food are in Berea, Manchester, and McKee.

Nearby attractions: Levi Jackson Wilderness Road State Park (see Drive 10).

 The drive

The drive begins in Manchester at the junction of KY 80 and U.S. 421. Take U.S. 421 north through town. Just before the road enters the old part of town, there is a very high limestone cliff on the left. At 5.0 miles, the road is down in a hollow surrounded by tree-covered hills. At 5.8 miles, you will pass the post office at Fall Rock, a small community named for the falls on nearby Laurel Creek. At 6.9 miles, KY 11 goes right. Stay to the left on U.S. 421 and head toward Burning Springs. This small community was named for the natural gas wells in the area. They were first discovered around 1798, and the story is that one or more of them burned for many years.

For the next couple of miles, the road meanders through the wooded mountains. There are a number of unmarked and unnamed communities along the way. By 10.7 miles, the canyon has widened out and the views, especially to the left, are longer. In another mile, the canyon is even wider. The wooded mountains have moved back quite a bit. At 13.5 miles, you will pass Possum Trot Road. At 14.1 miles there is an old coal-loading chute. At 19.1 miles, the road enters Tyner. According to the map, between Tyner and

Manchester to Berea

Along U.S. Highway 421

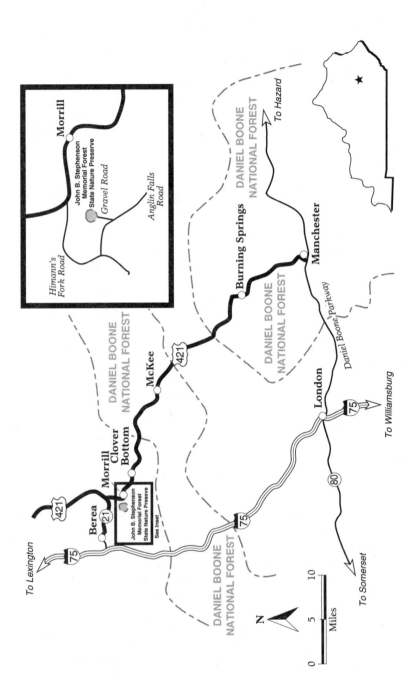

Burning Springs is Egypt. We didn't see any signs. Maybe the pyramids are hidden in the trees. All along U.S. 421 the road is mostly in the trees, but in most places they are not really close to the road, so the views are relatively unobstructed. It is a pretty drive. At 22.5 miles, you will enter Gray Hawk. It may have been named for the gray hawks in the area, or, as some old-timers tell it, the name came from two gentlemen named Gray and Hawk who owned the land at the time the post office was established.

At 26.2 miles, the road goes sharp left at the Jackson County High School. At 26.2 miles, there is a beautiful broad view off to the left. After winding downhill through the trees for a couple of miles, the road passes the city limits sign for McKee at 28.1 miles. In the middle of McKee, you will come to the junction of KY 89. Keep straight ahead on U.S. 421. At 30.1 miles, you will pass St. Paul's Catholic Church on the left. One of the buildings is sitting up on built-up stone pillars about six feet in the air. At 32.5 miles, the road leaves the Daniel Boone National Forest. At 33.8 miles, you pass through Waneta. At 36.0 miles the road crosses a small ridge as you enter Sand Gap. On each side of the ridge are houses sitting in the middle of beautiful lawns. At 37.3 miles, you will be in the center of Sand Gap, and at 37.6 miles, you will have left Sand Gap behind you. Beyond Sand Gap, the road meanders through rolling farmland and, at 39 miles, it passes a truss factory. Folks around here must do a lot of heavy lifting.

At 40.2 miles, you enter Clover Bottom, a little town named for the stream that flows through a rich limestone bottom with a heavy growth of clover. In about 3.5 more miles, you will arrive in Morrill. There is an interesting side trip to the John B. Stephenson Memorial Forest State Nature Preserve which starts about 0.2 mile beyond Morrill. Go left on Himanns Fork Road for about 4 miles to Anglin Falls Road. Go left on Anglin Falls Road for 1 mile and turn left onto a gravel road for a short distance to the preserve. Park on the right at the end of the road. The preserve is a 124-acre wooded gorge with two waterfalls. There is a beautiful wildflower display in the spring. It is a great spot for photography and bird watching. A moderate to strenuous mile-long trail leads to the preserve.

When you return to U.S. 421, turn left and continue the main drive. At 45.5 miles from the junction of KY 80 and U.S. 421 in Manchester, you will pass along a high ledge road. There is a very long drop-off to the right and beautiful long views across the valley to the mountains. There is a guardrail on the drop-off side. At 48.1 miles, go left on KY 21 toward Berea. In the next 4.9 miles, the road winds up the mountain through the trees, crosses a wide valley with great wide views and enters Berea at 53 miles.

Berea is one of the most unique communities in Kentucky. Back in 1850, the area was known as the Glade, and was just a conglomeration of farms. It differed from most of the surrounding areas in that most of the citizens were sympathetic to the abolitionist cause. Cassius Marcellus Clay,

The Berea College Log House Craft Gallery.

a politician and sometime abolitionist and one of Kentucky's more colorful figures, was eager to start a community in the Glade to use as a base for both his political ambitions and the abolitionist cause. In 1853, he persuaded John G. Fee to accept a free tract of land and to move to the Glade. Local supporters and missionaries from the American Missionary Association joined Fee and built a small village with a church and a school. He named the village Berea after the biblical town.

Under Fee, the village became the center of an abolitionist mission. It was never a major player in the movement, but it was enough of a burr under the saddle of the slave owners that they drove Fee and his supporters from the state. During the years of the Civil War, Fee, in exile from Berea, spent his time raising funds for the school he knew he would one day build. With the end of slavery after the war, Fee and some of his exiled followers returned to Berea and reestablished their interracial community.

When the Berea Literary Institute opened in January of 1866, the prevailing wisdom said that admission of black students would destroy the school, but during the last half of the nineteenth century, much of Fee's vision became a reality. By 1899, the school included primary, secondary, and college sections. The enrollment was almost 500, and about half of the students were black. The school actively recruited black students, the church welcomed black members, and the college even sold lots in the town on the condition that owners live next to a family of a different race. Former slaves were quick to take advantage of the opportunity for an education, and a large number of black graduates went on to have distinguished careers throughout the United States. The percentage of black-owned farms in the county was three times the state average, most black men outside of town owned their own farms, and only a small percentage of black women worked as domestic help.

Despite the obvious tremendous success of his experiment, Fee's vision was soon to pass into history. In 1904, the Kentucky legislature passed a law that forbade interracial education.With the passage of this law, the school turned its attention to poor whites from the mountains who had no other opportunities to get an education. The founders of the school had as one of their original goals to provide a complete education at the least possible cost. In the early years, a small tuition was charged, but by 1892, the finances were in good shape, and a student labor program was working well, so the tuition charge was eliminated.

Today, students at Berea College are responsible only for their room and board and personal expenses based on their ability to pay. No one who is accepted is denied an education, and, since 1917, each student is required to work at least 10 hours per week in one of the areas of the student labor program. There are more than 140 labor departments ranging from broom-craft, woodcraft, ceramics, weaving, and wrought iron to working in the cafeteria, the bookstore, Boone Tavern Hotel, the library, the Berea Hospital, academic offices, laboratories, or the computer center. Some students work as custodians, some work in the dormitories, and some work as tutors in the adult literacy program.

Works of the students are on display and for sale in the Log House Sales Room. Some of the finest woodworking you will see anywhere can be found here. Everything from pens to fine furniture is on display. Of course, many other crafts from ceramics to quilts may be found here, too. One of the most prominent examples of student participation in the labor program may be found at the famous Boone Tavern Hotel. The hotel was built, originally as a guest house, in 1909 under the direction of William G. Frost, the president of the college from 1892 to 1920. He acted on the urging of his wife, Nellie, who had been given the unenviable task of entertaining 300 guests of the college in the summer of 1908. Today, after a number of renovations over its 90 years of operation, the hotel boasts 59 air-conditioned rooms furnished with Early American reproduction furniture and other items from the college's crafts programs. It is still owned by the college, and 80 percent of the staff is made up of students in the Student Labor Program.

You should not miss The Appalachian History Museum in town. It is operated by the college and contains thousands of objects, photographs, and volumes of printed material on the southern Appalachian region. Could there be a more fitting place to visit after a beautiful drive through the mountains?

10
Williamsburg to Levi Jackson Wilderness Road State Park

Through the Mountains to McHargue's Mill

General description: This 46.5-mile drive begins in Williamsburg on KY 92 just east of Interstate 75, and winds its way along KY 92 through some great mountain scenery to Barbourville. Here is the site of the first Civil War skirmish fought in Kentucky. This is also home to a museum and the Dr. Thomas Walker State Historic Site. North of Barbourville, KY 229 picks its way through mountains and farmland to Levi Jackson Wilderness Road State Park.

Special attractions: Knox Historical Museum, Dr. Thomas Walker State Historic Site, Levi Jackson Wilderness Road State Park.

Location: East-central.

Drive route numbers: KY 92, 11, 229; U.S. 25E.

Travel season: Spring and fall are best.

Camping: Campgrounds at Levi Jackson State Park, London, and Williamsburg.

Services: Motels in Williamsburg, Barbourville, and London. Restaurants and fast food in Williamsburg, Barbourville, and London.

Nearby attractions: Big South Fork National River and Recreation Area, Big South Fork Scenic Railway, Blue Heron Mining Community, Cumberland Falls (see Drive 17).

The drive

We begin this drive at Williamsburg, the county seat of Whitley County, which, as was the town, was named for one of Kentucky's more famous Indian fighters, Colonel William Whitley. The town was established as the county seat in 1818. In 1819, the post office was established as Whitley Court House. In 1882, the name was changed to Williamsburgh. The "h" was dropped in 1890.

There are a number of things to see in Williamsburg before hitting the road, including Cumberland College. A student-guided walking tour of the campus may be arranged by contacting the reservation desk (see appendix). The college also owns and operates the Cumberland Museum. The museum, which opened in 1992, houses a number of very interesting collections.

Drive 10: Williamsburg to Levi Jackson Wilderness Road State Park

Through the Mountains to McHargue's Mill

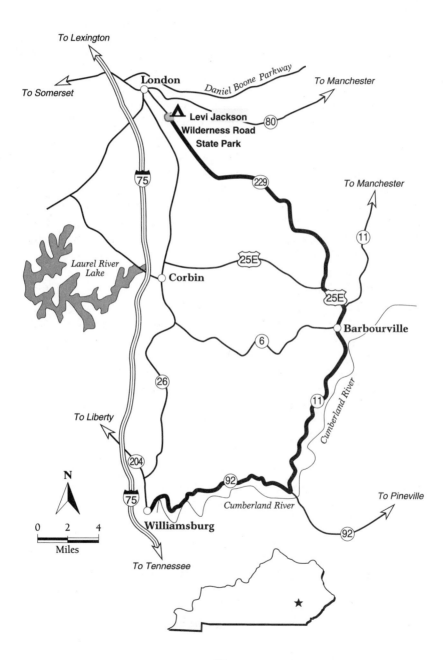

To Lexington

To Somerset

London

Daniel Boone Parkway

To Manchester

Levi Jackson
Wilderness Road
State Park

80

75

To Manchester

229

11

Laurel River
Lake

25E

Corbin

25E

Barbourville

6

Cumberland River

26

11

To Liberty

204

92

To Pineville

N

Cumberland River

92

0 2 4

Miles

75

Williamsburg

To Tennessee

The Henkelmann Life Science Collection contains specimens ranging from the tiny short-tailed shrew to a giant polar bear that Henry and Mary Henkelmann gathered on their world wide expeditions. The museum also houses an exhibit of the Appalachian life style. Displays include furniture, tools, glassware, spoons, stamps, coins, thimbles, prints, Lincoln memorabilia, and a Norman Rockwell plate collection.

About halfway through this drive, you will come to Barbourville, the county seat of Knox County. The town was named for James Barbour, the man who donated the land for the first county court house. You can visit the Dr. Thomas Walker State Historic Site just 5 miles south of Barbourville on KY 459. Dr. Thomas Walker discovered and marked the Cumberland Gap. There is a replica of Dr. Walker's cabin, a picnic area, a gift shop, and more. See the appendix for where to write for more information.

The drive begins at the junction of U.S. 25W and KY 92. Head east on KY 92. For the first couple of miles or so, you will be paralleling the Cumberland River. At 2.3 miles from the junction, the road makes a sharp curve to the left and starts to climb past a high cliff with tall trees on the top. The road is two-lane blacktop. There is no shoulder, but there is a guardrail on the right. At 3.9 miles, there is another sharp left turn. The road is still climbing and there are occasional long views of the mountains framed by the trees. At 5.5 miles, there is a broad view over the mountains to the right and rolling fields to the left. At 9.1 miles, you will enter Louden.

At 10 miles, you will cross a bridge and be treated to a great, long view down across the valley and the rolling hills. Just beyond the bridge, the road climbs into a deep canopy of trees. By 10.6 miles, you will be out of the canopy of trees. The road is still good two-lane blacktop with no shoulders, but the guard rails are there when necessary. At 12 miles you arrive at Mossy Gap and a pretty white church on the left. At 12.4, you will find the junction with KY 11. Go left on KY 11 toward Barbourville. At 15.0 miles, there are hills to the right and a broad view of the distant mountains to the left. By 16.2 miles, you will be back in walls of trees on both sides of the road. The road wanders back and forth through the mountain scenery, and at 21 miles, ducks back into the tree canopies again. At 21.7 miles, you will find yourself on top of a little hill with a long view of the mountains and a shorter view of a beautiful brick home on a knoll a hundred yards or so from the road. At 23.3 miles, KY 3441 goes right. There is a big elementary school on the right. Just past the school, there is a beautiful view of the tree-covered mountains in the distance. At 24.5 miles, you will come to a stop sign in Barbourville.

Turn right at the stop sign, staying on KY 11 heading north. At 24.9 miles, you will come to the junction of KY 11 and U.S. 25E. Go left on U.S. 25E/KY 11 (the Cumberland Gap Parkway). At 25.6 miles, KY 11 goes right. Stay on U.S. 25E. At 28.5 miles, go right on KY 229. This junction comes up

A relaxing day at Levi Jackson Wilderness Road State Park.

McHargue's Mill at Levi Jackson Wilderness Road State Park.

suddenly, so don't get so engrossed in the beautiful scenery along the parkway that you miss it. You will follow KY 229 all the way to the end of the drive. For the first 4 or 5 miles, the road winds through mountain meadows with long views to the left. At 32 miles, you will pass the "Big Daddy and Son" store on the right. For a few miles after the store, the road climbs up into the mountains. There are some big views along the way. At 40.5 miles, you pass through a small town. We didn't see a sign, but we believe this is Boreing. This small hamlet was originally called Camp Ground after a religious meeting place that existed here long ago. The town was not named after its lack of excitement, but for Vincent Boreing, a local school superintendent in the late 1800s. For the next 5 miles or so to the entrance to Levi Jackson Wilderness Road State Park, you will be treated to beautiful views to both the left and the right. At 45.6 miles, the entrance to the park goes off to the left.

It was on the grounds of what is now Levi Jackson Wilderness Road Park that the worst pioneer massacre in Kentucky history took place. On the night of October 3, 1786, a party of about 30 people including the McNitt, Ford, and Barnes families and their servants from Virginia had camped by a spring. Some time during the night, a band of Chickamauga Indians raided the camp and killed and scalped 21 persons. In addition, they took five women prisoners and stole all of the cattle, horses, and belongings.

There is a story that a woman hid in a hollow tree and gave birth to a baby during the night. The story continues that she was found the next day and reunited with her husband, who had escaped. The story of this tragic affair is found in the history books as the McNitt Defeat. A memorial to the party was established in the park.

There is much to be seen in this beautiful and peaceful park, but our favorite is the McHargue Mill. This working replica of the original gristmill stands on the banks of the Little Laurel River in stands of beech and poplar. The mill with its pond and trees is a favorite spot for photographers. The curving walkway to the mill is lined with the largest display of old millstones in the country.

You can camp in one of the 146 sites surrounded by stately oaks. There are utility hookups, a grocery store, a dump station, and three central service buildings with rest rooms, showers, and laundry facilities.

Hikers have a unique treat at this park. There are 8.5 miles of trails that retrace portions of the old Wilderness Road and Boone's Trace. If you would like to walk in the footsteps of the early pioneers, then Levi Jackson Wilderness Road State Park is your spot.

11

Mount Vernon to Winchester
Spectacular Scenery along KY 89

General description: All driving in Kentucky is scenic, but some drives are better than others. This 89.5-mile drive is one of the best. It begins in Mount Vernon and winds along about 8 miles of pretty scenery along U.S. 25 to Livingston. Here it traverses a short stretch of KY 490 to KY 89, which it follows the rest of the way. Part of KY 89 is designated as a Kentucky Scenic Byway. You will see canopies of trees, creeks, farms, rolling bluegrass hills as well as several mountain towns.

Special attractions: Kentucky River.

Location: East-central.

Drive route numbers: U.S. 25; KY 490, 89

Travel season: Fall would be number one, with spring a close second. Summer would be fine, but winter on those narrow stretches might be hazardous.

Camping: Campgrounds at McKee and Renfro Valley.

Services: There are motels at Winchester, Irvine, McKee, Mount Vernon, and Renfro Valley. Bed and breakfasts can be found at Winchester and Renfro Valley. Restaurants and fast food in Winchester, Irvine, McKee, Mount Vernon, and Renfro Valley.

Nearby attractions: Fort Boonesborough State Park, Red River Gorge Area (see Drive 7), Daniel Boone National Forest.

 The drive

The drive begins just south of Mount Vernon on U.S. 25 where it passes under I-75. Set your odometer at zero here and drive southeast on U.S. 25 toward Livingston. For the next 6.7 miles to the Livingston city limits, you will travel through rolling hills with nice views to both sides. Just past the city limits sign at 7.0 miles, KY 490 goes left. This junction appears suddenly, so be on the lookout. After the sharp left, you will cross a concrete bridge over some railroad tracks. At the end of the bridge, you will reach a T intersection. KY 1955 goes left and KY 490 goes right. Stay on KY 490 to the right. Just a few miles south of here, at Wildcat Mountain, the earliest major battle of the Civil War took place.

KY 490 meanders along, past homes and by rolling farmland until, at 12.9 miles, it makes a very sharp turn to the right and passes the Pleasant

Drive 11: Mount Vernon to Winchester

Spectacular Scenery along KY 89

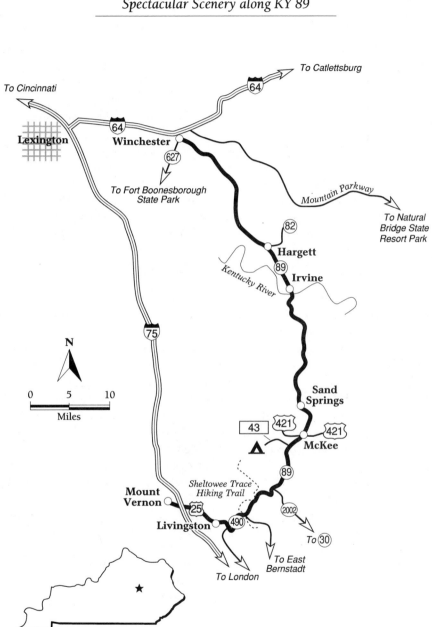

Run Baptist Church on the left. At 14.4 miles, it reaches the junction of KY 89. Turn left on KY 89 and you will see a sign for the start of a Kentucky Scenic Byway. The Sheltowee Trace hiking trail crosses the road at the junction.

Sheltowee means Big Turtle in the Shawnee language, and is the name that the Shawnee Chief Blackfish gave Daniel Boone when he was adopted into their tribe. Over the more than 200 years since Daniel Boone walked the trail, countless other explorers and adventurers, including John Muir, have retraced Boone's steps. Today, anyone can do the same along this more than 250-mile National Recreation Trail. The trail was built by a partnership between the government and volunteers and was dedicated on June 23, 1979. It begins in Pickett State Park, Tennessee (only the initial ten miles of the trail are in Tennessee), and ends near Morehead, Kentucky. Along the way, hikers will see the Big South Fork of the Cumberland River, Daniel Boone National Forest, Cumberland Falls, Natural Bridge State Park, and the Red River Gorge area. About 10 miles from the end of the trail at Morehead, Sheltowee intersects the Jenny Wiley Trail that runs north to Portsmouth, Ohio, or south to Jenny Wiley State Resort Park. If you have the time, energy, and inclination, you can walk from Tennessee to Ohio.

Continue north on KY 89, and as soon as you pass the Scenic Byway sign, you will see why this stretch of road was awarded the designation. You will start into the first of many canopies of oak and beech, but you will also be on a very narrow road. It is good blacktop, but it has no center stripe and no shoulders. At times the road is barely more than one lane, and there are several blind curves. Drive with care, and you will have no problems, but if you are late for an appointment in McKee, don't go this way.

At 17.0 miles, you will come to a one-lane bridge. There is a dirt road going left, which makes a good place to pull over and park. You can get nice pictures of the bridge, the stream, and the beech and oak canopy over the road looking south. If you walk down the dirt road, you will see many of the oak, beech, sycamore, sweet gum, and poplar trees that cover the whole area from the beginning of the drive all the way to McKee. When you are ready to go, cross the bridge and continue north. At 19.2 miles there is a curious site on the left side of the road. It is a roofed-over barbecue that looks a little like a pagoda. The curious part is that there are no tables or benches, and there is no place to park. Maybe you can figure it out. At 23.2 miles, you will come to the junction of KY 2002 going right. From the map, this looks like it might make a nice side trip.

Just beyond the junction, there are wide fields to the right and trees on the left. At 23.6 miles, the road curves to the left, and on the right you will see a house and barn and, down below, a church. Beyond this point, the road makes a shallow "S" past a little house and a barn on the left. At 27.5 miles there are a picturesque house and barn on a hillside to the left. A few

Along KY 89 north of Livingston.

tenths of a mile beyond here, you will pass by (and under) a big sand and gravel operation. There is a conveyor going over the road and you can see two tunnels back into the mountain. At 29.5 miles, there is a turnoff on Forest Road 43 to the S-Tree National Forest Campground. For the next few miles you will still see nice mountain scenery, but you will also see more and more signs of civilization. At 32.9 miles, you will cross a bridge and enter McKee.

Go right onto KY 89 at the junction of KY 421 and KY 89. In half a mile, KY 89 goes left. This spot is a little confusing, since the sign makes it look as though you go another block to the traffic light to turn. If you miss the turn, don't despair. You can go to the light, turn left, and go around the block back to KY 89. McKee is not Manhattan. Out of McKee to the north, the road gets wider as do the views. The drive along this half of KY 89 is much different from the first half. It is very pretty, but in a different way. The views are wider, the trees are farther back from the road, and it passes more signs of civilization. At 43.0 miles, there is a long view to the left across a wooded valley as you enter Sand Springs. By 45.5 miles, the road narrows some and drops down through a canopy of trees. At 47.3 miles, the road swings to the right and crosses a concrete bridge over a creek. In another mile, you will be back in a canopy of trees in a dip in the road. This is a beautiful spot. In about a mile, you will pass Uncle Joe's General Store on the left.

Winchester's claim to fame: Ale-8-One.

Just beyond the store, there are beautiful, long views as far as you can see both to the right and to the left. In about a mile, you will have views looking up at the mountains through the trees and more views of the distant mountains across the valley. There was also a turtle in the road, but he may be gone by the time you get there. At 60.7 miles, you will cross the high steel bridge over the Kentucky River and enter Irvine, the county seat of Estill County. Irvine was founded in 1812 on 20.5 acres of land owned by General Green Clay. It was named for Colonel William Irvine who had been wounded in the hand-to-hand fighting at the Battle of Little Mountain near the site of present day Mount Sterling. In this battle in 1782, Captain James Estill, for whom the county was named, and seven others in his group of 25 frontiersmen were killed by Wyandot (Wyandotte) Indians. The battle is commonly called Estill's Defeat.

Continue north on KY 89. At 5.9 miles from the high bridge, you will arrive at the junction of KY 82 and the town of Hargett. On down the road at 10.6 miles, a steel bridge crosses a small grassy meadow. We suspect that in wet weather this may be quite a stream. At 15.4 miles, the road passes through Trapp. The name is rumored to have come from the array of animal traps that hung in the store housing the post office. Where the second "p" came from is anyone's guess. By 18.0 miles, the scenery has become rolling blue-grass hills with some tree-covered hillsides. At 26.5 miles, you will come to a traffic light at the junction of U.S. 60 in Winchester.

For history buffs, there is a lot to look over in Winchester, but if you have been driving on a hot day and are thirsty, you may want to investigate one of Winchester's more modern claims to fame: Ale-8-One. This soft drink in the bright green bottles and cans is a Winchester treasure, and the taste is something that is hard to describe. To some, it is a little like ginger ale, while to others, it is closer to 7-UP. You will just have to try one and see for yourself. Back in the 1920s, a gentleman by the name of G. L. Wainscott conceived the formula for the drink. Since he didn't have a name for it at hand, he had a name-the-drink contest. We don't know the name of the winner, but the name of the drink, "Ale-8-One - A Late One," has hung on for a long time. The bottling plant in Winchester has been here since 1926, and until recently was the only one. The drink now comes in both plastic (ugh!) and aluminum (yuk!). True Ale-8-One aficionados will tell you that only the green bottles have the true taste.

If you have a little extra time, you might want to take a short drive down KY 627 to Fort Boonesborough State Park. This interesting park is built on the site of the original Boonesborough, which was established in 1775 by Daniel Boone and Richard Henderson. It served as a stopping point for the traffic on the Kentucky River for more than 50 years, but declined as the need for a fort lessened after peace had been established with the Indians and the British. By 1820, it was no longer a town. Early in the twentieth century, it was used for a time as a mineral spring resort.

If you visit today, you will see a reconstructed fort with blockhouses, cabins, and furnishings of the period. Various artisans live on site and give demonstrations of pioneer crafts with eighteenth-century antique tools. You can also enjoy a campground, gift shop, or a museum tour, get in a little fishing, launch your boat on the river, play some miniature golf, have a picnic, or just take a walk along the river while drinking an Ale-8-One.

12

Jackson to Richmond
Along KY 52

General description: You will begin this 67-mile drive in the mountain town of Jackson, wind along KY 52 through the mountains, pass through Beattyville and Irvine, and end at historic Richmond.
Special attractions: Daniel Boone National Forest, Breathitt County Museum (Jackson); Richmond is a treasure chest of Kentucky history.
Location: East-central.
Drive route number: Kentucky Highway 52.
Travel season: Spring and Fall are prettiest, but any time of year would be nice.
Camping: There are campgrounds at Richmond.
Services: Motels in Beattyville, Jackson, and Richmond. Restaurants and fast food in Jackson, Beattyville, Irvine, and Richmond.
Nearby attractions: White Hall State Historic Site, the Battle of Richmond site, the Hummel Planetarium, and Bybee Pottery.

 The drive

Jackson, the county seat of Breathitt County, lies on the North Fork of the Kentucky River at the junction of KY 15 and KY 30. It was founded in 1839 on 10 acres of land that had been donated by Simon Cockrell, Sr. Until 1845, it was known as Breathitt after the county, but supporters of former president Andrew Jackson persuaded the citizens to rename the town.

In the very early years, the isolation of this area was such that little contact with the rest of the state was possible. This isolation was so pronounced, that the WPA Guide to Kentucky states that ". . .its inhabitants retained for many years the customs and peculiarities of speech of their English ancestors." In the early days, the major industry was the making of salt. We tend to forget the importance of salt in the days before refrigeration and canned goods, when salt was the only means of preserving food. The area around Jackson was blessed with many "licks," which are just brine springs. Of course, salt was essential not only for preserving meat, but a part of basic nutritional need for both humans and animals. The animals that came to the licks provided a ready food source for the citizens of Jackson.

The extracting of the salt from the brine was relatively simple. A large

Drive 12: Jackson to Richmond
Along KY 52

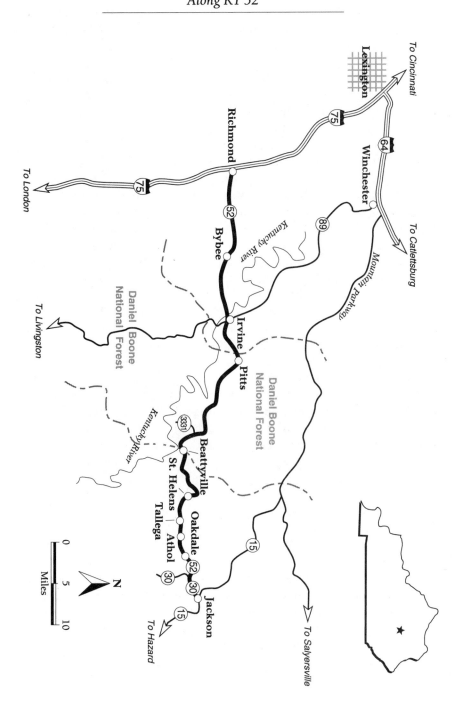

pot was filled with the brine and boiled dry. The clumps of salt remaining were broken up into crystals and sold. As more people came into the region, this method of reducing the brine could not keep up with the demand. At this point, human ingenuity took over, and wells were drilled to get a greater source of brine.

To look around Jackson today, it is hard to imagine that it was once the county seat of "Bloody Breathitt," also known as the "Feud County." Family feuds were common in the period during the end of the 19th and beginning of the twentieth century. By the early 1900s, somewhere in the vicinity of 150 people had been killed in the Breathitt County feuds.

We just can't move along until you've read this story of early Breathitt County. It may or may not be true, but it certainly is fun to contemplate. It seems that back in the early 1800s, a gentleman by the name of Jeremiah Lovelace professed to being a prophet and having both supernatural and divine powers. He assured those who would follow him that he could perform miracles, heal the sick, restore sight, relieve pain, and walk on water. This last boast proved to be his undoing. Although he did "prove" some of his powers before an audience, there were those who took his claims with more than a grain of salt. In fact, some of them would not have believed him with a whole bushel of brine salt. They would not be convinced until they saw him walk on water. To prove his claim, Jeremiah the Prophet made an appointment to meet the doubters at Frozen Creek one evening in the following week. (No, he didn't walk on frozen water. The name of the creek was just a coincidence.) Jeremiah spent a bit of time fashioning some lumber into three trestles each about 10 feet long, which, when placed in the creek, would be about six inches under water. On top of each, he laid a plank and ran the whole works toward the middle of the creek.

Unknown to him, some of the town boys spied on his labors, and when he left, they removed the middle plank. At the appointed time, a crowd had gathered to watch the Prophet perform. He was outfitted in a long, flowing white robe. After a short prayer and encouraging the crowd to sing a familiar hymn, he began his walk. No doubt the crowd was in awe for the first 10 feet, but when he stepped into the gap where the second plank should have been, his water walking days came to an abrupt, wet, and undoubtedly humiliating end. History makes no further mention of Jeremiah the Prophet.

If you have an interest in Kentucky history, drop in at the office of *The Kentucky Explorer* at 1248 Highway 15N in Jackson. This magazine is published 10 times a year and is filled with historical tales of Kentucky.

To begin the drive, go to the north end of town to the junction of KY 30 and KY 15 and set your odometer to zero. Drive west on KY 30 for 1.5 miles to the junction of KY 52. Go right on KY 52, cross the bridge over the

Lindon Fork of Cane Creek and enter Elkatawa. The post office here was established in 1891. Local lore says that the town was named by the railroad, which had reached the area in 1890, but just why they would have chosen such a name is a mystery. The story is that the name came from Tenskwautawa, the brother of Chief Tecumseh. This was supposed to have been corrupted to Ellskwatawa and then to Elkatawa. That sounds like a lot of corruption.

For the next few miles, the road runs down a little hollow with wooded hillsides on both sides of the road. On the right, the railroad tracks sit on a shelf part way up the hillside. At 4.5 miles, there is a rugged limestone road cut on the left. At 4.7 miles, you will pass through Yeadon, and at 5.4 miles, you will pass through Chenowee. At 6.1 miles, there is an unusual building on the left. The bottom half of it is made of railroad ties, and the top is vertical barn wood. At 6.4 miles, you will pass Oakdale. Here, the road is still running parallel to the railroad tracks. At 8.0 miles, the hollow widens out, the road crosses the railroad tracks, and there are fields on both sides of the road. At 9.0 miles, there is a modern brick house with a collapsing barn on either side of it. The road still parallels the railroad track, but the track is now on the left. At 10.2 miles you will enter Athol.

At 13.6 miles, the road passes under a modern railroad bridge, and in another mile, you will see a high limestone wall on the left. At 15.5 miles, there is a high wall of trees to the right and a little meadow off to the left. At 16.3 miles, the road makes a horseshoe turn to the right, and you will have a long view across the valley to the left. Just past the horseshoe turn, you will pass through a canopy of trees. At 18.2 miles, you will drive through St. Helens, and in less than half a mile, you will cross a bridge over the middle fork of the Kentucky River. At 20 miles, the road curves downhill past a wall of trees on the left and the middle fork of the Kentucky River on the right. About a half mile farther, there is an old cabin disappearing into the vines and undergrowth. At 22.5 miles, you will enter Beattyville. The name was from Samuel Beatty who arrived in 1843 and is given credit for founding the town. In 1870, he donated the land for the new county seat.

At Beattyville, keep to the right on KY 52 and cross the high bridge over the middle fork of the Kentucky River. At 22.7 miles, KY 52 goes left. At 23 miles you will pass the Beattyville post office on the left. Just past the post office, the road ducks under a railroad bridge, and at 23.9 miles, it makes a sharp right turn followed by a sharp left turn and begins a climb into the trees. At 24.1 miles, there is another sharp right turn followed by a steep climb. At 25.5 miles you will be at the top of the hill, and the land flattens out and KY 3331 goes left.

At 27.9 miles, you will come to a few houses and a pretty white church on the left. In the next couple of miles, you will pass rolling bluegrass fields, some homes, another church, and a small unmarked community. At 31.5 miles, the road winds downhill through the trees. The road is good two-lane blacktop with a double yellow centerline, white shoulder markers, and guard-rails where necessary. At 36.1 miles, there is a pretty meadow downhill and to the left, and at 38.0 miles there are several very old buildings on the left disappearing into the undergrowth. In less than half a mile, there is a beautiful farm over to the left against the hills. This is a good picture possibility. At 39.2 miles, KY 975 goes north to a rather amazing piece of nearly forgotten history: the Fitchburg iron furnace.

When most people think of Kentucky, they think of the Kentucky Derby, coal, tobacco, and— maybe—moonshine, but they don't think of iron. Yet at one time, Kentucky was one of the largest producers of iron in the United States. When one realizes what is needed to make iron, it is logical that Kentucky would have fit the bill. It had iron ore, which could easily be strip-mined, limestone for removing impurities, and forests to make charcoal to fuel the furnaces.

By 41.5 miles, you will be winding through Pitts. At 42 miles, you pass a sand and gravel operation, and by 45.5 miles, you will be in Irvine (see Drive 11). It is just 20 miles from Irvine to Richmond, and this stretch of KY 52 is an excellent road.

In 9 miles from Irvine, you will come to one of Kentucky's most visited spots. In the little town of Bybee, you can visit Bybee Pottery, the oldest existing pottery west of the Alleghenies. For more than 100 years, the old log building has contained the equipment and business of the pottery. Folklore says that it was established in 1809, but even if this is not accurate, actual sales records show that it has been a thriving business since 1845. Visitors are welcome to watch the whole process Monday through Friday. See the appendix for where to write for more information.

When you finish at Bybee, continue on down KY 52 for another 11 miles to Richmond. Here you will be in one of Kentucky's oldest cities. First established in 1784, Richmond was named by Colonel John Miller, a veteran of the Revolutionary War. It was not the Revolutionary War, but the Civil War that left indelible marks on Richmond. The Battle of Richmond was one of the most fiercely fought battles of the war and was the first Confederate victory in Kentucky.

It is estimated that of the 5,650 men killed in the Battle of Richmond, 4,900 were in the Union forces and 750 in the Confederate. If your interest has been tweaked, you can take a self-guided driving tour of the battle area. (See the appendix for further information.)

You might also want to go to the campus of Eastern Kentucky University and rub the foot of the Daniel Boone statue for luck. Located at Eastern Kentucky University is the Hummel Planetarium, one of the largest and most sophisticated planetariums in the country, and the second largest planetarium in the world located on a college or university campus. (See the appendix for further information.)

Or if you are interested in something more down to earth, you could just wander around downtown and visit some of the 65 buildings on the National Register of Historic Places. If you have seen all that you wish of Richmond, you might want to head either up or down Interstate 75 to some of the other drives. There is still a lot of Kentucky to be seen.

13

Georgetown/Maysville Loop
Rambling through the Bluegrass

General description: The 115.6-mile drive begins in the historic city of Georgetown and follows U.S. 460 through some beautiful bluegrass country to Paris. Here the drive heads north along U.S. 68, the old "Buffalo Trace" toward Maysville. Along the way is the Blue Licks Battlefield State Park and the town of Old Washington, which is now on the National Register of Historic Places. Just before Maysville, the drive heads back south on U.S. 62. It winds through tunnels of trees that reach out to touch each other across the road as it passes Mount Olivet and Cynthiana, where a famous Civil War battle was fought.

Special attractions: Georgetown antique shops and historic buildings, Blue Licks Battlefield.

Location: North-central.

Drive route numbers: U.S. Highways 460, 68, 62.

Travel season: Any time spring through fall is good.

Camping: Campgrounds in Maysville, Blue Licks Battlefield State Park, and Lexington.

Services: Motels are plentiful in the area. Good ones can be found in Lexington, Georgetown, Paris, Mount Olivet, Maysville, and Cynthiana. Bed and breakfasts are available in Georgetown, Paris, Maysville, Cynthiana, and Lexington. Restaurants or fast food in Lexington, Georgetown, Paris, Maysville, Mount Olivet, and Cynthiana.

Nearby attractions: Kentucky Horse Park (Lexington), Kincaid Lake State Park, Mason County Museum, the Underground Railroad Museum, Double Stink Hog Farm. (If you visit the area in the fall, you can attend the Double Stink Pumpkin Festival.)

 The drive

Our drive begins in historic old Georgetown, the county seat of 286 square-mile Scott County. Although humans have inhabited this area for at least 15,000 years, our more modern ancestors did not show up until the late 1700s. In 1774, a surveyor named John Floyd, who was with a party scouting land for French and Indian War veterans, found the famous Big Spring in what today is Georgetown. He named his find Royal Spring and remarked that "the spring is the largest I have seen in the whole country, and forms a

Drive 13: Georgetown/Maysville Loop
Rambling through the Bluegrass

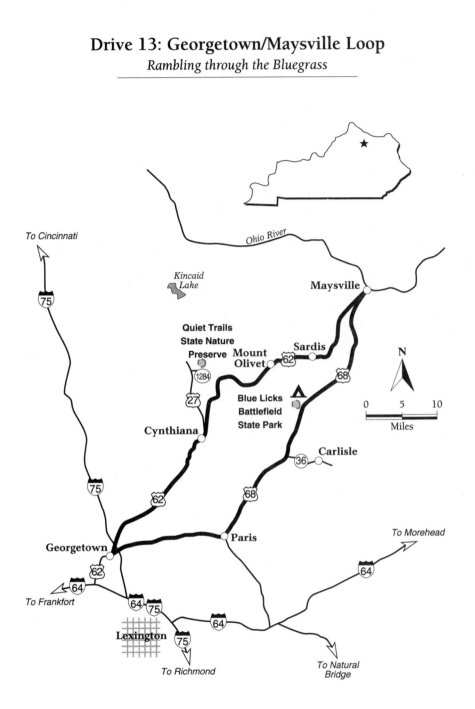

To Cincinnati

Ohio River

Kincaid Lake

Maysville

Quiet Trails State Nature Preserve

Mount Olivet

Sardis

75

1284

27

68

62

N

0   5   10

Miles

Blue Licks Battlefield State Park

Cynthiana

Carlisle

36

75

62

68

To Morehead

Georgetown

Paris

64

62

64

To Frankfort

64   75

64

To Natural Bridge

Lexington

75

To Richmond

creek in itself." Floyd claimed 1,000 acres at the spring, but he never settled there. It is generally thought that the first permanent settlers were the John McClelland family from Pennsylvania who bought the land from Floyd and built a cabin on the site around 1776.

The area around the spring was pretty much ignored until some time around 1782 or 1784, when Reverend Elijah Craig, a preacher from Spotsylvania County, Virginia, who, by some accounts, had been jailed for preaching without an Episcopal license, arrived with some members of his Baptist congregation to found a settlement he called Lebanon. The town was incorporated in 1784 and was renamed George Town after George Washington in 1790. In 1846, the name was officially changed again to the present Georgetown.

Mr. Craig was evidently something of an entrepreneur. Between sermons, he seems to have found time to establish a school that would be absorbed by Rittenhouse Academy, which would in turn be absorbed by Georgetown College. He also built a sawmill, a gristmill, a fulling mill, a paper mill, and the first ropewalk in Kentucky. As if this weren't enough, he grew hemp, and, according to many, developed the first bourbon whiskey using corn, rye, barley malt, and, of course, water from the spring. It is interesting to note that in the place where bourbon was invented, none is made today. Scott County is dry.

Be sure to visit the spring while you are in Georgetown. It is in a small park just off Main Street near Water Street and College. It is not only pretty to look at, but a truly historic site that has been providing water for this area since 1775.

To begin the drive, head for the east side of town, and set your odometer at zero at the point where U.S. 460 crosses over Interstate 75. Continue east on U.S. 460 toward Paris. Between Georgetown and Paris, you will pass a number of beautiful horse farms with fencing and cross fencing, great barns, and lots of rolling fields of bluegrass. At 7.9 miles, there is a four-way stop at the intersection with KY 353. Keep straight ahead on U.S. 460. At 11.0 miles, the fence on the left has been replaced by hedge. There are lots of great bluegrass views. At 12.3 miles, you will be in a canopy of trees, but there is no undergrowth, so you will still have nice views of the bluegrass between the trunks. At 14.0 miles, you will come to the intersection with U.S. 68 and U.S. 27. At this point, you will need to make a decision. If you would like to go into Paris and look around, stay straight ahead on U.S. 460; you can pick up U.S. 68 in town and go north toward Maysville. If you choose to bypass town, go left at the intersection on U.S. 68/27. At 14.4 miles, U.S. 27 goes left to Cynthiana, and U.S. 68 goes right toward Maysville. Stay on U.S. 68 to the right.

If you decided to look around Paris, there is a lot to see: the Eiffel Tower, the Seine, and the Mingua Brothers Beef Jerky processing plant. Oh

A fine old home in Georgetown.

well, we just couldn't resist one little Paris joke. Seriously, if racehorses happen to be one of your interests, then this is the area for you. The Claiborne Farm is probably most famous for Secretariat, a Triple Crown winner. Other Kentucky Derby winners from Claiborne were Johnstown in 1939, Jet Pilot in 1947, Swale in 1984, and Ferdinand in 1986. Stone Farm is home to Derby winners Gato del Sol in 1982 and Sunday Silence in 1989. Dust Commander, winner of the 96th Kentucky Derby in 1970, called Golden Chance Farm home.

Around 1822, a young man on a break from Washington College taught school for a short time in Paris. He later went on to be president of several colleges and universities, but he is much better known for a series of books he wrote that revolutionized education in America. William Holmes McGuffey wrote the famous McGuffey Eclectic Readers that sold more than 125,000,000 copies. For this major contribution, he was paid a total of $1,000.

If you bypassed Paris, continue on U.S. 68 to a stop sign at 16.8 miles. This is the junction of U.S. 68 and the U.S. 68 Bypass. If you visited Paris, take U.S. 68 north out of town to the point where the U.S. 68 bypass comes in from the left. Continue north on U.S. 68. At 2.2 miles from the junction of U.S. 68 and U.S. 68 Bypass, you will see the Paris Stockyards on the right. This is a center for hog and cattle sales, and, if the wind is right, you may know you are approaching it even before you see it. At 5.2 miles, there is a pretty limestone fence on the left. At 6.9 miles, the road crosses a bridge over Hinkston Creek and enters Millersburg, a small town named for Major John Miller who founded the town in 1798 on 100 acres of his farm. At 8.2 miles, there is a long view of the rolling bluegrass fields to the left. At 10.9 miles, U.S. 68 makes a sharp left turn. KY 36 goes straight ahead to Carlisle a couple of miles away.

If you enjoy old homes and buildings and would like to get a sense of Kentucky life in the 1800s and early 1900s, you might want to take the short side trip to Carlisle. Here you will find a small town with 350 buildings on the National Register of Historic Places. Among the many structures on Main Street is the 1893 courthouse, which features the original tin ceiling in the courtroom. There are also many old churches with stained-glass windows.

After you have seen Carlisle, head back to U.S. 68 and turn right toward Blue Licks. At 13.2 miles look to the left at the ostrich and emu farm. One can only imagine what Daniel Boone would have thought about this. At 17.1 miles, you will enter Ellisville. James Ellis, a Revolutionary War veteran, established Ellis's Station here sometime before 1782. He built a log stagecoach station and a tavern on the site. The town was born in 1805 and declared the county seat. In 1816, the county seat was moved to Carlisle since it was closer to most of the population of the area. At 19.8 miles, you will cross a high bridge over the Licking River. There is a picturesque group of houses down the hill and to the left. In less than a mile, you will be at the entrance to Blue Licks Battlefield State Park. The Battle of Blue Licks was the last battle of the Revolutionary War in Kentucky.

Long, long before it was a battleground, Blue Licks held an important place in the lives of such diverse groups as prehistoric mammoths, American Indians, frontiersmen, including Daniel Boone, and nineteenth century spa lovers. The salt springs provided that needed mineral for centuries of animals and humans. Indians once captured Daniel Boone while he was operating a salt works at Blue Licks. In the 1800s, the licks were used as a health resort. Over the course of history, the salt was undoubtedly more important, but it is the Battle of Blue Licks that draws our attention to the area today.

The park offers cottages, a 51-site campground, a museum, a pool, a miniature golf course, picnic areas, and, of course, a gift shop. It will soon have a lodge. There are two main hiking trails, the Buffalo Trace Trail and the River Trail. The park is also home to Short's Goldenrod, a wildflower endemic to Kentucky that is a federally listed endangered species. If you have the time, you can wander among the oaks, elms, dogwood, and redbud trees or picnic in one of the provided areas.

When you leave the park, go left on U.S. 68 toward Maysville. For the next few miles, the road winds through nice open lightly wooded hills. By 7.8 miles, the view has widened out, and there are rolling hills of bluegrass all the way to the horizon on both sides of the road. In the next few miles, you will pass two turnoffs to the historic town of Mays Lick. At 15.4 miles, you will pass through a high limestone road cut. The walls are on both sides of the road. In a couple of miles, there will be two turnoffs to Old Washington (see Drive 15). At 18 miles, you will reach the junction of U.S. 62 on the left. You turn left here to return to Georgetown, but you might want to go on to Maysville for supplies or lunch. If you have the time, you might want to take Drive 15 before you head back.

Begin the return to Georgetown at the junction of U.S. 68/62 and head south toward Mount Olivet. At 9.0 miles from the junction, there is a three-way stop. Go right on U.S. 62. At 12.5 miles, you will be in Sardis. At 17.3 miles, there is another stop sign, where you will go right on U.S. 62. In just 0.4 mile you enter Mount Olivet. The name is of biblical origin, but how and why it was named seems to be a mystery. In any case, the town was founded somewhere around 1820, was incorporated in 1851, and designated the county seat of the newly formed Robertson County in 1867.

Beyond Mount Olivet, the road twists and turns past beautiful views of rolling wooded hills to the right. All along this part of the drive, you should look for oak, osage orange, and canopies of locust. By about 40 miles, you will enter Cynthiana. Keep a sharp eye out for highway signs, since U.S. 62 zigs and zags through town. It isn't really difficult, but there are a number of right and left turns to watch for. As you wind through this pretty, peaceful town, it is hard to imagine that this was the site of the Civil War Battle of Cynthiana.

At dawn on June 11, 1864, General John Hunt Morgan approached Cynthiana with 1,200 troops. The Union forces consisted of only 300 men of the home guard and the 168th Regiment of the Ohio Volunteer Infantry under the command of Colonel Conrad Garis. Morgan surrounded the town and attacked the Union forces at the covered bridge. The Confederates drove the Union troops back toward the depot and north along the railroad. The Confederates then set fire to the town. As the fighting continued in Cynthiana, about 750 men of the 171st Ohio National Guard under the command of General Edward Hobson arrived on the train at Kellar's Bridge north of town. Morgan's men trapped this force in a bend of the Licking River and, after a brief battle, forced them to surrender. Morgan had taken about 1,300 prisoners. At dawn on June 12, General Stephen Gano Burbridge with 2,400 men from Ohio, Kentucky, and Michigan, attacked Morgan's troops and drove them back into town where many were either killed or captured. The estimated casualties were 1,092 Union and 1,000 Confederate, though the battle was listed as a Union victory.

That sad chapter in America's history is long behind you as you follow

U.S. 62 across the bridge over the South Fork of the Licking River at the south end of town. At 1.5 miles from the bridge, you come to the junction of U.S. 27. If you would like to spend a pleasant hour or so hiking, bird watching, or just relaxing in a peaceful part of the bluegrass region, head right on U.S. 27 to the Quiet Trails State Nature Preserve. To reach the preserve, take U.S. 27 north for about 10 miles to KY 1284. Go right on KY 1284 to Sunrise. After passing through the four-way intersection, go straight ahead on Pugh's Ferry Road for 1.8 miles. There is parking for four cars on the right. In the preserve is a great diversity of trees, wildflowers, birds, and 3.1 miles of moderate hiking.

It is hard to leave Quiet Trails, but Georgetown awaits. Head back to Cynthiana and turn right on U.S. 62. At 8 miles from the junction of U.S. 62 and U.S. 27, you will pass through Leesburg, a town that has been here since the 1790s. At 9.7 miles you will see another great weathered barn. From here to Oxford, you will pass some nice views and go through some more beautiful tree canopies. At 13.2 miles, you will go through Oxford and enjoy bluegrass views for a couple of more miles until you come to a traffic light at about 14.8 miles. U.S. 62 goes left here past the Toyota plant. If you have a reservation, you can take a tram tour of the plant. If you don't, see the appendix for information on where to write. In about 3 miles, you will be back in Georgetown.

14

Covered Bridge Tour
History with a Roof

General description: This 85-mile drive will take you to four of the best covered bridges in Kentucky that are still standing.
Special attractions: Covered bridges.
Location: North-central.
Drive route numbers: KY 11, 32, 1895, 158, 111, 57, 984; Cabin Creek Road.
Travel season: Spring and fall are best, though summer is fine, too.
Camping: Campgrounds in Maysville.
Services: Motels in Maysville, Flemingsburg, and Morehead. Restaurants and fast food in Flemingsburg and Tollesboro.
Nearby attractions: Old Town of Washington, Mason County Museum, Underground Railroad Museum.

The drive

Our drive begins in Flemingsburg, a town founded in 1797 that has many buildings on the National Register of Historic Places. Set your odometer at zero at the junction of KY 32/57 just west of Flemingsburg. Drive south on KY 32. At 1.0 miles, KY 11 joins KY 32. Continue south on KY 32/11. At 3.3 miles, KY 32 business route goes left. Keep straight ahead on KY 32/11. At 4.1 miles, KY 11 goes off to the right to Hillsboro. Keep straight ahead on KY 32. At 8 miles, there is an especially pretty view of a tree-covered hill straight ahead. At 8.8 miles the first of our covered bridges appears on the left. This is the Goddard Bridge, one of the few covered bridges still open to traffic. Most have either become unsafe due to time, weather, and neglect, or stand on roads that are no longer used. In the early 1900s, there were about 400 covered bridges in Kentucky, and one can only imagine how many there were before the Civil War when raiders burned bridges by the score. By 1924, only 200 still existed. In 1952, there were only 43 left, and today there are only about a dozen still standing. There are a number of types of construction for wooden bridges. The earliest designs were the kingpost, the queenpost, and the multiple kingpost. No other designs of any merit appeared from the 1500s to 1797 when Timothy Palmer patented a combined kingpost and arch design with an arched roadway. He used this general

Drive 14: Covered Bridge Tour
History with a Roof

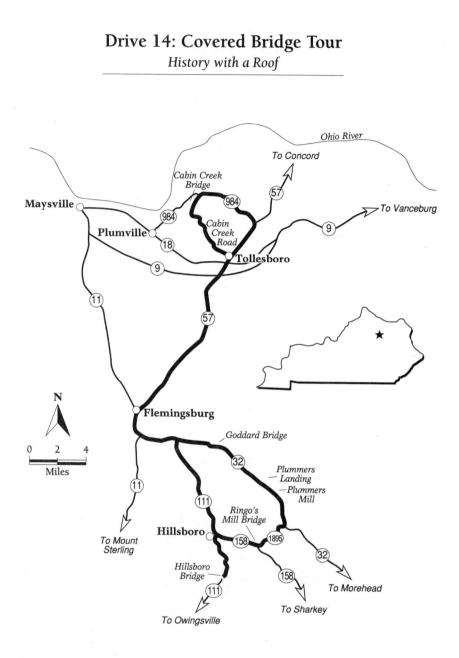

plan for the country's first covered bridge, which was built in Philadelphia in 1805. Just one year earlier, Theodore Burr patented a similar design using the combined arch and kingpost, but with a level roadway. About 1812, Lewis Wernwag built a bridge named The Colossus that used a double arch with flared kingposts.

In 1820, Ithiel Town designed a unique bridge with lattice-like trusses resembling a garden trellis. Finally, Colonel Stephen H. Long developed a truss made up of a series of boxed Xs in each panel. Three or more panels were needed to complete the truss. William Howe copied Long's design, but used an iron rod in the wooden trusses. His design became the favorite of the railroads. While any of these designs would make a very nice and dependable bridge, the alternating effects of rain, snow, and hot sun could rot the timbers and reduce the life of a bridge to 10 or 15 years. This is where the covered bridge stepped in and saved the day. Contrary to myth, the covered bridge was not developed for lovers. Nor was it built to protect travelers from the weather. Quite simply, wooden bridges were covered to protect the main timbers from rot, and many covered bridges have stood with only routine maintenance for more than 100 years. Most of the lost bridges were torn down to make way for concrete ones or were destroyed by storms, fire, vandalism, and/or floods. (For a more complete discussion of bridge construction, see the appendix for the Kentucky Covered Bridge Association.)

The Goddard Bridge is built on Ithiel Town's lattice design and is the only one of this type left in Kentucky. The exact date of construction is not known, but this type of truss was patented in 1820. It was restored after a fire some years ago, and steel supports have been placed under it. For the

A sign notes the historical significance of covered bridges near the Hillsboro Bridge.

The Goddard Bridge is one of the few covered bridges still open to traffic.

photographer, the most important thing about this bridge is its location relative to the little white church down the road. If the light is right, you can get a great picture of the church framed in the opening of the bridge. Remember, however, when you are taking photographs that the bridge is open to traffic. When you finish admiring the bridge, you might want to go across KY 32 and look around the craft store you find there. It is filled with the work of local artisans.

Continue the drive by heading south on KY 32. At 3.3 miles from the Goddard Bridge, there is a pretty view ahead and to the right of a wooded valley with houses and weathered barns. At 4.1 miles, a road goes left to Plummer's Landing. At 5.1 miles, you will enter Plummer's Mill.

At 9.5 miles, turn right on KY 1895. Keep a sharp eye out for KY 1895; it is easy to miss. After the turn, you will pass some nice homes, make a very sharp right turn, and begin climbing. By 10.2 miles, you will be over the top of the hill and dropping down through the trees. In the next mile, you will pass a couple of ponds and barns. For the next 4.7 miles, you will twist and turn through canopies of trees while dropping down hill. At 14.9 miles, you will come to a stop at the junction of KY 158. When we were there last, the 158 sign was missing, but trust us, that's what it is. Turn right and drive 0.3 mile to the Ringo's Mill Bridge.

Ringo's Mill Bridge was built over Fox Creek in 1869–70. The creek, by the way, was named for a man named Fox who had fallen into the creek and drowned long before the bridge was built. The 81-foot span is a multiple kingpost truss design.

To reach the Hillsboro Bridge, continue north on KY 158. At 18.6 miles, you will come to a stop sign at the junction of KY 158 and KY 111 in Hillsboro. Turn left on KY 111. Within a mile, you will be treated to a beautiful long view to the left across the valley to the distant wooded hills. At 19.8 miles, the road will curve to the left and expose even more long views as the road continues to dip and curve. There are very few trees along here, just undulating fields of bluegrass. At 21.4 miles, the Hillsboro Bridge will appear on the right. Hillsboro, which is sometimes referred to as the Grange City Bridge, is almost a twin of Ringo's Mill. The 86-foot span is also a multiple kingpost truss design and it crosses Fox Creek just as Ringo's Mill does. In the 1930s, the wood shingle roof and the horizontal wood siding were replaced with galvanized steel. The bridge was retired from service in 1968 after 100 years. In 1984, the badly rusted roof and siding were replaced with white oak planking and a new metal roof. If you look, you will see a water line mark left by the big flood in 1997. Many homes in the area were washed away and many lives were lost in this flood. It is amazing that the bridge has only a high water mark to show for it.

Now head back north on KY 111 to Hillsboro. At 2.8 miles from the bridge, you will be back at the junction of KY 158/111. Continue along KY

An inside look at the Cabin Creek Bridge.

111 through the rolling farmland. At 7.6 miles, you will be in Poplar Plains, a settlement that dates back to sometime before 1792. The original settler, William Pearce, wanted the settlement to be named Pearceville, but he was outvoted by those who wanted The Poplar Plains after the nearby grove of yellow poplars. The name was subsequently shortened to Poplar Plains.

Beyond Poplar Plains, there are long views of the rolling hills all the way to the horizon. At 10.2 miles, you will come to the junction with KY 32. Go left toward Flemingsburg. For the next 3 miles, you will be treated to great views of the hills in all directions. At 13.3 miles, you will come to the junction with the KY 11 business route to the right. Take the business route into town. At 14.0 miles, you will come to a traffic light in Flemingsburg. Go left on KY 11. In 0.1 mile, there is another traffic light at the junction with KY 57. Go right on KY 57. Just after you turn, you will see the old courthouse sitting right in the middle of the road. Fortunately, someone thought to build a road around it, so just swing around it and continue on along KY 57.

In the next few miles, you will see a big white church on a knoll to the left and a big home and farm buildings down in a valley to the left. At 27 miles, you will come to Tollesboro. At 27.4 miles, you will come to the intersection of KY 57 and KY 9. Continue straight ahead across KY 9 to the junction of KY 57/10. Turn left on KY 57/10, travel a couple of blocks and turn right on KY 57. There is a big white church on the corner. For the next 5 miles or so, you will pass through some beautiful farmland and rolling hills. At one point, you will drive along a ridge with a spectacular view of rolling farmland and wooded hills to the left. At 33.4 miles, you will come to the junction with KY 984. Go left on KY 984. Within several miles you will pass houses, farms, wooded areas, old barns, and great views of rolling farmland. At 39.7 miles, you will see the Cabin Creek Bridge on the left on Cabin Creek Road.

The Cabin Creek Bridge was built in 1867 and has a 114-foot-long span with a multiple kingpost truss design. Iron tension rods were added in 1914, and structural steel was added to reinforce the trusses in the 1970s. A new road bypassed it in 1983.

To return to the twentieth century, you have two options. If you continue on along the Cabin Creek road, you will wind along past farms and rolling land for about 5 miles to the junction with KY 57. Turn right on KY 57 for 2 more miles and you will be back in Tollesboro. If you continue on along KY 984, you will wind through more pretty farmland for 1.7 miles to the junction with Springdale Road. Go left on Springdale Road for just under 2 miles to the junction with KY 10 in Plumville. Turn right on KY 10, and in about 6 miles you will be in Maysville.

15

Dover/Walcott Covered Bridge Loop
Ohio River Country

General description: On this 45-mile drive, you will begin in Maysville and follow the Ohio River west through Augusta to Wellsburg. At Wellsburg, the drive drops southeast to Brooksville, then heads back east through Germantown to Maysville. Along the way, it passes two covered bridges. The first of the bridges is at Dover and is just 0.1 mile off the highway on a local road. It is a very pretty bridge and is one of the few that is still in use. A little farther on, just south of Wellsburg, is the Walcott Bridge.

Special attractions: Covered bridges, Ohio River.

Location: North-central.

Drive route numbers: KY 8, 1159, 10.

Travel season: All year.

Camping: Campgrounds at Maysville and Kincaid State Park.

Services: Motels in Maysville. There are several bed and breakfasts in Augusta. Restaurants and fast food in Maysville, Augusta, Brooksville, and Germantown.

Nearby attractions: Close to or on the drive route are the towns of Old Washington and Maysville, Mays Lick, the Mason County Museum, the Underground Railroad Museum, and Kincaid Lake State Park.

The drive

This drive begins in the old Ohio River town of Maysville, which lies where Limestone Creek flows into the Ohio. This drive will take you past some more nice scenery and to two more covered bridges. Set your odometer at zero at the junction of KY 8 and Bridge Street in Maysville. Follow KY 8 west past some great old buildings. As you leave the downtown area, there are some more old houses on the terraced hillside to the left. At 3.2 miles, there is a very old house on a hill to the left. At 5 miles, you will see the Spurlock Power Plant on the right. At 5.6 miles, you will pass under a new, green railroad bridge. This is probably for the trains carrying coal to the power plant.

For the next 5 miles or so, you will enjoy the trees on both sides of the road and occasional views of the Ohio River to the right. At 10.6 miles, a sign points to the right to Dover. It is a little difficult to see, so be on the

Drive 15: Dover/Walcott Covered Bridge Loop
Ohio River Country

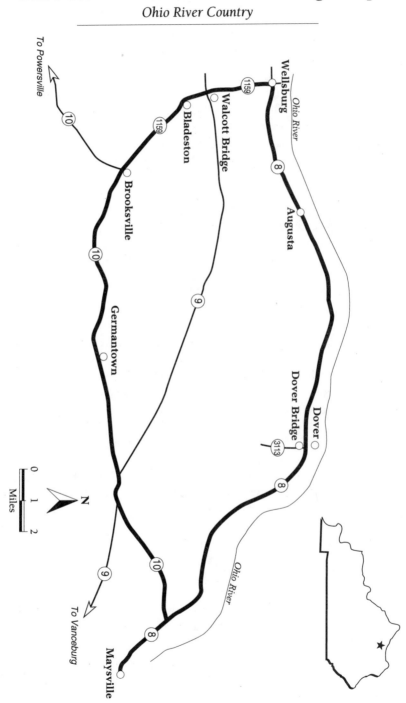

lookout. You have to go back about a third of a mile to the bridge, but it is almost impossible to see the turn when you are driving west. As long as you are on the road to Dover, you may as well drive through town and get a look at the river. There is an interesting tobacco barn on the west side of the road behind the church.

To get to the Dover Bridge, drive back toward Maysville on KY 8 for 0.4 mile. A road goes right at this point. There was no sign when we were there, but it is KY 3113. There is a historical marker next to a tree at the junction, but it, too, is hard to see. Go right on KY 3113 for 0.1 mile to the bridge. The Dover Bridge is one of the oldest remaining in the state. The 63-foot long span is of modified queenpost truss design and was built in 1835. This 1835 bridge replaced an even earlier bridge that had burned. The Dover Bridge was also originally a toll bridge. By 1965, the bridge had deteriorated to the point that it was touch and go as to whether it would be torn down and replaced with a new concrete or steel bridge. The Kentucky Covered Bridge Association (see the appendix) was instrumental in saving the bridge. It was rebuilt, and in the early 1980s, steel beams were added to the underside to withstand the traffic loads. This is one of the old bridges that is still open to traffic. The load limit is 11 tons.

From the Dover turnoff, head west toward Augusta on KY 8. For the next 5 miles, KY 8 follows the Ohio River, and you will get broken views of the river through the trees. At 5.0 miles, the road turns away from the river a bit, then tops a rise at 5.7 miles where you will get a great view across the river to the wooded hills in Ohio. At 6.3 miles, you will come to the city limits sign for Augusta, a pretty, old Ohio River town. Augusta was part of a large Revolutionary War Grant assigned to Captain Phillip Buckner by the state of Virginia. He selected 600 acres for the town and put it on sale at public auction in 1795. The purchasers petitioned the Kentucky legislature for the right to establish a town named Augusta. The name may have come from the Virginia county that at one time covered all of what is now Kentucky. It is said that the town was built on an old Indian burial ground.

The name Kentucky brings forth images of racehorses, tobacco, coal, and whiskey from moonshine to fine bourbon; but, to most of us, it does not impart an image of wine. We can picture the rolling hills of bluegrass. We can see fields of corn, but it is hard to imagine vineyards on the rolling hills. Such was the case, though, in Bracken County in the 1870s. In fact, at one time, Bracken County was one of the leading wine-producing regions in the United States, furnishing half of the entire national production of wine. The rolling hills reminded the German immigrants in the area of the Rhine River country in their native land. Their dreams of making Bracken County the "Rhineland of America" were dashed by some disastrous winters, a tornado, and crop blight. At the junction of KY 8 and KY 19, you can see an old winery, a reminder of days gone by and dreams gone awry.

The Dover Bridge.

Although Augusta did not play a major role in the Civil War, there was a Battle of Augusta. It is hard to find in the history books, and takes some digging, but it is there. It seems that in September 1862, a group of General John Hunt Morgan's Confederate raiders under the command of General Basil W. Duke attacked the Union Home Guards under the command of Colonel Joshua T. Bradford. Duke's plan was to take the town and then cross the Ohio River and march to Cincinnati. Bradford's men holed up in the many brick houses and fought a valiant battle, but they were overpowered and finally surrendered. Two gunboats that had been stationed on the river to protect the town saw the Confederate cannons pointing at them and decided to take a river cruise somewhere out of range. Duke's was a Pyrrhic victory, however, for, since he had lost so many men in the fierce fighting, he was unable to proceed.

Augusta's fame is not limited to past centuries. It is the boyhood home of TV and movie star George Clooney, and it was the site for the Saint Louis scenes in the mini-series *Centennial.* Many other films were shot here, including *Huckleberry Finn* and Neil Simon's *Lost in Yonkers.* You can spend many delightful hours in Augusta, but you won't think you are in Yonkers, and you won't get lost. If you are longing to see what's in Ohio, you can take one of the few remaining ferries across the river. Hurry back, though, since we have to get on to the Walcott Bridge.

To get to the Walcott Bridge, go west on KY 8 at the junction with KY

19 and wind through the trees for a couple of miles where you will see a high limestone cliff on your left. At 2.6 miles, the river appears back on the right. There are broken views of the river through the trees. At 4.3 miles, the road bends to the left and there is a nice view of the river to the right. At 5.9 miles, you will come to the junction of KY 1159. Turn left and start winding uphill toward Brooksville. At 7.5 miles, the road drops down and you have a fine view of the hills. At 7.6 miles, you will come to a stop sign. Go left on KY 1159. At 8.6 miles you will be at the junction of KY 1159 and KY 9. You will also be at the Walcott Bridge. The bridges we have seen thus far have been in more peaceful settings than the Walcott Bridge. They were usually well off the beaten track and, in summer, were covered with shrubs and vines. The Walcott Bridge is only a stone's throw from the AA highway, which is the next best thing to an interstate in this area. It is a pretty bridge, but it seems as out of place as King Kong on the Empire State Building. The span over Locust Creek is 74 feet, and it is a combination of kingpost and queenpost truss design. It was built in the 1880s and probably replaced a similar bridge that was built much earlier. The bridge was bypassed and abandoned in 1954 when KY 1159 was realigned.

If you are in a hurry, you can just go left on KY 9 and drive back to Maysville, but our way is a lot prettier, if a little slower. From the bridge, cross KY 9 on KY 1159 and head south. In just a mile from KY 9, you will come to a stop at the junction with KY 1011 in Bladeston. As you pass the junction, you will be treated to some beautiful views of tree-studded hills to the left and rolling bluegrass-covered hills to the right. At 3.7 miles, you will enter Brooksville, the county seat of Bracken County. At the junction of KY 19 and KY 10 in town, go straight ahead on KY 10 toward Germantown. After about 6.5 miles of rolling farmland, farmhouses and barns, and generally pretty rural scenery, you will come to Germantown. In 1794-95, a group led by Whitfield Craig laid out Germantown on 320 acres. It was settled by Pennsylvanians of German descent and was incorporated as Germantown in 1795. Beyond Germantown, you will traverse about 4 miles of rolling farmland until, at 14.7 miles, you come to the junction with KY 9. Go right on KY 9 and enjoy the 4 miles or so back to Maysville.

16

Frankfort to Florence

The State Capital to Big Bone Lick, with a Sidetrip to Rabbit Hash

General description: This 128.5-mile drive begins in Frankfort, Kentucky's capital, visits a town with the unlikely name of Rabbit Hash, and ends in Florence at I-75. From Frankfort, the drive heads northwest through Campbellsburg to Milton on the Ohio River north of Louisville. From Milton to just beyond Warsaw, a distance of 30 miles or so, the road follows the river. At Beaverlick, it heads northwest, makes a semicircle to Rabbit Hash, and goes on across the Boone County Scenic Byway to Florence at I-75.

Special attractions: Rabbit Hash, Big Bone Lick State Park. (Big Bone Lick State Park has bones of prehistoric animals that used to congregate at the salt licks at the end of the last Ice Age.)

Location: North-central.

Drive route numbers: U.S. 421, 42; KY 36, 338, 536, 18; Riddles Run Road.

Travel season: All year.

Camping: Campgrounds in Frankfort, Carrollton, Rabbit Hash, and Big Bone Lick State Park.

Services: Motels in Frankfort, Carrollton, and Florence. Bed and breakfasts can be found in Frankfort. Restaurants and/or fast food in Frankfort, New Castle, Bedford, Carrollton, Warsaw, and Florence.

Nearby attractions: Old Governor's Mansion, the Old State Capitol, General Butler State Resort Park, The Floral Clock in Frankfort, the Frankfort Cemetery, Dinsmore Homestead near Florence, Curtis Gates Lloyd Wildlife Management Area.

The drive

The drive starts in the beautiful city of Frankfort, tucked into a lush valley on big loops of the Kentucky River. White men visited this picturesque spot as early as 1751.

The Old Capitol Building has been the home of the Kentucky Historical Society since 1920. Extensive restoration work in the 1970s has returned the building to the way it must have looked in the 1850s. You may take a guided tour of the building, but small groups and individuals may roam on their own.

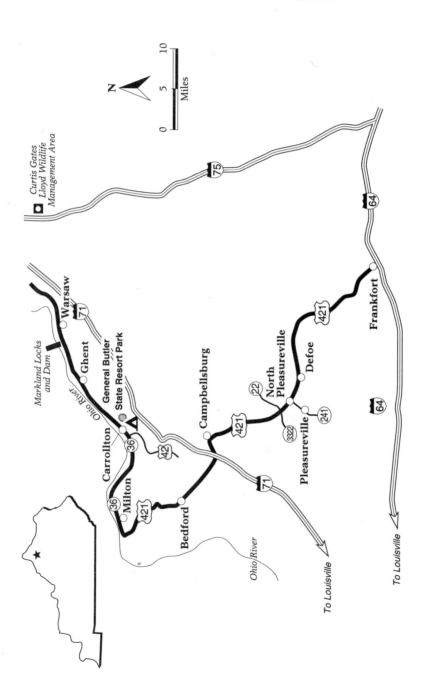

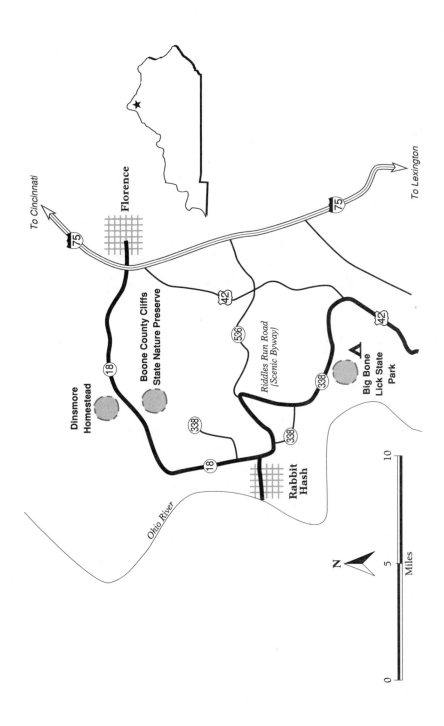

To Cincinnati

Florence

To Lexington

75

75

18

Dinsmore Homestead

Boone County Cliffs State Nature Preserve

42

536

Riddles Run Road (Scenic Byway)

42

338

338

338

338

Big Bone Lick State Park

18

Rabbit Hash

Ohio River

N

0   5   10
Miles

Frankfort hidden in the trees.

If you like antiques, you should see the Liberty Hall Historic Site. Here in a Federalist-style mansion, you can see local antiques owned by four generations of the Brown family who have lived in the house. Next door is the Orlando Brown House, a Greek Revival building designed by Gideon Shyrock. It is filled with antiques as well as portraits and water colors.

Lovers of architecture can see the Zeigler-Brockman House, the only house in Kentucky designed by Frank Lloyd Wright. The famed architect designed this house during his prairie period in 1910 for the Reverend Jesse R. Zeigler. There is a lighted, stained-glass case surrounding the fireplace.

Don't leave Frankfort without a trip to the floral clock. Thousands of flowering plants cover the 34-foot diameter of this unique clock. You can throw a coin into the fountain for good luck. If your luck is good, you will have time to see the Salato Wildlife Education Center and Game Farm. Inside, you will see three large aquariums containing several species of Kentucky fish. You will also see an exhibit of Kentucky trophy fish and watch a working beehive. Outside, there are trails that wind past captive bald eagles, buffalo (North American bison), white-tailed deer, elk, wild turkeys, bobcats, river otters, black bears, and much more.

Drive over to the junction of U.S. 421 and U.S. 127. Be careful here, since there are two places where these roads join. One is at the north end of town, and U.S. 127 goes north. Don't take this one. The second junction is at the west end of town by the bridges, and U.S. 421 (Bald Knob Road) goes northwest. Set your odometer at zero at the junction and head north on KY 421. For about 12 miles, you will climb, twist, turn, and drop through the trees and pass limestone road cuts. By 12.8 miles, you will be on top of the hill and will be treated to beautiful long views of the rolling farmlands in all directions. At 14 miles, you will cross a bridge over a fair-sized creek and plunge back into a canopy of trees. The most common trees that form the canopies in the area are locust, and, occasionally, Osage orange. In the next 3 miles, the road winds past well-kept farms and rolling fields and views spread out on both sides. At 17.5 miles, it enters Defoe. At 17.6 miles, as the road turns right, the Defoe General Store pops up on the left. From Defoe to Pleasureville, there are grand views of the trees and rolling hills to the left. At 21.2 miles, you will enter North Pleasureville.

At 24.1 miles, you will come to a stop at the junction of KY 22 and KY 3322. Keep straight ahead on U.S. 421. After more beautiful rolling farmland, you will come to another stop at the junction of KY 55. Go right on U.S. 421/KY 55. At 28 miles, you will enter New Castle, the county seat of Henry County since 1798. Continue along U.S. 421 and enjoy the farms and the rolling hills. At 34.7 miles, you will be in Campbellsburg.

Originally called Campbellsville for a local family, the legislature changed the name to Chiltonsville in 1840, after the family of an official by the name of Charles J. Chilton. Three weeks later, another act changed the name to Campbellsburg. The name of the post office, which had been established as Benevola in 1830, was also changed to Campbellsburg. In 1869, the railroad built a depot about a half-mile away, and the resulting population shift split the town into Old Campbellsburg and New Campbellsburg. Over the years, the two have grown together, and the area is now called Campbellsburg. At 35.0 miles, the road goes left, and at 35.7 miles, you will see the Campbellsburg post office on the right. At 37.5 miles U.S. 421 crosses over Interstate 71.

From I-71 to Bedford, you will enjoy twists and turns, walls of hardwood trees, long views across the fields, wooded hills, and a couple of creeks. At 44.7 miles, you will be in Bedford, the county seat of Trimble County. At 45.0 miles, U.S. 421 goes right at a traffic light. In about two blocks, the road goes left. At 46.2 miles, you will see Trimble County High School on your left. Continue along U.S. 421 to Milton at 53.8 miles.

Beyond Milton, you will leave the open land for a while and duck back into the trees. At 56.9 miles, you will come to a junction. U.S. 421 goes left across the Ohio River to Indiana. Keep going straight ahead on KY 36. For about 10 miles, you will be paralleling the Ohio River. There are a number of spots where you get a terrific view both up and down the river.

At 68.2 miles, you will cross a turquoise blue steel bridge over the Kentucky River and enter Carrollton. This old river town sits at the confluence of the Kentucky and the Ohio Rivers.

Benjamin Craig and James Hawkins laid out the town in 1792. It was part of more than 600 acres that they had purchased from a 2,000-acre grant that Colonel William Peachy had received for service in the French and

Indian War. The town was initially called Port William and was formally established by the Kentucky legislature on December 13, 1794. In 1798, Port William became the county seat of newly formed Gallatin County, and a post office of the same name was established in 1807. Both the town and the post office became Carrollton when Carroll County was formed in 1838. The name was given in honor of Charles Carroll of Maryland, the last surviving signer of the Declaration of Independence.

If you are tired of driving and would like a break, you might want to try the General Butler State Resort Park just east of town, named for General Orlando Butler, a writer, lawyer, statesman, philanthropist, poet, and hero of the War of 1812. At the park you can dine in the 176-seat dining room and enjoy a view of the Ohio River Valley at the same time. If your energy level is up, you can play a little golf on the regulation 9-hole course, do a little fishing, or take a hike on the 0.25-mile trail from the lodge to the campground or the 0.5-mile loop trail in the campground. After all of that, you may be ready for a room in the lodge with a private balcony overlooking the pool or the hillside. Or maybe you had better just get back in the car and get going. Don't forget, you still have to see Rabbit Hash.

The junction of KY 42 and KY 36 is at 69.7 miles. Go straight ahead on KY 42. At 75.7 miles, you will enter Ghent. The town was originally called McCool's Creek Settlement after one of the members of the party that first settled the area in 1795. The story is that the name Ghent was given to the town by Henry Clay, who was one of the signers of the Treaty of Ghent, which officially ended the War of 1812.

At 76.6 miles, you will have a really nice view of the Ohio River. At 81.9 miles, you will be at the Markland Dam and Locks on the Ohio River. There is a nice picnic ground, clean rest rooms, a beautiful river view, and an observation deck where you can take a break and watch the river traffic.

At 1.6 miles from the locks, you will cross a bridge with the Ohio River on the left and a pretty marina on the right. At 3.3 miles, you will be in Warsaw. Another of the old river towns, Warsaw was settled sometime around 1800 by several families from Virginia and Pennsylvania. It was originally called Great Landing or Johnson's Landing. In any case, the name was officially changed to Fredericksburg in 1831. Unfortunately, there was another Fredericksburg in Washington County, so just five days later, the name was changed again, this time to Warsaw. It is thought that the name came from *Thaddeus of Warsaw*, a popular novel of the time by Jane Porter.

At 8.5 miles, U.S. 127 will come in from the right and join you. At the junction, U.S. 42/127 begins to swing inland away from the river. The scenery changes from views of the Ohio to views of wooded hillsides. By 14.5 miles, the road is winding up into the hills, and by 17.7 miles, it is on top of the hills and offering broad views of the distant hills. At 18.8 miles, turn left on KY 338 toward Big Bone Lick State Park. At 2.7 miles from the junction,

The Rabbit Hash General Store.

you will be at the entrance to the park.

While walking these beautiful rolling hills today, it is almost impossible to imagine this area as a salty bog where mastodons, mammoths, arctic musk ox, and many other prehistoric mammals roamed dating back to the end of the Ice Age between 12,000 and 20,000 years ago. Yet such was the case. This was a place where animals through the centuries came to lick the ground for the salt so necessary to life. It is ironic that a place that provided one of the essentials to life also provided a means for death. These huge animals would get mired in the bog and die of starvation or suffocation. As they sank in the mire, their bones were preserved much as the bones of other prehistoric animals were preserved in the La Brea Tar Pits in Los Angeles, California.

As the centuries passed and more and more bones accumulated, the scene must have been like something out of a horror movie. Into this amazing pile of gigantic bones came a French-Canadian explorer by the name of Charles Lemoyne de Longueil. The year was 1729, and he was in a group providing protection for a surveying party. It is probable that he was taken to the big bones by Indians, since they had used the spot for salt-making and hunting for many years. The path to the bones from the Ohio River was well trodden, though, since the modern buffalo and other animals of the time used the lick for the same purpose as the mastodons and mammoths. In fact, many of the uppermost bones taken from the lick were of bison, elk, and deer.

A riverboat docked across the Ohio River from Rabbit Hash.

Following de Longueil's discovery, a long procession of frontiersmen, traders, collectors, statesmen, and scientists made the trek to the big bones and hauled away as much as they could carry. Some of the bones went to museums or universities, while others were sold as curiosities. Some undoubtedly ended up in attics or basements. It is not hard to imagine a mastodon tooth with "souvenir of Kentucky" stenciled on it. The result of all of this unchecked frenzy of collection is that today there are no visible bones at Big Bone Lick. What would have been an amazing sight for all to see and wonder at is reduced to rolling grassy hills. The marshes, too, are gone, and the sulfur springs are drying up. At the park, you can see a small museum with fossilized bones or walk the 1-mile trail to see some life-sized models of the prehistoric animals and the last of the sulfur springs. You can also fish, hike, picnic, and golf, but you will have to close your eyes and imagine what de Longueil must have seen and felt on that day so long ago when the huge bones littered the ground.

Drive back down the park road to the junction with KY 338 and turn left. You will wind along for 3.2 miles to Riddles Run where you will turn right. Riddles Run Road is part of one of the Kentucky Scenic Byways. Within a mile, you will see a wall of trees on your right and a steep drop off to your left. On the drop-off side, there is a beautiful view across the fields to the wooded hills beyond. After dipping and climbing through the trees for another mile, you will come to a stop sign at the junction of KY 536. Turn left and wind along some more until you come to another stop sign at the junction of KY 338 at 9.8 miles. Across the road, you will see a sign to Rabbit Hash. Go 0.9 mile and make a sharp turn across a little bridge. You are in Rabbit Hash. The general store is on the right. There are a lot of stories around about how the town got its name, and one is about as good as another. One that seems plausible is that due to flooding along the Ohio River, rabbits were being driven out of their condos in droves. The local folks killed them for food, but like any good thing, it got to be too much. The town at that time was called Rising Sun, and the story goes on that two travelers met along the road and one asked the other if he could get anything to eat in town. The reply was "Yes, plenty of rabbit hash." It's a good thing he didn't answer "Yes, plenty of corned beef and cabbage."

Drive back to the junction of KY 536 and KY 338. Go north on KY 338 for a half-mile or so to the junction of KY 18. Take KY 18 to the left. At 4 miles from the junction, KY 20 goes left. Keep straight ahead on KY 18. At 4.8 miles, you will see the entrance to the Dinsmore Homestead. Here you can tour an 1842 country house filled with the memorabilia of five generations of the Dinsmore family. The Dinsmores were influential Kentuckians who were close friends of Theodore Roosevelt, Eleanor Roosevelt, B. F. Goodrich, and many other famous personages of their time.

Just beyond the Dinsmore Homestead, Middle Creek Road goes right to the Boone County Cliffs State Nature Preserve. The parking area is on the left at about 1.5 miles from the junction with KY 18. The 74-acre preserve was set aside to preserve the unique 20- to 40-foot conglomerate cliffs along a tributary of Middle Creek. Access from the parking area is over a 2.4-mile uneven trail that is rated as moderate. In the area, you can hike, do a little bird watching, or study the unique geology.

Drive back to KY 18 and turn right. From here to the four-way stop in Burlington, you will pass through rolling hills, through lush woods, and past beautiful homes. From Burlington to I-75, a distance of just under 5 miles, you will have a nice four-lane highway. When you reach the interstate, you will be in Florence.

If you are heading south on I-75, you might want to stop at the Curtis Gates Lloyd Wildlife Management Area. Here you can walk a nature trail through one of the state's oldest virgin hardwood stands. You may also see numerous animals and birds, including deer, turkey, dove, red and gray fox, bluebirds, and the pileated woodpecker. To reach the area, drive south on I-75 for about 18 miles to the Crittenden exit. Go left at the exit to U.S. 25S and turn right. Follow U.S. 25S a short distance to a left turn across the railroad tracks. Parking is at the entrance to the area.

17

Somerset/London Loop
Farms, Mountains, and Whitewater

General description: This drive is 65 miles of some of Kentucky's finest scenery. From Somerset to London, KY 192 twists and turns, dips and climbs through some of the prettiest wooded hills in this part of the state. The drive begins outside of Somerset and passes through a wide, flat area with homes and farms and a wide vista. The road then drops down with trees on each side of the road reaching out to shake hands high above. Unfortunately, there are few places to pull over and park to take the photos. The second half of the loop, from London back to Somerset, follows KY 80 through more beautiful scenery.

Special attractions: Daniel Boone National Forest.

Location: East-central.

Drive route numbers: KY 192, 80; I-75.

Travel season: The best time for this trip would be fall. Spring would be a close second, but any time would be worth the trip.

Camping: Campgrounds can be found at Laurel River Lake, Levi Jackson State Park, Lake Cumberland, Daniel Boone National Forest, General Burnside Island State Park, and London.

Services: There are a number of motels in both London and Somerset. Restaurants and fast food in London and Somerset.

Nearby attractions: Laurel River Lake, Levi Jackson State Park, and General Burnside State Park are all within a few miles of the drive.

The drive

The drive begins in Somerset, the county seat of Pulaski County since 1801. To begin the drive, head northeast on KY 80 to the eastern edge of town where a sign at a little junction will point to KY 192/914. Set your odometer at zero at the junction and go 0.1 mile on this road to a stop sign. Turn left at the stop sign and drive 0.6 mile to a traffic light at the junction of KY 192 and KY 914. Keep straight ahead on KY 192. At about 1.2 miles, you will be passing nice well-kept homes on both sides of the road. There are intermittent views between the houses of a big grassy valley and wooded hillsides beyond. By 3 miles, you will be down in a dip with trees on both sides. Beyond the trees are rolling fields with an occasional limestone road cut to block the view. At 3.8 miles, you will have a view to the right of wooded

Drive 17: Somerset/London Loop
Farms, Mountains, and Whitewater

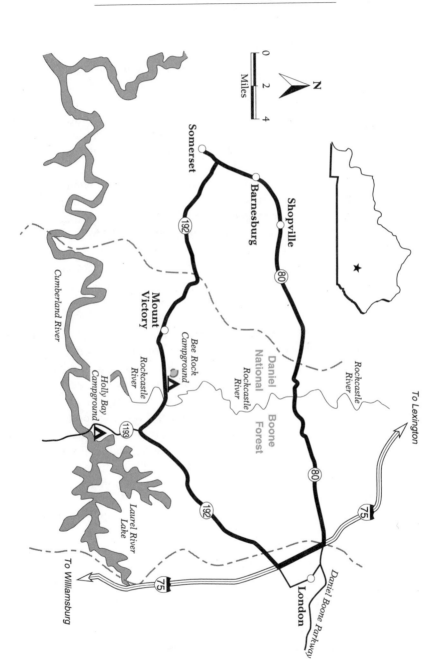

hills beyond the rolling farmland. By 5 miles, the road swings gently back and forth through walls of trees. In another half mile, you will be passing a wall of green on your left and more rolling farmland and wooded hills on your right. At almost 6 miles, the road climbs upward to the left through a canopy of trees. For the next 2 or 3 miles, you will pass by more walls of trees and some canopies. At 9.6 miles, there is a nice farmhouse and an old gray-weathered barn. At 10.5 miles, you will cross a high bridge over a creek. By 12.2 miles, the road will be dropping down and curving left through a wall of trees. All along this drive you will see black and white oak, pine, cedar, redbud, dogwood, and poplar. In several spots, the contrast between the dark green of the pines and cedars contrasts nicely with the lighter green of the hardwoods. Just past the trees is a nice old barn with an interesting rusty roof. At 14.8 miles, you will be in Mount Victory.

This little town has many stories about how it was named. The first one goes that Lieutenant Nathan McClure, with a small patrol escorting settlers through the area, engaged in a skirmish with some renegade Indians. He was killed in the action, but his men defeated the Indians on a ridge between the Rockcastle River and Buck Creek. A Victory! There are those who say that Ella P. Darr, the wife of Methodist minister Timothy T. Darr, and a group of her colleagues established a church and a school here. They considered that a religious Victory! Some think that it was named for a successful religious revival that was once held here. Another Victory! Some, but not many, believe that two schoolteachers agreed to carry the mail free for a year if they could get a post office. They got the post office. One more Victory! Maybe you would like to come up with a story and add it to the list. Or maybe the town should be named Mount Victories.

Beyond Mount Victory the road dives back down into a wall of hardwood trees. The oaks are beautiful in the fall, and the dogwood and redbud make a beautiful display in the spring. At 17.7 miles, the road is still in the trees and a sign announces that you are entering the Daniel Boone National Forest. At 18.2 miles, the road makes a sharp right turn across a bridge over the Rockcastle River. Just before the turn is the turnoff to the Bee Rock Campground.

The Rockcastle River is one of three in Kentucky that has been given "Wild and Scenic" status. The section from the bridge at KY 80 to the backwaters of Lake Cumberland is a designated wild river and one of Kentucky's most popular white-water runs. This section is 16.9 miles long, and is classified as Class III and Class IV. Some of the interesting spots along this stretch are the Loop, the S-Turn, the Stair Steps, and the Narrows. These areas include blind turns, drops, undercut rocks, and in-stream obstacles. They are obviously not intended for the weak at heart or the first-time canoeist. The experts say that camping at Bee Rock and hiking along the river will give you an idea of what to expect should you want to try it. Of course, if you are not a white-water enthusiast, you might like to hike along there just to see if you can watch the canoes coming down.

After you cross the bridge, the road makes another sharp right turn and climbs up through the trees. At 22.2 miles, you will reach the junction with KY 1193 that goes down to Laurel River Lake and the Holly Bay campground. At Holly Bay, you can even rent a pontoon boat or fishing boat and enjoy some time on one of the prettiest lakes in the south. You can even rent a houseboat that is equipped like a condo in Hawaii. The boats come in all sizes and rental prices. You can cruise the 300-foot deep, 5,000-acre lake, explore the 200 miles of shoreline, try for a record walleye, or just swim in water as clear as that in a swimming pool—without the chlorine.

After you have seen the lake, continue along KY 192. At 26.7 miles, you will see the Bald Rock Picnic Ground on your left. At 29.5 miles, you will see the sign telling you that you are leaving the Daniel Boone National Forest. From here to London, you will be more out in the open, and more and more farms and homes will show up as you approach the city. At 36.1 miles, you will be at the intersection of KY 192 and I-75 at exit 38 just outside of London, the county seat of Laurel County. Looking down on the traffic moving along I-75, it is hard to imagine that once this was a part of the Wilderness Road, barely a track, which Daniel Boone followed from Virginia through the Cumberland Gap all the way to the Ohio River. It is almost as hard to imagine the wagon toll road that ran from Crab Orchard to the north to Cumberland Gap in the south. If it is difficult to imagine what this looked like 200 years ago, it is impossible to dream of what it will be like 200 years in the future.

Turn onto I-75 heading north and drive to exit 41. Leave the interstate and head west on KY 80. For a few miles, you will be spoiled by a four-lane divided highway. It will drop down to two lanes, but is a beautiful road all the way to Somerset. At 3.3 miles from I-75, you will see few homes and lots of nice rolling farmland. At 6.2 miles, scattered homes are visible through the trees that line the road. At 7 miles, the road curves downward to the left and the hills are higher with more trees. More of the trees here are evergreens rather than hardwoods. By 8.7 miles, you will pass many more trees, a few limestone road cuts, and have a number of beautiful, long views through the trees of the rolling hills beyond. At 9.3 miles, KY 80 goes through a dip and there is a great long view of a tree-studded valley to the right. At 10.7 miles, you will cross the bridge over the Rockcastle River. This is the beginning of the white-water run that goes by the Bee Spring Campground and under KY 192. At 11 miles, you will pass through a rock road cut that looks like sandstone. In any case, it is not the typical limestone that you have seen so much of throughout Kentucky. At 14.7 miles, there are nice views of wooded hillsides ahead and to the left. At 16.6 miles, there are a couple of houses, an old gray barn, and green rolling hills beyond in both directions.

The Laurel Rock Quarry shows up on the right at 17.7 miles. It is a big quarry. At 22.0 miles, you will pass the Shopville Elementary School. By 23.2 miles, the four-lane divided highway has returned. At 23.5 miles, you will pass through a big limestone road cut, and at 25 miles, you will enter Barnesburg. Beyond Barnesburg, there are peaceful views of the trees, farms, and a pretty little town down in the valley. At 29 miles you will be back at the junction of KY 192 where you started.

18

Somerset to Mill Springs Via Russell Springs

Around Lake Cumberland

General description: This 80-mile drive begins in Somerset and rambles along old KY 80 across an arm of Lake Cumberland to Russell Springs. There, it turns south and passes more of Lake Cumberland, winds by the Wolf Creek Fish Hatchery, crosses Wolf Creek Dam where it turns east on KY 90, passes Monticello, and ends at the old mill at Mill Springs.
Special attractions: Old Mill Springs Mill, The Wolf Creek National Fish Hatchery.
Location: South-central
Drive route numbers: KY 90, 1275; Old Kentucky Highway 80; U.S. 127.
Travel season: All year.
Camping: Campgrounds at Somerset, Jamestown, General Burnside Island State Park, Lake Cumberland State Resort Park, and Russell Springs.
Services: Motels in Somerset, Jamestown, Monticello, and Russell Springs. There is a bed and breakfast at Mill Springs. Restaurants and/or fast food in Somerset, Jamestown, Russell Springs, and Monticello.
Nearby attractions: Zollicoffer Park, site of the Civil War Battle of Mill Springs.

The drive

This drive will take you past the site of the Battle of Mill Springs, one of the more important battles of the Civil War. The famed Confederate General Felix K. Zollicoffer had been guarding the Cumberland Gap against Union attempts to enter Tennessee. Part of his strategy had been to send about 4,000 men to establish a fortified camp near the town of Mill Springs. In January 1862, General George B. Crittenden took over command of the Confederate forces. At the same time, the Union forces were advancing under the command of General George B. Thomas.

Because the camp at Mill Springs was so near the river, it was in a very vulnerable position. If the troops should have to retreat, crossing the river, with its swift currents, would make the move extremely hazardous. Consequently, Crittenden decided to launch a preemptive strike on Thomas's troops. On January 17, Thomas had reached Logan's Crossroads (Nancy) about 10

Drive 18: Somerset to Mill Springs Via Russell Springs

Around Lake Cumberland

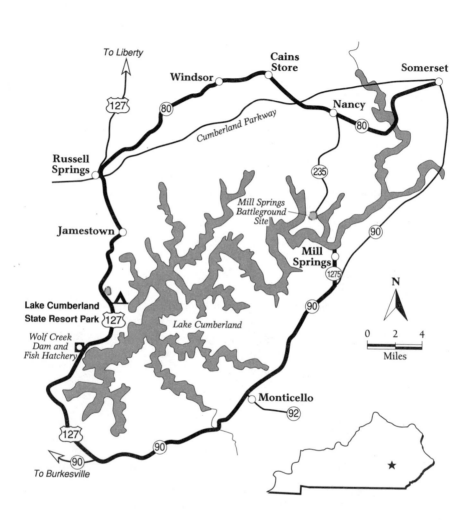

miles north of the camp at Mill Springs. General Crittenden realized that a lot was at stake. He knew that a Union victory could cause Kentuckians who were on the fence to shift their allegiance to the Union. Further, if the defense of Cumberland Gap weakened, it could mean the loss of much of Tennessee. Seeing no alternative, he ordered Generals Zollicoffer and William H. Carroll to attack the Union forces at Logan's Crossroads.

At midnight on January 18, the Confederate forces left their camp and marched through mud and darkness for the 9 miles or so toward the Union camp. The first skirmishing began when the Confederates came upon the Union pickets under the command of Colonel Frank Wolford. The Union soldiers, who were just getting out of bed, were warned of the impending attack and soon were in the thick of it. General Zollicoffer had deployed his troops in a ravine from which they were able to fire at will on the exposed Union troops. During a lull in the battle, one of the strangest incidents in the war took place.

Union Colonel Speed S. Fry rode a short distance from the battle lines to try and get a better look at the Confederate position. The day was wet and the battlefield was nearly obscured by the smoke from the rifles. Out of the haze, Fry saw a solitary figure riding toward him from the trees. The rider was none other than General Felix K. Zollicoffer! The general, who was nearsighted to begin with, was further confused by all of the haze and smoke. He approached Fry, thinking that he was another Confederate, and warned him that his men had been firing on their own troops. About the time that the astounded Fry realized what was happening, another Confederate soldier came out to warn Zollicoffer that he was talking to the enemy. When Fry saw the soldier approaching, he turned to flee, but as he did so, he fired his pistol and killed Zollicoffer. When Fry was told whom he had shot, he was understandably elated. It isn't every soldier who gets to shoot an enemy general. On the other hand, it isn't every general who wanders out of the mist of battle to talk to the enemy.

General Zollicoffer had fallen near a large oak tree, and for many years, it was an unofficial monument to the Confederate hero. In 1902, Dorotha Burton began a tradition of placing a wreath around its trunk. Henry Trimble, a Union veteran, donated an acre of land that contained the tree and a mass grave of more than 100 Confederate soldiers. In 1910, this was officially designated as Zollicoffer Park and monuments were placed there in honor of Zollicoffer and the men who gave their lives at the Battle of Mill Springs. On June 6, 1995, the tree, affectionately known as the "Zollie Tree," was downed by lightning. A seedling, descended from the original tree, was planted on the spot in May 1996.

The battle raged on, and finally ended in a Union triumph with Confederate soldiers deserting and running for the relative safety of Tennessee. Although Thomas had broken the defense of the Cumberland Gap, a lack of

Lake Cumberland at Wolf Creek Dam.

supplies and bad winter weather kept him from advancing until spring.

The drive begins at the intersection of U.S. 27 and Old KY 80 at the north end of Somerset. Go west on Old KY 80. In just over a mile, you will come to the junction with KY 80 Bypass, which will take you over to the Cumberland Parkway. The parkway replaced Old KY 80, and it is a beautiful drive in itself, but parkways by their very nature are designed to get you from point A to point B as quickly as possible. We have chosen the slower, kinder, gentler way, so keep on straight ahead on Old KY 80. In about three miles, the houses will be slowly giving way to trees and fields. At 4.9 miles, you will cross the high bridge over Fishing Creek, an arm of Lake Cumberland. On the water below, you will see houseboats tied up to a dock on the left. Beyond Fishing Creek, the houses have almost completely disappeared and have been replaced with rolling hills and stands of hardwood trees. You are out in the country. At 8.7 miles, you enter the town of Nancy. The town was originally called Logan's Crossroads after William Harrison Logan, who was the first postmaster. The post office, however, was established in 1865 as Lincolnville. It was decommissioned in 1875 and recommissioned again in 1884, and given the new name of Nancy for Logan's wife, Nancy Lester Logan. Just after you enter Nancy, you will see the junction of KY 235 going left to the site of the Battle of Mill Springs.

Just beyond Nancy, Old KY 80 crosses over the Cumberland Parkway and gives you a view of some beautiful hilly farmland. At about 20 miles, you will enter Cains Store.

A couple of miles further along, you will pass through Windsor. Beyond Windsor, Old KY 80 drops down for a while, twists and turns as though it can't decide where to go, then crosses a creek and climbs back into the trees. At 25.2 miles, there is a very pretty brick church sitting all by itself in the middle of a green lawn on your right. In about 5 more miles, you will come to a stop at the junction of U.S. 127 just east of Russell Springs. Russell Springs was a health resort as far back as the early 1800s. Known for a long time as Big Boiling Springs, the spring had a high content of iron that was supposed to have curative properties.

In Russell Springs, turn south on U.S. 127. In 1 mile from the junction of U.S. 127 and Old KY 80, you will cross over the Cumberland Parkway again, and at 3.5 miles, you will be in Jamestown, the county seat of Russell County. In the middle of Jamestown, there is a traffic circle. Follow U.S. 127 to the right. Beyond Jamestown, the road curves to the right, drops downhill through the trees, curves back to the left, then makes a sweeping turn to the right and crosses over Perkins Creek on a concrete bridge. Beyond the bridge, the road climbs back up into the trees until it comes out on top where you will have a grand view of broad, rolling fields. By 10 miles, U.S. 127 is winding back and forth through gently rolling farmland studded with stands of hardwood trees. At 13.7 miles the entrance to Lake Cumberland State Resort Park appears on the left. The park, on beautiful Lake Cumberland, offers a couple of lodges, cottages, a 147-site campground, and a dining room where you can enjoy breakfast, lunch, and dinner. When you have finished in the dining room, you can rent a fishing boat, a pontoon boat, a houseboat, or even a ski boat for a little recreation on the water. There is also an indoor pool complex at the Lure Lodge. There you have your choice of a pool, a hot tub, an exercise room, or a game room. Hikers might like to try the four-mile loop hike through forests of beech, oak, and hickory. If you would like to trade the car for a horse for a while, trail rides depart every hour.

From the turnoff to the state park, the road winds down through more hardwoods to the Wolf Creek Dam. There is a nice parking area at the north end of the dam. Our favorite parking spot is across the dam just before the road turns left. There is only room for a couple of cars, but you have a nice view of both sides of the dam. Look down the length of the lake and realize that even with the long view you have, you are seeing only a fraction of this huge lake. It is actually 101 miles long and has 1,255 miles of shoreline. That's a lot of water. The project was authorized by the Flood Control Act of 1938, and construction began in 1941. World War II slowed construction down, but the dam was ready for flood control use in 1950, and for full use in August 1952. The six hydroelectric generators produce enough power to supply a city of 575,000 people.

Shell fossil found in road cut at Wolf Creek Dam.

A definite plus at this site is the high limestone cliffs next to the parking place. The rubble that has tumbled from the steep cliff contains some nice fossil shells. A little careful searching will get you something to take home and show the neighbors. There is no climbing or hard work to do. Just sift through the little pieces of shale that litter the ground.

At the base of the dam is the Wolf Creek Fish Hatchery. This facility, one of the newest in the federal system, produces more than 1,000,000 brown and rainbow trout with a total weight of about 230,000 pounds each year. Although they cooperate with state fish and wildlife agencies, most of the fish are stocked into federal waters in Kentucky, Tennessee, and Georgia. The water to the hatchery is taken from Lake Cumberland at a depth of 25 to 100 feet and at a temperature of 40 to 65 degrees. The water flows through the hatchery at a rate of up to 10,000 gallons per minute. Hatchery Creek is randomly stocked two or three times a week and is wheelchair-accessible.

Beyond the dam, the road climbs again, and winds up through the trees. From here, all the way to the junction of U.S. 127 and KY 90, you will climb through trees, break out into wide meadows, and pass lots of rolling hills and woodland. The junction will appear at 29 miles. Turn left at the junction on KY 90 and drive about 10 miles or so toward Monticello. From the traffic light where KY 90 and KY 92 meet just outside Monticello, it is just 8 miles to the junction with KY 1275. Go left on KY 1275 for 1.2 miles to the parking lot at the Mill Springs Mill.

This is a really beautiful old gristmill that will reward you with history, great views across Lake Cumberland, and some outstanding photo opportunities. Photographing the mill wheel is a little tough, since you cannot get back very far because of the hillside and the trees.

The millstones at Mill Springs are interesting in their own right. From stone that was quarried in France, wheels 48 inches in diameter are made up of thirteen pieces each, all fitted painstakingly and held together with two metal bands. The stones are made up in sets consisting of a stationary bottom stone and a rotating top stone. The outside workings of the mill are unique, too. The 40 foot in diameter overshot water wheel is thought to be the largest in the world still operating. Unlike most gristmills that get their power from dammed up river water, Mill Springs gets its water power from thirteen springs on the hill above. The mill produced both corn meal and flour, which were loaded onto flatboats and shipped down the Cumberland River as far as Nashville. This is a fascinating place, and we hope you can spend some time here and absorb a bit of the history.

19

Somerset to Russell Springs
The Knobs Area

General description: This 86.7-mile drive begins in Somerset and runs north through limestone road cuts and bluegrass along U.S. 27 and U.S. 150 for a little more than 40 miles to the historic city of Danville. Here, it turns south on U.S. 127 and continues on to Russell Springs through some really grand scenery. There are farms, old barns, limestone road cuts, knobs, densely wooded areas, and rolling hills.

Special attractions: Constitution Square and the McDowell House in Danville.

Location: South-central.

Drive route numbers: U.S. Highways 27,150,127.

Travel season: All year.

Camping: Campgrounds at Danville, Russell Springs, General Burnside Island State Park, and Somerset.

Services: Motels in Danville, Somerset, and Russell Springs. Restaurant and fast food in Danville, Somerset, Russell Springs, and Liberty.

Nearby attractions: General Burnside Island State Park, Lake Cumberland State Resort Park, The Isaac Shelby Cemetery Historical Site, William Whitley House State Historic Site, Crab Orchard, Central Kentucky Wildlife Refuge.

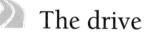 ## The drive

This is the third and final of our drives beginning in Somerset. Along the way, you will have a chance to take a side trip to the William Whitley House State Historic Site near Crab Orchard. William Whitley was a famed Indian fighter in the early days of Kentucky. Visitors to the area can see the unique estate, which Whitley called Sportsman's Hill, and marvel at its architectural features. The bricks in this first brick home in Kentucky were laid in a Flemish bond, which gave the walls great strength. The walnut and pine paneling along with the moldings and carvings show that everything on the frontier wasn't done with an ax. There were skilled craftsmen, and the William Whitley House is proof. The racetrack is also a unique feature. It was the first to be built in a circular design, it used clay instead of turf, and it was the first in which the horses ran in a counterclockwise direction. Speculation is that this latter practice was in response to the anti-British feelings at

Drive 19: Somerset to Russell Springs
The Knobs Area

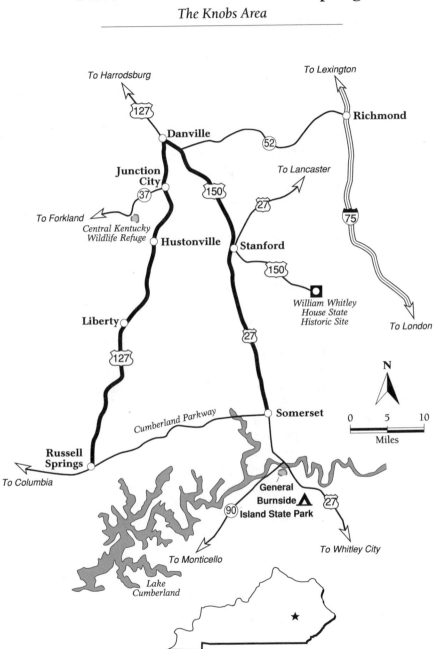

To Harrodsburg

127

Danville

52

Richmond

To Lexington

Junction City

37

150

To Lancaster

To Forkland

Central Kentucky Wildlife Refuge

27

Hustonville

Stanford

150

William Whitley House State Historic Site

75

To London

Liberty

27

127

N

0   5   10
Miles

Cumberland Parkway

Somerset

Russell Springs

To Columbia

General Burnside Island State Park

90

27

To Monticello

To Whitley City

Lake Cumberland

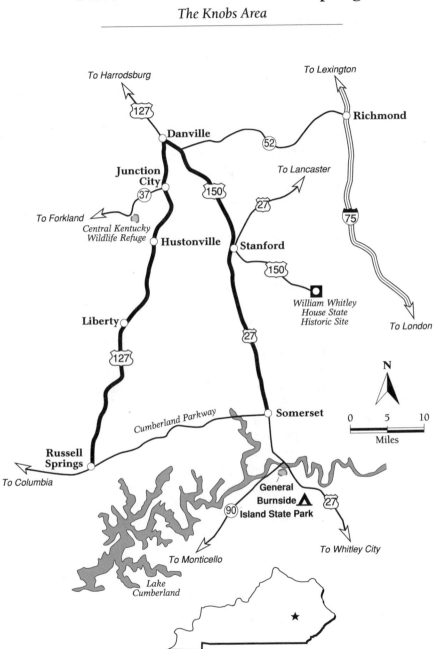

the time. British horses ran in a clockwise direction. There is a picnic ground on the site, and, of course, a gift shop.

The drive begins on U.S. 27 at the northern city limits. Go north on U.S. 27 toward Danville. For the first couple of miles, businesses and homes are slowly replaced with nice Kentucky scenery. In a little more than 4.0 miles, you will pass Science Hill. The name was given to the area by William J. Bobbitt, a scientist who engaged in some geological research there. At about 25 miles, the road passes through a large, limestone road cut with a lot of foliage both on the walls and on the top. At the bottom of the cut, looking back toward Somerset, you will see a giant, green V. With some big clouds in the sky, it would make a nice picture.

In a few more miles, you will see some of The "Knobs" off to the left. These cone-shaped hills are erosional remnants. Originally a part of the Mississippian Plateau, erosion caused by streams has carried away the softer material and left The Knobs. The base of these hills is usually a black shale, and the upper portions a sandstone or erosion resistant-limestone. If you take Drive 22, you will see many more examples of this interesting geological feature.

At about 30 miles, you will come to Stanford and the junction with U.S. 150. Turn right here if you want to visit the William Whitley House. Go left if you are continuing on toward Danville. Between Stanford and Danville, you will pass some very nice bluegrass scenery. There are wooded hills, wide-open rolling fields, and distant mountain views to enjoy. At about 40 miles, you will be in Danville. There is so much to see here, that you will have to take a couple of days to do it right. A quick tour should begin in Constitution Square.

In Courthouse Square, you will see a replica of the original log courthouse where, between 1784 and 1792, 10 constitutional conventions were held. At the time, Kentucky was a county in Virginia, but on June 1, 1792, Kentucky became the 15th state in the Union. You can also see a replica of the original jail, built with 9-inch diameter logs. On Fisher's Row, there are two, 2-story brick houses which were built by Jeremiah Fisher in 1817 to be used as rentals. The units were joined by a common wall much as our town homes, today. Were they "Towne Homes"?

Danville, Kentucky, in the early 1800s seems an unlikely place for one of the greatest advancements in medicine, but such a place it was on Christmas morning in 1809. Tom Crawford had taken his 45-year-old wife, Jane, to see Dr. Ephraim McDowell about her abdominal pain. He saw her distended abdomen and the blue-green spots on her skin and diagnosed the problem as a large ovarian cyst. Today, a routine surgery would have been scheduled, but in 1809, surgery was limited to amputations and a very few other procedures. Internal surgery was unknown. The wisdom of the time was that if the abdominal cavity were opened, the air rushing in would immediately cause an infection that would be fatal. It was felt that God had placed a limit upon surgeons and that if they performed such an operation, the surgeons were "an assassins." Still, there were those who believed in the theoretical possibility of such a procedure. Dr. McDowell believed that it could be done, and on that morning he and his nephew, James, prepared a large oak table by covering it with a white linen cloth and tying cords to the legs which would be used to restrain Mrs. Crawford. She was given some opium pills, which were sometimes known to relieve a "little pain," and the operation began.

Without benefit of anesthetic or sterilization techniques, a 21-pound tumor was removed from Mrs. Crawford's abdomen. She was stitched up and taken to a bedroom where she remained for several days while Dr. McDowell waited and watched for infection, but none showed up. On the fifth day, Dr. McDowell entered the room and found Mrs. Crawford up and making the bed. Jane Crawford lived for 33 more years and died in March of 1842 at the age of 78. The word "tough" doesn't even come close. Dr. McDowell, who became known as "the father of abdominal surgery," went on to perform 12 more ovariotomies, 11 of which were successful. Ironically, he died in 1830 at the age of 59 of a perforated appendix.

To continue the drive, go south on U.S. 127. We began at the junction of U.S. 127, U.S. 150, and KY 52. This is on the U.S. 150 Bypass at the west end of town. Go south on U.S. 127. At two miles or so south of Danville, you will come to Junction City. The town was probably founded in about 1866, which is when the Louisville and Nashville Railroad reached the site. The town was originally called Goresburg after the two Gore brothers who ran the local hotel. When the Cincinnati Southern Railroad made connection with the L&N Railroad just a month later, the name was changed to Junction City. If you think that is confusing, just hear this. At Junction City, you can go south on KY 37 to the beautiful Central Kentucky Wildlife Refuge. This refuge, which is run entirely by volunteers, is home to such wildflower species as lady's-slippers, bluebells, bird's-foot violets, bloodroot, and trilliums, as well as many ferns and mosses. Wildlife includes deer, foxes, muskrats, flying squirrels, and woodchucks. For bird watchers, there are purple finches, house finches, evening grosbeaks, cardinals, towhees, flickers, and nuthatches among others. If you would just like a nice hike, there are several trails ranging from easy to strenuous. To find the refuge, go south out of Junction City on KY 37 for about 7 miles to Carpenter Creek Road. Go left on Carpenter Creek Road for 0.6 mile to the refuge.

Retrace your route to Junction City and head south again on U.S. 127. For the next 8 miles or so, the billboards and other signs of the twentieth century will begin to fade and be replaced with rolling fields, stands of trees, and more nice views of some of the knobs. Soon Hustonville will show up on your left. Once it was called Cross Roads because of its location at the junction of the trail between the Kentucky and Green Rivers and the trail between Stanford and Louisville. Later on, it was known as Farmington, and the post office was named Hanging Fork. For 3 months in 1826 it was called New Store, then changed back to Hanging Fork. Maybe after 3 months the local folks thought the store wasn't new anymore. The story of the name Hanging Fork is interesting. It is told that a couple of bad guys from Virginia had been captured and were being taken back to be hanged. The story goes on that they were giving their captors a lot of trouble, so the captors decided that they didn't need the grief and hanged them, then and there. "Then and there" happened to be at the forks of a nearby stream. Now don't you think that Hanging Fork is a lot more romantic than Hustonville, which the town became in 1837?

From Hustonville, continue on down U.S. 127 through more of the knobs and more oak and hickory-covered hills. Notice how densely wooded some of the knobs are. It looks as though it would be hard just to walk through the woods. At a little more than 20 miles, you will cross the Green River and enter Liberty, the county seat of Casey County. Liberty was founded by a group of Revolutionary War veterans in 1791, reportedly on land that had been granted them for war service. Even earlier, a station had been built on the Dix River by Colonel William Casey. He was a member of the second Constitutional Convention in 1799, and was probably the great grandfather of Mark Twain. Liberty is also on the headwaters of the Green River.

Beyond Liberty, the road climbs up through a large limestone road cut. At about 33 miles, you will pass through a small town with the distinction of being the home of the "Dog Walk Market." At around 36 miles, there is a gray-weathered barn on the left. From here to Russell Springs, enjoy the hills, farms, limestone cuts, and rolling oak-studded hills.

20

Corbin to Parker's Lake
Past the Home of the Moonbow

General description: This is one of the shortest drives in the book, just 27.2 miles, but it is also one of the best. It begins in Corbin, the home of Colonel Sanders' Kentucky Fried Chicken, follows U.S. 25W to KY 90, winds past Cumberland Falls, twists and turns through a part of the Daniel Boone National Forest, and ends at the junction of KY 90 and U.S. 27 in Parker's Lake.
Special attractions: Cumberland Falls, Daniel Boone National Forest.
Location: East-central
Drive route numbers: U.S. 25W; KY 90.
Travel season: All year.
Camping: There are campgrounds at Corbin and Cumberland Falls State Resort Park.
Services: There are both a lodge and cabins at Cumberland Falls State Resort Park, and motels in Corbin. Restaurants and fast food in Corbin.
Nearby attractions: Laurel River Lake, Beaver Creek Wilderness.

The drive

We begin this drive in Corbin, a town which, for many years, was just a small collection of farms that were collectively called Lynn Camp. The camp was named for Lynn Creek, which, in turn, was named for William Lynn, a pioneer who arrived in the area in about 1800. When the Louisville and Nashville Railroad reached the area in 1882, they named their station Lynn Camp. In 1883, the post office was established and called Cummins for Nelson Cummins who had been instrumental in getting the railroad to come to the area. In 1885, both the post office and the railroad station were re-named Corbin after Reverend James Corbin Floyd. The town was incorporated in 1902.

Corbin is not known for the Lynns, the Cummins, or the Corbins, though. It is known as the home of "Colonel Harlan Sanders' Kentucky Fried Chicken." A lot of jokes have been made about KFC, and many folks have made light of it, but Harlan Sanders may well be the epitome of the entrepreneurial spirit in America. He was born on September 9, 1890, on a farm near Henryville, Indiana. His father died when young Harlan was just

Drive 20: Corbin to Parker's Lake

Past the Home of the Moonbow

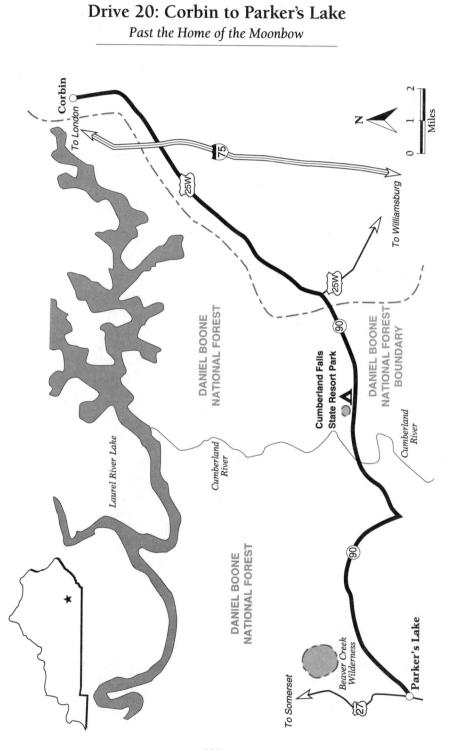

six, and he was forced to stay home and care for his three-year-old brother and baby sister while his mother worked to support the family. Part of his family responsibility was to cook for the family, and by the time he was seven, he had mastered a number of dishes. When he was around ten years old, he got his first job working on a neighbor's farm. By the time he was twelve, his mother remarried and he left home to work on a farm in Greenwood, Indiana.

Over the next few years, he held a number of jobs. He was a street-car conductor in New Albany, Indiana, and a sixteen-year-old soldier in Cuba. After his army service, he was a railroad laborer, a fireman, a cook, and an insurance salesman as well as a tire salesman. While on the road in Kentucky selling tires, he was crossing a bridge when a cable broke and sent him, his car, and the bridge crashing into the river 42 feet below. He survived without any ill effects, but his car did not. Without transportation, he could not continue as a traveling tire salesman, so he opened up a service station in nearby Nicholasville, Kentucky. He did so well in this business that a major oil company built him a new station on U.S. 25 in Corbin.

To bring in some more money, he started serving meals at the service station. He had no restaurant, but used the dining table in the living quarters at the station. During this time, he experimented with different seasonings for his fried chicken. The travelers who ate there loved it, and it was not long before word of mouth had made his chicken famous. He capitalized on this by moving across the street where he had a motel and restaurant that seated 142 people. In 1936, Governor Ruby Lafoon conferred upon Harlan Sanders the honorary title of Kentucky Colonel. There have been many such honorary Colonels, but none of them made it pay off like Harlan. It was after this that he began wearing the white suit and the mustache and goatee that one day would become the symbol of his enterprise and make him famous. There were bad times ahead, however, and it would take a lot more work to make the dream come true.

By 1955, his restaurant and motel were booming. He was even offered $164,000 for the business. Within a year, though, his business was so bad that it was sold at public auction for far less than he had been offered just the previous year. The reason for this setback was all too common throughout the country in those days. The new I-75 was built, bypassing all of the businesses along U.S. 25. Not one to give up and sit on the porch sulking at his misfortune, the 65-year-old Colonel took the money he made from the auction and his $105 per month social security check and hit the road once again. He and his wife would go into restaurants and cook for the owners and employees. He would be in his "Colonel uniform," and his wife would be in an ante-bellum dress. If the owners liked the recipe, he would make a handshake agreement that they would pay him a nickel for each chicken

Cumberland Falls is one of only two known places in the world where the spectacular and unique moonbow occurs.

sold. By 1964, he had more than 600 franchises. He sold his interest in the United States operations later in that year for $2,000,000. Colonel Harlan Sanders died of leukemia in 1980 at the age of 90.

On your way to Parker's Lake, you will probably want to stop at the famous and beautiful Cumberland Falls. It is fascinating to learn just how these beautiful falls came into being. As the Cumberland River eroded away the softer rock in its course, it kept cutting deeper and deeper, creating canyons as it went. When it contacted a particularly hard layer known as the Rockcastle Conglomerate, the cutting action slowed down. At a spot where there was a break in the conglomerate, the downcutting resumed and as it cut down, the falls were created. Actually, the process is still going on, and the falls are continually moving upstream. As the erosion under the falls continues, shelf areas are formed which, when they become heavy enough, fall off. It has been estimated by geologists that Cumberland Falls was originally about 40 miles downstream from where it is today. Geologists also estimate that as the falls move upstream, they get smaller. The projection is that one day they will only be a small rapids far upstream. This will take a while, though, so if you go off to lunch and come back in an hour or so, the falls will probably be right where you left them.

In fact, they are probably within tiny fractions of an inch from where they were in 1780 when Zachariah Green, with his brother and 2 companions, became the first white men to see the falls. These long hunters (a name that may be for the long rifles they carried or the long hunting and exploring trips they took) came down the Cumberland in a small boat. Since they were in unexplored territory, they had no idea that they were coming up on a waterfall. Consequently, they had to abandon their boat, which went over the falls, and swim for shore. One of the party did manage to get below the falls and retrieve the boat.

This was rugged country, and the settlers coming through the Cumberland Gap just kept on to the Bluegrass where farming was a whole lot easier. By the 1800s, though, the word had gotten around about the beauty of the falls and in particular its spectacular and unique "moonbow." This phenomenon occurs on clear nights with a full moon as the moon rises above the surrounding hills and shines through the mist above the falls. The only other documented place on earth where this occurs is on the Zambezi River in Zimbabwe.

Cumberland Falls State Resort Park was dedicated on August 21, 1931, becoming Kentucky's third state park. It is a jewel in the Kentucky State Park System. To reach Cumberland Falls and Parker's Lake, set your odometer at zero on U.S. 25W where it goes under Interstate 75 at exit 25 just southwest of town. Go west on U.S. 25W. In a couple of miles, you will be away from town and into the trees that line the road. Look for oak, maple, hemlock, and pine. At 3.8 miles, you will be driving through a wide valley with views of farms in the distance. In another mile, you will see the road to the Grove Recreation Area going off to the right. This leads to Laurel River Lake, where you will find a campground and boat ramp. At 6.3 miles, the road curves gently to the left, dips down through a canopy of trees, and climbs up to a beautiful view of hardwood-covered hillsides to the right. At 7.3 miles, you will come to a Y intersection with KY 90.

Go right on KY 90. In about 2 miles, a sign announces your arrival in the Daniel Boone National Forest. For the next 5 miles, you will drive through beautiful forest with white and red oaks, hemlocks, and tulip poplars right next to the road on both sides. At 14.4 miles, the Cumberland Falls State Park campgrounds are on the left. There are 50 campsites with electric and water hookups, a central service building with showers and rest rooms, a grocery, and a dump station. In another 0.3 mile, you will see the Park lodge with 52 rooms, massive stone fireplaces, beautiful views, hemlock beams, and pine paneling. There are also cottages available with 1 or 2 bedrooms, fireplaces, tableware, cooking utensils, and linen. Next to the lodge are duplex rooms that offer the privacy of a cottage, but with daily maid service, wet bars, and small refrigerators. There is also a gift shop, a coffee shop, 17 miles of nature trails, fishing in the Cumberland River, tennis, horseshoes, shuffleboard, swimming, horseback riding, and white-water rafting. Beyond the lodge, the road makes a sweep to the right, followed by a sweep to the left, and drops down deeper into the trees. At 15.3 miles, you will be at the parking area for Cumberland Falls.

To proceed on to Parker's Lake, turn right onto KY 90 from the parking area and cross the beautiful old limestone bridge. As soon as you cross the bridge, you will start to climb uphill through the tulip poplars and oaks on either side of the road. At 5.2 miles, you will pass Honeybee and continue winding through the trees of the Daniel Boone National Forest. At 6 miles, the road bends to the right and you have a long, beautiful view to the right across the valley below. At 11.4 miles, you will see the big Parker's Lake water tank on your left, and at 11.9 miles, you will be at the junction of KY 90 and U.S. 27 at Parker's Lake.

You can drive north on U.S. 27 for about 3.0 miles to Greenwood. Near here you will find access to the Beaver Creek Wilderness. In this wilderness area, you can hike through forests of oaks, tulip poplars, red maples, yellow southern pines, redbuds, dogwoods, and many others. There are opportunities for wilderness camping, horseback riding, and backpacking in this primitive area. For more information and maps, see the Daniel Boone National Forest listing in the appendix.

21

Lincoln's Birthplace to Lexington
Along the Bluegrass Parkway

General description: This 84-mile drive begins at the Abraham Lincoln Birthplace National Historic Site just south of Hodgenville. From there, it follows U.S. 31E (part of the old Louisville to Nashville Turnpike), north to Bardstown and My Old Kentucky Home State Park at Federal Hill where Stephen Foster is said to have received the inspiration for his famous song. From Bardstown, the drive runs along the Bluegrass Parkway to Lexington, with a side trip on the way to visit the old Beech Fork Covered Bridge outside Mooresville on KY 458. Unlike many of the Kentucky covered bridges that are hidden in trees and other foliage, Beech Fork is right out in the open so you can appreciate its size and get photographs of it from several angles.

Special attractions: Be sure to take the side trips to the Beech Fork Bridge and My Old Kentucky Home State Park.

Location: North-central

Drive route numbers: KY 31E, 55, 458; Bluegrass Parkway.

Travel season: All year.

Camping: Campgrounds in Lexington, Bardstown, and My Old Kentucky Home State Park.

Services: Motels in Lexington, Bardstown, and Hodgenville. Bed and breakfasts can be found in Lexington and Bardstown. Restaurants and/or fast food in Lexington, Bardstown, New Haven, and Hodgenville.

Nearby attractions: Bernheim Arboretum and Research Forest (Near Bardstown), Taylorsville Lake State Park, Kentucky Horse Park, Schmidt's Museum of Coca-Cola Memorabilia (Elizabethtown).

The drive

The drive begins at the Abraham Lincoln Birthplace National Historic Site south of Hodgenville. In 1808, Thomas Lincoln bought the Sinking Spring Farm and moved his wife and daughter there. On the western edge of the 348-acre farm was a beautiful white oak tree. In those days, landmarks such as boulders and trees were commonly used as survey and boundary markers. Such was the case with this tree, which came to be known as "the Boundary Oak." It was first used in the original 1805 survey of the farm. In addition to its use as a boundary marker, the tree was used by untold numbers of

Drive 21: Lincoln's Birthplace to Lexington
Along the Bluegrass Parkway

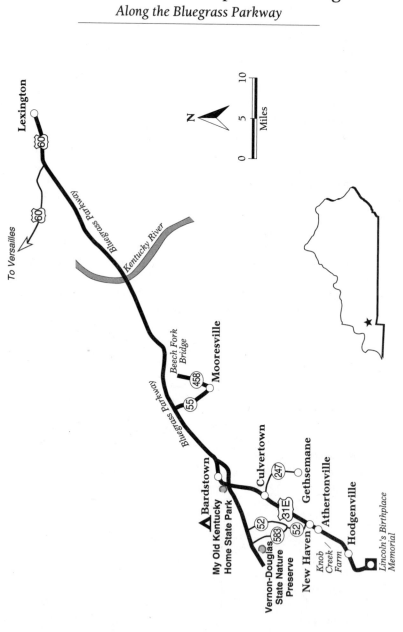

Previous Page: *Peaceful woodland brook offers a tempting respite from the road.*

Immediate Page: *Rich pasturage produces the fine horses for which the state is known.*

Facing Page: *Handsplit rail fence at Hensley Settlement near Corydon bespeaks simpler times.*

Facing Page: *The bounty of the harvest explodes in a patch of plump pumpkins.*

Above: *Trillium livens up a spring meadow.*

Left: *Autumn maples glorify a manicured field.*

Facing Page: This mill house at Levi Jackson State Park exhibits classic dovetail log construction. (Drive 10)

Above: Red River Gorge, Daniel Boone National Park. (Drive 7)

Right: Cumberland Falls. (Drive 20)

Following Page: Cypress trees stand sentinel over a pond in Pennyrile State Park. (Drive 34)

early travelers as a landmark to help guide them on their journeys. When Abraham was born on the farm in 1809, the oak, which was estimated to have been about 28 years old at the time, stood less than 150 yards from the cabin. Sadly, the effects of time, weather, insects, and disease took their toll on the old landmark, and in 1976, it died. At the end of its long life, it was 6 feet in diameter, 90 feet high, and had a spread at the crown of 115 feet.

The Lincoln family lived at Sinking Spring until 1811, when they lost the farm due to a defective land title. Thomas then moved his family to Knob Creek Farm, about 10 miles north. It was while he was living at Knob Hill Farm that Lincoln first saw slaves being driven along the road to be sold in the south. At this historic site, you can listen to interpretive talks, view exhibits, watch a film, hike or picnic, and visit the memorial building or the environmental study area. The most striking feature on the site is, of course, the beautiful neo-classical marble and granite memorial building that houses a nineteenth century log cabin. This cabin was placed in the memorial building almost 100 years after Thomas Lincoln moved his family, including young Abe, from the Sinking Spring Farm to Knob Creek. At first, it was accepted that this was the authentic cabin in which Lincoln had been born, but extensive research has failed to verify that it is, indeed, authentic. The original cabin had been moved, dismantled and reassembled, and exhibited in many cities over the years, and records don't exist to follow its trail. The cabin on display is a nineteenth-century structure, though, and probably very similar to the one in which Lincoln was born. The movement to create the memorial began around 1900, when Robert Collier, Mark Twain, William Jennings Bryan, and Samuel Gompers, among others, formed the Lincoln Farm Association to preserve the birthplace and establish a memorial to Abraham Lincoln. In 1905, they bought the farm, and in 1906, they purchased the cabin. More than 100,000 Americans contributed a total of $350,000 to complete the project. Theodore Roosevelt laid the cornerstone in 1909, and two years later, President William Howard Taft dedicated the memorial.

Before you leave, you might want to visit the environmental study area. We sometimes don't stop to realize just how unbelievably different our lives are from those who lived in the wilderness of Kentucky more than 100 years ago. Without the benefit of supermarkets, pharmacies, Home Depots, HMOs, and fast food, these people were dependent upon the land for virtually everything required to stay alive. They made tea from sassafras, rose hips, and mint. Their salads were made with pokeweed, dandelions, and wild lettuce, and berries perked up desert. Medicinal herbs were used for healing, nettles were used to make thread for weaving, and lamp wicks were made from milkweed and moss. Opossum, rabbit, elk, deer, and bison provided meat. Oak and hickory trees were used for everything from tool handles to log cabins, and acorns could even be eaten in an emergency.

Abraham Lincoln's Birthplace Memorial.

If you set your odometer at zero in the parking lot at the Birthplace Site and drive north on U.S. 31 for 1.4 miles, you will enter Hodgenville, the county seat of LaRue County. In Hodgenville, U.S. 31E becomes one of Kentucky's State Scenic Byways as it follows the route of the old Louisville-to-Nashville Turnpike. At 3.1 miles, U.S. 31E makes a sharp right turn and emerges from a tunnel of trees into rolling farmland. At 7.8 miles, there is a gray weathered barn on the left disappearing into the vines and undergrowth. In the next mile or so, the road drops down past wooded hillsides and through limestone road cuts. At 9.5 miles, there is another photogenic gray barn on the right. In about a half mile, a road goes left to the Lincoln Boyhood Home site near Knob Creek, where you can see a reproduction of a cabin in which Lincoln lived. There are guided tours, a museum, and a picnic area. In a little more than 2 miles, you will pass through Athertonville. Beyond the town are wide fields reaching over to the wooded hills on the left and a wall of trees on the right. At 13.8 miles, the road crosses a bridge over the Rolling Fork River and enters New Haven.

New Haven is the current home of the Kentucky Railway Museum. Here is a place where you can have a cool drink, browse in the gift shop, wander through the museum, or even take a break from driving with a train ride into history (see the appendix for more information). At the Museum, you can board a train and take an hour-and-a-half ride through the forests, farms, and fields of the Rolling Fork River Valley. If you are lucky, you may take your ride on one of the days when the restored Louisville and Nashville Railroad steam locomotive No. 152 is in service. This locomotive, built in 1905, pulled passenger trains on the L&N's Lebanon Branch, once one of the major routes in central Kentucky. The Lebanon Branch was vital to the Civil War effort, which made it a target for Confederate raiders. A number of skirmishes were fought along the line, and the bridge at New Haven was destroyed at least once. From time to time during the year, a group of Civil War re-enactors stage skirmishes along the line.

It took volunteers 13 years to completely restore the engine. When old No. 152 isn't on the job, the trains are pulled by early diesel engines. In addition to the ride, there is a museum containing railroad artifacts and memorabilia housed in a replica of the original New Haven Depot.

If you would like a nice side trip to the Vernon-Douglas State Nature Preserve, take KY 52 northwest about 3 miles to the junction with KY 583. Go left on KY 583 about 7 miles. Just before you reach the Bluegrass Parkway, turn left on a gravel road and go 1 mile to the parking area for the preserve. It is a 2.6-mile hike over a moderate to strenuous trail to the preserve. The preserve features a beautiful show of wildflowers in the spring and some of the oldest second-growth forest stands of sugar maple, beech, and tulip poplar in the region.

You could just get on the Bluegrass Parkway and head for Bardstown, but we think that retracing your route back to New Haven and continuing up U.S. 31E will be a more peaceful and scenic drive.

At New Haven, turn left on U.S. 31E and head toward Bardstown. At Culvertown, KY 247 goes south for 4 miles to the Abbey of Gethsemane. The Abbey of Gethsemane is the largest and oldest order of Cisterian Monks in the United States. The Abbey, founded in 1848, was home to Thomas Merton, the author of the 1948 best seller *Seven Storey Mountain*. You might get some great photos of the Abbey, and you can get some world famous fruitcake and cheese. And it's only an 8-mile round-trip excursion.

At 20.3 miles, the road is curving back and forth downhill through a tunnel of trees. At 25 miles, you will come to the junction with the Bluegrass Parkway. Go right on the Parkway for about 3 miles to exit #25. Leave the Parkway at exit #25 and head left toward Bardstown.

Bardstown is the county seat of Nelson County and the second oldest city in Kentucky. There is much to see and do in the Bardstown area, but one place you must see is My Old Kentucky Home State Park. It is easy to find, just keep straight ahead after you leave the parkway and in a half-mile or so the entrance will appear on your left. The park is on the grounds of Federal Hill, the estate of Judge John Rowan, a prominent political figure of the 1800s. The home, which sits on 285 acres, was completed in 1818, and was visited by such dignitaries of the day as Henry Clay and Aaron Burr. Of all of the guests that this stately mansion must have seen in all of its years as a social and political center, the most remembered, if not the most famous, must be Stephen Foster. He was a cousin of the Rowans and, it is believed, got the inspiration for his ballad "My Old Kentucky Home" while on a visit to Federal Hill in 1852. The connection between Federal Hill and "My Old Kentucky Home" went pretty much unnoticed until the Civil War when soldiers in the area learned of the origin of the now popular song. People began to come from miles around to see Federal Hill because of the song, and even began to call Federal Hill "My Old Kentucky Home." The estate was deeded to the Commonwealth of Kentucky in 1922, and "My Old Kentucky Home" was adopted as the state song in 1928.

If you should want to tour the home, guides in ante-bellum costume will guide you on a tour of the stately, 2-story brick mansion where you will see the beautiful furnishings and accessories in a mansion that is authentic in the smallest detail. If you would just like to roam the beautiful grounds, you can go down the hill in front of the mansion to the old log building built over the stone spring. For many years, this building served as Rowan's law office, where many cases were prepared, and where several young lawyers received their training. There is a gift shop and a 39-site campground with hookups, showers, and a dump station. The grounds at the park are a tree-lover's dream. Here you will find sugar maples, walnuts, elms, buckeye, dogwoods, redbuds, cedars, pines, pin oaks, and sycamores. The flowering trees are gorgeous in the spring and the fall is a riot of color.

To continue the drive, go back to the Bluegrass Parkway and head east toward Lexington. In a little more than 8 miles from Bardstown, take exit 34 to KY 55 going south. You are on your way to the covered bridge near Mooresville, and for the next 6 miles, you will have a very pretty ride down a great rural road past lots of hardwood trees and rolling farmland. Just after you enter the city limits of Mooresville, you will come to the junction of KY 458. This is called the Mount Zion Road, and sometimes, Tunnel Mill Road. Go left on KY 458 for 2.5 miles and you will see the bridge on the left.

The Beech Fork Bridge, which is sometimes called Little Beech Creek Bridge or the Mooresville Bridge, spans the Beech Fork of the Chaplin River. It was built in 1865 by Henry Cornelius Barnes and consists of two 102-foot Burr Truss spans, which makes it the longest covered bridge in Kentucky.

Retrace your route back to the Bluegrass Parkway and continue on to Lexington. This is a really pleasant part of the drive. You can relax, engage the cruise control, and enjoy the next 37 miles of rolling farmland, bluegrass views, limestone road cuts, a beautiful view of the oak, hickory, and maple-covered hillsides up and down the river from the high bridge over the Kentucky River. At 37 miles, the Bluegrass Parkway ends. Going right takes you into Lexington, and going left takes you to Versailles.

22

Lexington to Green River Lake
There's Lots of History along U.S. 68

General description: This 85-mile drive begins in Lexington and follows U.S. 68 past the Shaker Village at Pleasant Hill, through Harrodsburg, past the Perryville Battlefield Site, past some of the best views of the knobs—a unique geological feature—through Lebanon and Campbellsville, and ends at Green River Lake.

Special attractions: Perryville Battlefield State Historic Site, Green River Lake State Park.

Location: South-central

Drive route numbers: U.S. 68; KY55,1061.

Travel season: All year.

Camping: Campgrounds at Harrodsburg, Campbellsville, and Green River Lake State Park.

Services: Motels in Lexington, Harrodsburg, Lebanon, and Campbellsville. There are bed and breakfasts in Danville and Campbellsville. Restaurants and/or fast food in Lexington, Harrodsburg, Lebanon, and Campbellsville.

Nearby attractions: Shaker Village at Pleasant Hill, Old Fort Harrod, Perryville Battlefield State Historic Site, Historic Danville (see Drive 19.)

The drive

The drive begins in Lexington at the junction of U.S. 68 and Man-o-War Boulevard and goes south on U.S. 68 toward Harrodsburg. In 0.9 mile, the road crosses South Elkhorn Creek. On your left at 2.8 miles is a very large church, and on your right is one of the many beautiful horse farms for which the Bluegrass area is world famous. Right here, you will also see the sign for the beginning of one of Kentucky's Scenic Byways. For the next 6 miles, you will be treated to more of the wide rolling Bluegrass views and scattered farms and stands of trees. At 9 miles, there is a Y intersection with KY 29. Keep to the right on U.S. 68. At 11.3 miles, you will see some of the many old limestone fences that line this drive. There are sections crumbling away, and you can see places where trees have moved the blocks out of line as they grew. For the next 2 miles, the road winds down through the trees past tall limestone walls. U.S. 68 is a little narrow along here. At 13.4 miles, it crosses a high bridge over the Kentucky River. For a little less than 2 miles, the twisting and turning through the trees continues. At that point, you will

Drive 22: Lexington to Green River Lake

There's Lots of History along U.S. 68

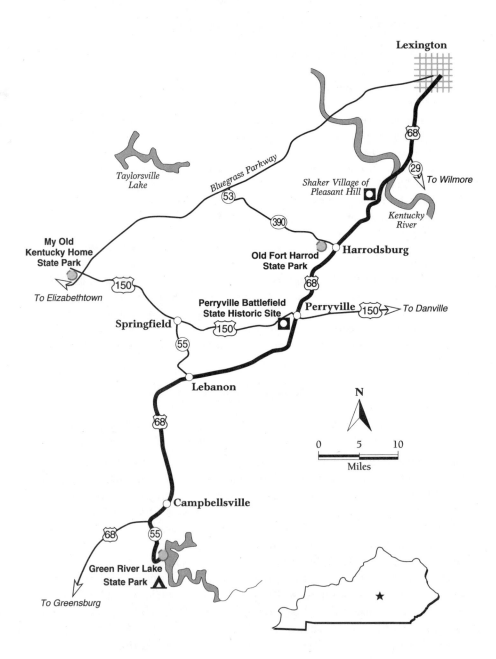

emerge from the trees, and for the next three miles you can enjoy more open views of the rolling grassland and see a lot more of the old limestone fences. At 19 miles the Shakertown Road goes right to the restored Shaker Village of Pleasant Hill.

During the early 1800s, Kentucky was in a frenzy of religious revival. Into this steaming cauldron of people speaking in tongues, barking like dogs, falling into trances, and even handling snakes came three Shaker missionaries. In August of 1805, these missionaries converted Elisha Thomas, Samuel Banta, and Henry Banta. A year later, there were scattered believers around the area, and before long, a small community was taking shape on the farm of Elisha Thomas about a mile and a half from the present village at Pleasant Hill. The community grew very rapidly, and by 1823, there were almost 500 Shakers who were buying up the land around them as fast as they could. Eventually, they would hold about 4,500 acres on which they grew corn and potatoes and had fruit orchards. The Shakers were as ingenious as they were devout. Some have likened them to the Amish, but the Shakers were always interested in any new tools and machinery.

Restoration of the village began in 1966 and included finding original colors, replacing missing walkways, and rerouting U.S. 68 around the village and restoring the old road to look as it did in the nineteenth century. Today, you can take a leisurely self-guided tour of the village, dine at the Trustee's Office Inn, visit craftsmen using the tools of the nineteenth century, take a riverboat ride, shop in the gift shops, or even schedule a workshop, seminar, or retreat in the meeting rooms.

If you stopped to visit the village, get back on U.S. 68 and turn right to Harrodsburg. Along the way, you will see farms, rolling hills, stands of trees in the meadows and, at 23.7 miles, a huge mansion far off on the right across the fields. When you enter Harrodsburg, you will be in the first permanent white settlement in Kentucky and the first English settlement west of the Alleghenies. The settlement began in June of 1774, when James Harrod and a band of 30 pioneers built cabins and a stockade at the headwaters of the Salt River near what they called a boiling spring.

As the drive continues, U.S. 68 makes a sharp left turn in town. About 0.5 mile, it makes a sharp right turn and goes 0.7 mile to a Y at the junction with KY 152. Keep to the left on U.S. 68. From here to Perryville at a little more than 10 miles, you will drive through more rolling hills and farmland. At 10.4 miles, U.S. 68 goes right and in about a block goes left. If you would like to visit the Perryville Battlefield State Historic Site, keep straight ahead here instead of following U.S. 68. It is just 2 miles to the site.

If you visited the Perryville Battlefield State Historic Site, retrace your route back to the junction of U.S. 68 and U.S. 150. Follow U.S. 68 west toward Lebanon. At 3.7 miles from the junction, look to your left and you will see a long view of the rolling hills and some more of the knobs (see

Along U.S. Highway 68 north of Harrodsburg.

Drive 19). At 4.9 miles, you will be getting closer views of the knobs on your left. There are rolling hills with a few trees leading up to the knobs. At 9.8 miles, the road drops down through a wooded area with houses and barns on both sides. For the next 7 miles or so, you will enjoy more rolling hills, some more of the knobs, and nice Bluegrass country. At 16.6 miles, you will enter Lebanon.

The Kentucky Scenic Byway ends at the junction with KY 55 in Lebanon. At 21.1 miles, look to your right and you will see something to tell the folks back home about: the "Whistling Pig General Store." At 22.2 miles, you will be driving between some of the knobs, and you can get a good look at just how dense the oaks and hickories are on their flanks. From here to Campbellsville, you will get great looks at The Knobs in this wide valley. At one point, you will climb a hill right between them. Here you can almost verify the story about the trees in Kentucky being so thick that a squirrel could cross the state and not touch the ground. It looks as though it would be extremely difficult just to walk through a stand of these trees. At 35.6 miles the city limits of Campbellsville pop up. At 38 miles, KY 55 goes left toward Green River Lake. At 41.7 miles, KY 1061 goes left to the lake. At 43.2 miles, go left to Green River Lake State Park. In 2.5 miles you will be at the parking area at the park.

Green River Lake is an 8,200-acre jewel. You can camp in the 156-site campground with a grocery, dump station, showers, rest rooms, and a laundry facility. There are pontoon boats, houseboats, fishing boats, ski boats, and personal water craft for rent. If you brought your gear, you can try for bass, crappie, muskie, and bluegill. If you don't want to catch the fish, you can swim with them or just relax on the beach. There is also a 20-mile trail for hiking and mountain biking.

23

Glasgow to Burkesville
Scenic Driving at its Best

General description: This 54.8- or 91.6-mile drive offers two options. Option A twists and turns through the hills and past small towns along KY 63 from Glasgow to Tompkinsville. The scenery is beautiful and is up close and personal. Option B leaves Glasgow and follows U.S. 31E across the Barren River Lake area to Scottsville. From Scottsville, it meanders along KY 100 to Tompkinsville. Both options follow KY 100 from Tompkinsville to Burkesville, a road that snakes its way through backcountry Kentucky and some unmatched rural beauty.

Special attractions: Barren River Lake, historic West Main Street in Scottsville, Scottsville Historical Museum.

Location: South-central.

Drive route numbers: Option A: KY 63, 100, 90; Option B: U.S. 31E; KY 101, 100, 90.

Travel season: All year.

Camping: Campgrounds at Barren River Lake State Resort Park, Scottsville, Glasgow, Dale Hollow Lake State Park, Sulfur Creek, and Wolf River.

Services: A lodge and cottages are available at Barren River State Resort Park. Motels can be found in Burkesville, Glasgow, Scottsville, Dale Hollow Lake, and Tompkinsville. Bed and breakfasts can be found in Dale Hollow Lake and Glasgow. Restaurants and/or fast food in Glasgow, Scottsville, Gamaliel, Tompkinsville, and Burkesville.

Nearby attractions: A few miles from the route will take you to Dale Hollow Lake and the Old Mulkey Meetinghouse. Just to the north is Lake Cumberland (see Drive 18), Old Mulkey Meetinghouse State Historic Site.

The drive

If you like the leisurely pace of a country road that wanders slowly through the hills, then Option A is for you. If you like some of your scenery wide open, and like to make a little more speed, then choose Option B.

Option A
There is a traffic light at the junction of U.S. 31E and KY 90 in Glasgow. Set your odometer at zero at this intersection and go south on U.S. 31E. At 0.6 mile, turn left onto KY 80/90. This is marked as a Kentucky Scenic Byway.

Drive 23: Glasgow to Burkesville
Scenic Driving at its Best

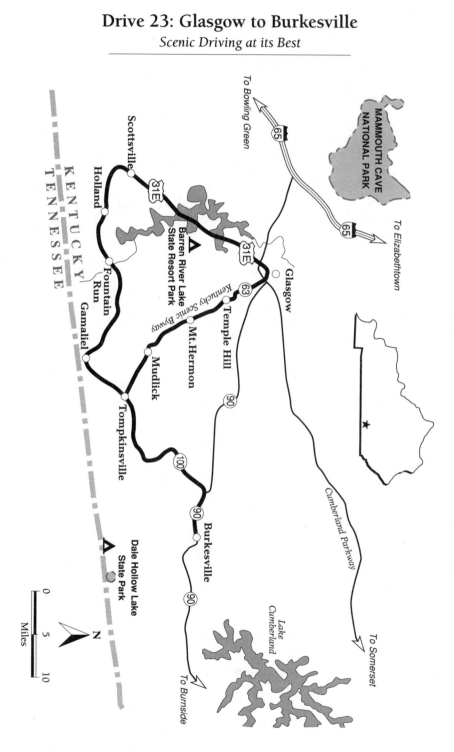

You will wind through old Glasgow for about a mile, then come to a stop sign at U.S. 31E. Turn right on U.S. 31E, then left on KY 63. KY 63 is a part of this Kentucky Scenic Byway, so just follow the signs through a few more turns and you will be out of town. At 2.1 miles, the road makes a left turn, crosses Beaver Creek, and begins a climb into the trees. For the next 3 miles, KY 63 twists and turns past some pretty homes and acres of lawn. At 5.1 miles you will cross Boyd's Creek. In the next mile, you will climb past a limestone road cut to the top of a hill where you will be treated to beautiful views to your left. At 7.6 miles, you will cross Falling Timber Creek. At 9 miles, there is a really nice little roadside park on the right and a spectacular long view toward the wooded hills to the left. A little over half a mile from the park, you will enter Temple Hill, a pretty village named for its location on the hill once owned by a family named Temple. Temple Hill runs along the road for about a mile.

At the end of town, KY 63 makes a right turn and continues on past more fields, farms and barns, crosses Skaggs Creek, Shoals Creek, and continues on to Mount Hermon at 16.2 miles. Beyond Mount Hermon, the road makes a gentle sweep to the left and exposes views of rolling hills and red barns. Look to your right at 20.4 miles and you will see a nice weathered gray barn. In just 0.3 mile farther, you will enter Mud Lick, a tiny hamlet named for a local salt stream that was kept muddy by the animals stomping around in it when they came to drink. The road continues to snake its way along and by 21.2 miles is on top of a hill where you can enjoy a long view to the left of houses, trees, and rolling Kentucky landscape. In about 5.5 miles, you will be in Tompkinsville.

Option B

Set your odometer at zero at the traffic light at the junction of U.S. 31E and KY 90. Head south on U.S. 31E. By 5.6 miles, most of the views are of gently rolling farmland. Look to your right at 7.6 miles and you will see a home sitting in the middle of more fenced lawn than the average small town anywhere else would have in total. Just beyond, the road drops downhill and crosses an arm of Barren River Lake. In the next 4 miles, the road drops downhill some more and passes rolling fields and red barns. The drive continues to drop down through stands of mixed hardwoods until it crosses another arm of Barren River Lake at 12.3 miles near the entrance to Barren River Lake State Resort Park.

At the park, you can check into one of the 51 rooms at the Louie B. Nunn Lodge that overlooks the 10,000-acre lake, or perhaps you might prefer one of the two-bedroom, two-bath cottages, which include tableware, linens, and cooking utensils. There is also a 99-site campground. At the campground, you will find utility hookups, a dump station, showers and rest rooms, and parking for RVs. There are also spots to pitch a tent. When

Along KY 90 east of Burkesville.

you are settled, look around at the dining room, the swimming pool, the 18-hole regulation golf course, the horse stables, the 4 miles of hiking trails, or even the lighted tennis and basketball courts. For more information on Barren River Lake State Resort Park and for specific directions, see the appendix.

Designed, built, and operated by the U.S. Army Corps of Engineers, Barren River Lake was created to reduce flooding and damage along the Barren, Green, and Ohio Rivers. The project was begun in 1960 and became operational in 1964. During the periods of maximum rainfall in the fall and winter, the lake is kept at a fairly low level so that surface runoff can be stored to protect the downstream areas. The secondary uses of boating, fishing, camping, hunting, picnicking, and swimming are an added benefit both for the users and the local economy.

You may have wondered how this area, which seems lush to us, ever got the name "barren." Some believe that the amount of rocky limestone in the soil kept trees from growing, and others feel that early logging stripped the land of its trees; but most historians seem to think that the Indians regularly burned it to make hunting game easier.

In the next 2 miles, you will pass a pretty picnic ground in the trees on the left and cross still another arm of the Lake. At 18.4 miles, there is a great long view to the right of the rolling hills covered with many of the hardwood species found throughout Kentucky. At 21.6 miles the views are to the left.

At 23 miles, there is a traffic light at the intersection with KY 101. Keep straight ahead on U.S. 31E. In 2 miles, there is another traffic light at the junction with U.S. 231. Keep straight ahead on U.S. 31E. At 26.1 miles, go left toward Scottsville at the intersection with KY 100. In less than 0.5 mile, KY 100 makes a sharp left into Scottsville.

There are a number of interesting things to see and do in Scottsville. Your first stop might be the Historical Society Museum on Fourth Street. Located in the 1900s home of Dr. Pellie Graves, it houses lots of items from the early days in the area and many genealogical records. There are many historic homes along Main Street, but the one on the corner of Welch has a Calacanthus bush on the front lawn that has been blooming since 1842. On Locust Street is the public spring that has provided a steady flow of water for more than 200 years.

Stay on KY 100 as it winds through town. At 29.3 miles you will be back in the trees again. At 33.5 miles, you will be passing more rolling farmland with many small farms along the way and trees in the distance. In the next 3 miles, you will travel through some especially pretty spots. You will drop downhill steeply and twist back and forth through the trees, and wind back uphill. As you come over the top of the hill, a big farmhouse will greet you on your right. Just beyond the farmhouse, you enter Holland. The small community grew up around a house built in 1810 by William Holland. After Holland, the road turns left, then makes a hairpin turn to the right, while hiding deep in the trees.

At 43.4 miles, you will come to a four-way-stop in Fountain Run, a town named for 7 nearby springs that residents said bubbled up like fountains. The town's first name of Jimtown was not acceptable to the Post Office Department. Keep straight ahead at the stop on KY 100. The road will drop downhill and twist and turn past some old log cabins on the left. The road continues through the trees, drops down past an old barn on the right, levels out some, and passes the Gamaliel City Limits sign at 56.4 miles.

Gamaliel was named for the teacher of the Apostle Paul, but it is not clear just who gave the town the name. Some think it was named by a Dr. Bobo, a physician who practiced in the area, while others think it was Samuel Dewitt, a local school teacher. In 0.4 mile, KY 63 joins KY 100, and the two go on into Tompkinsville together.

About 2 miles south of town on KY 1446 is the Old Mulkey Meetinghouse State Historic Site. This roughhewn log building is the oldest log meetinghouse in Kentucky. It was built in 1804 by a small band of Baptists from North and South Carolina. Their leader was Philip Mulkey, and the first preacher was John Mulkey. The building was made in the shape of a cross with 12 corners. Some say the 12 corners symbolize the 12 apostles, and others say they represent the 12 tribes of Israel. The truth might be more prosaic. The shape of the cross naturally dictated the 12 corners.

Both of your options for this drive come together at Tompkinsville, so no matter which drive you chose, you will continue your drive from the intersection of KY 63/100/163. Go east on KY 100. Beyond this junction, and all the way to the junction of KY 90 just outside of Burkesville, KY 100 has no road signs to let you know what road you are on. It is the only paved road on the route, though, so you won't get lost. This segment is less than 25 miles long, but it is spectacular. If you can imagine yourself in a horse and buggy, you could be in the 19th century. The road is a real snake, and it is lined much of the way with varieties of hardwood trees. They do not form canopies, though, so there is plenty of open sky to light the views. At 21.5 miles, you will come to the junction of KY 100 and KY 90. Go right on KY 90 for 6 miles to Burkesville.

Just south of Burkesville is Dale Hollow Lake State Resort Park. The bulk of the huge 28,000-acre lake lies in Tennessee, but there is plenty in Kentucky and plenty to see and do. The 30-room Mary Ray Oaken Lodge sits on a cliff 300 feet above the lake at one of its widest points. There is a 144-site campground with hookups, a dump station, showers, rest rooms, and a swimming pool. Twenty-four campsites are set aside for campers with horses. A 2-story-high dining area has walls of glass on three sides and a 37-foot-high stone fireplace. The meals feature Kentucky regional food, but international entrees are also on the menu. The marina rents pontoon boats, and there is a launching ramp in case you happen to have your own boat along. Crappie, bream, muskie, walleye, trout, catfish, and five species of bass should keep you busy if you like fishing. In addition, you can enjoy 13.4 miles of trails, horse camping, mountain biking, or picnicking. After all of this activity, maybe just a nap would be nice.

24

Monticello to Williamsburg

Along KY 92

General description: This 54.5-mile drive begins at the intersection of KY 90 and KY 92 in Monticello at the south end of Cumberland Lake. From there, it winds along KY 92 through the Daniel Boone National Forest and the Big South Fork National River and Recreation Area to historic Williamsburg on the Cumberland River.

Special attractions: Daniel Boone National Forest, Big South Fork National River and Recreation Area, Big South Fork Scenic Railway.

Location: South-central .

Drive route numbers: KY 92.

Travel season: Spring and fall are probably nicest because of the color. Summer is fine, too. Be aware that many of the attractions close at the end of October and do not open again until March or April. To find out where to write for further information, see Appendix A.

Camping: Campgrounds in Monticello, Williamsburg, and Big South Fork National River and Recreation Area.

Services: Motels in Williamsburg, Monticello, and Stearns. Restaurants and/or fast food in Monticello, Stearns, Pine Knot, and Williamsburg.

Nearby attractions: Lake Cumberland, Cumberland Falls State Park (see Drive 17), Blue Heron Mining Community (near Stearns).

The drive

About halfway through this drive, you will pass through Stearns, which was one of the old company coal towns. If you have the time, and really want to get the flavor of the old mining days, you can take tours of Blue Heron and Barthell. Both are restored mining camps and can be reached by driving about 10 miles from Stearns on KY 742.

Blue Heron, sometimes called Mine #18, was a part of the Stearns Coal and Lumber Company's operations. It is now a part of the Big South Fork National River and Recreation Area. Even though the mine operated from 1937 to 1962, there are virtually no written records of the day-to-day activities of the camp. Most of what is known about the town and the mine is from oral history. Fortunately, since it wasn't an old operation, there are still lots of folks around to contribute to an oral history.

Drive 24: Monticello to Williamsburg
Along KY 92

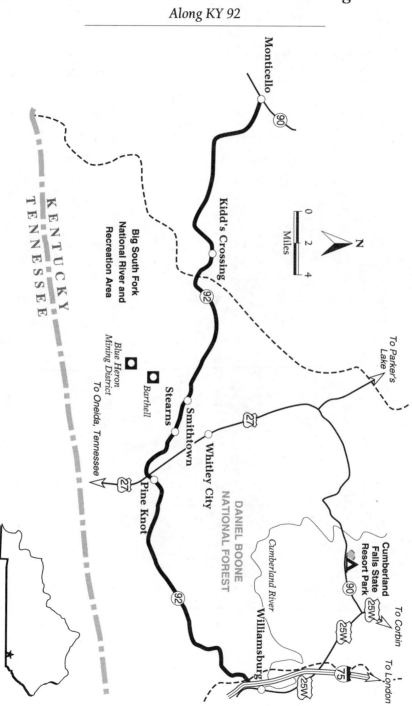

Along KY 92 east of Monticello.

When the mine and town were abandoned in 1962, all of the buildings were either removed or allowed just to rot away. When the "rebuilding" began, it was decided to make this an interpretive center rather than just a restored ghost town. The new buildings are on the sites of some of the old ones, but they are really just steel frameworks with roofs, referred to as "ghost structures." Each such structure has an audio station where you can hear tapes of some of the past residents talking about their memories. If you have access to the Internet, you can go to the Blue Heron website and listen to the tapes there (see the appendix for the website address).

You might also want to see the Barthell Mining Camp. Unlike Blue Heron with its ghost structures, Barthell is being rebuilt as close to its original state as possible. The University of Kentucky has researched the area to help keep the restoration authentic.

While you can drive to the two towns, an interesting change of pace would be to take the train. The Big South Fork Scenic Railway runs from Stearns along the original 11-mile route to the mines. The cars are open air, and a guide narrates the trip. Currently, the season is from April through October (see the appendix for more information).

To begin the drive, set your odometer to zero at the intersection of KY 90 and KY 92 at the northwest end of Monticello. Head southeast on KY 92 for 1.4 miles where the road goes left. You can't miss the turn, there is a monument in the middle of the intersection. In half a block, KY 92 goes right and continues to wind through town. By 2.5 miles, the houses are giving way to farms, fields, and some oak-covered knobs. The road winds back and forth through the farmland and wooded areas until it passes through a small community at 12 miles. The road continues to drop and climb and wind along for another 1.5 miles to the junction with KY 3286 at Kidd's Crossing. For the next 4 miles, you will enjoy wooded areas and some long views through breaks in the trees. At 18.8 miles, you will enter the Daniel Boone National Forest, and at 24.1 miles, you will be in the Big South Fork National River and Recreation Area. In less than a half mile, you will cross the bridge over the South Fork of the Cumberland River and twist and climb back up through the trees to Smithtown. For 5 more miles, the road continues to twist and turn, but the view widens out and the trees are not as dense. More and more homes and stores show up as you get closer to Stearns. At 29.5 miles, you will be at a stop sign in Stearns, a town that once was wholly owned by the Stearns Coal and Lumber Company. It was first settled in around 1840 by Riley and Bailey Sellers and was called Hemlock. Justus S. Stearns of Ludington, Michigan, officially founded the town and the company in 1902.

If your interests run more toward camping, hiking, canoeing, white-water rafting, kayaking, swimming, mountain biking, horseback riding, hunting and fishing, four-wheel-driving, or just absorbing scenery, then the 113,000 acres of the Big South Fork National River and Recreation Area is for you. The area stretches way down into Tennessee and offers just about any outdoor activity (see the appendix for more information).

At 1.2 miles from the stop sign in Stearns, there is a traffic light. Stay on KY 92 to the right. At 1.7 miles, you will come to Revelo. In a little under 2 miles, you will reach Pine Knot. Beyond Pine Knot, the road snakes its way downhill through the trees. It is two-lane blacktop with no shoulder, but there are guardrails in the appropriate places. At 16.2 miles, you will cross over a creek on a high bridge. At 17 miles, you will come over the top of a hill and find yourself in a bowl-shaped valley ringed by mountains. In only a mile, the road climbs out of the bowl and sneaks under some canopies of the typical Kentucky hardwood trees. At 19.6 miles, there is a sharp bend to the left and a nice long view of the valley through a break in the trees. At 24 miles you will cross over Interstate 75 and come to the junction of KY 92 and U.S. 25. Go left for about a half mile to Williamsburg.

25

Old Frankfort Pike

One of Kentucky's Best Scenic Byways

General description: This 16.9-mile drive is along Old Frankfort Pike that runs from Lexington to a point just southeast of Frankfort. This Kentucky Scenic Byway has been voted one of the 10 best scenic drives in the United States.

Special attractions: Old limestone rock walls, famous Thoroughbred farms, numerous buildings on the National Historic Register.

Location: North-central .

Drive route numbers: Kentucky Highway 1681.

Travel season: All year.

Camping: Campgrounds in Frankfort and Lexington.

Services: There are many motels in Frankfort and Lexington, and bed and breakfast establishments in Lexington, Frankfort, and Versailles. Restaurants and/or fast food in Frankfort and Lexington.

Nearby attractions: Keeneland Race Track. Both Lexington and Frankfort, as well as the towns between, are a tourist's and history buff's paradise. Check the web sites in the appendix or the section on where to write for more information to obtain a Kentucky Vacation Guide from the Kentucky Department of Tourism.

The drive

The drive begins at the junction of Old Frankfort Pike (KY 1681) and New Circle Road at the northwest edge of Lexington. Set your odometer at zero at the junction and get ready for a treat. Along KY 1681, you will pass many of the Thoroughbred farms for which Kentucky, and the Bluegrass area in particular, is famous. The breeding, racing, and sale of Thoroughbreds is a multibillion dollar business in Kentucky. Kentucky produces more Thoroughbred foals than any other state in the United States. Bordering the road for most of the drive are locusts, Osage orange, dogwood, redbud, red and white oak, and sugar maple. In the spring, the flowering redbud and dogwood make a spectacular display. There are also many canopies of trees along the route. Most of these are formed by either locust or Osage orange.

In just 0.5 mile from the junction, you will see a sign for the start of a Kentucky Scenic Byway. A short way beyond the sign is an old limestone fence on the left. At 1.5 miles, there is a scenic pull off where you can admire

Drive 25: Old Frankfort Pike
Drive 26: Pisgah Pike
Drive 27: Midway to Versailles

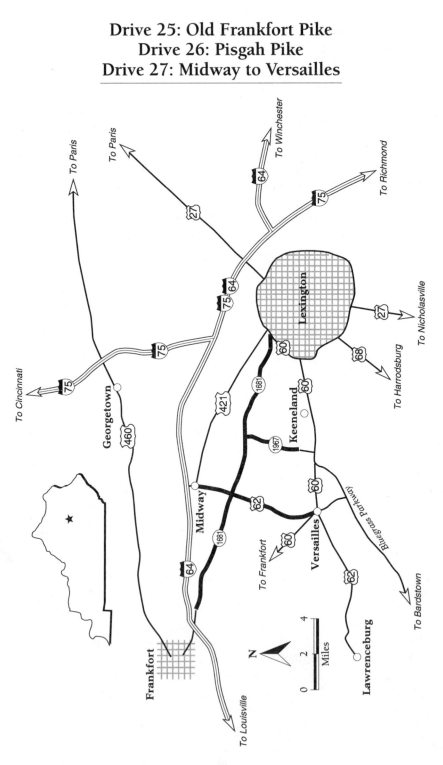

the farms and get a picture or two. Along the drive, some of the farms you will see are:

MARE HAVEN FARM—Owned by Dr. William O. Reed, veterinarian at Belmont Park, Aqueduct, and Hialeah. Mare Haven was once part of the same property that includes the Darby Dan Farm.

DARBY DAN FARM—Although Thoroughbreds did not appear at Darby Dan until 1905, the land has been farmed since 1788. In fact, the farm is part of a section that was surveyed by Daniel Boone. The Federal style house, known as Darby Manor, was built in 1823 by the son of Major Henry Payne, the original settler. Beginning in 1905, Colonel Edward Bradley developed the property into one of the most influential Thoroughbred farms in the history of the industry. His horses won four Kentucky Derbies: Behave Yourself in 1921, Bubbling Over in 1926, Burgoo King in 1932, and Brokers Tip in 1933. Twice his horses finished first and second in the derby. The Colonel gave his horses nothing but the best. He had a barn built with a roof that opened up so that the horses could get the benefit of sunshine. He even had some of his nearsighted horses fitted with glasses, a fine gesture which so startled one of them that he bolted and put the jockey in the hospital for a month. As a further protection for these valuable animals, he built a tunnel under the Old Frankfort Pike so that they would not have to compete with traffic.

BUCKRAM OAK FARM—This 469-acre farm came to the Thoroughbred industry far later than most of the others. It was originally a small cattle operation, but has been converted to a top notch Thoroughbred farm by Mahmoud Fustok and his family of Saudi Arabia. In addition to the main house and guest house, there are six houses for the farm workers. These are supplemented with a tennis court, a 5-acre lake spanned by 2 arched bridges, and a 1-acre island. For the horses, there are five 20-stall barns with slate roofs, ornate cupolas, and gold-veneered weather vanes. The stalls are paneled in red oak with stainless-steel hardware. If you drive by in the spring, you will see thousands of narcissus blooming around the lake and on the island. To line the 6.5 miles of paved roads on the farm, took three thousand trees.

DONAMIRE FARM—This beautifully landscaped farm has more than 13 miles of white fences, two lakes, several ponds, and hundreds of tulip poplar, pine, and walnut trees. There are two 15-stall barns for the broodmares, weanlings, and yearlings, a stallion barn with a breeding shed and seven stalls, and a 24-stall training barn. All of the structures are of Bedford stone with slate and copper roofs. The name comes from a combination of the first names of the owners: Don and Mira Ball.

View across the beautiful Keeneland Race Track.

THREE CHIMNEYS FARM—Among the stallions on this top farm are 1978 Triple-Crown winner Seattle Slew and two of his sons, Slew O' Gold and Capote. Fly So Free, Rahy, and Dynaformer also are in residence.

At 3.4 miles, you will pass through a short locust or Osage orange tree canopy, and at less than a mile farther, you will be at the entrance to the Headley-Whitney Museum. In 1968, George Headley, an artist-designer founded this small museum to display a diversified collection of fine arts. There are permanent displays as well as periodically changing collections. In the Jewel Room, you will be able to view one of the three finest collections of bibelot, small objects of beauty and rarity. This is the only contemporary collection of its kind in the world that is open to the public. Among the objects you will see are miniature plants, animals, gods and goddesses made of gold, bronze, ivory, coral, amber, and lapis lazuli and embellished with diamonds, sapphires, rubies, and other precious gems.

In the Shell Room, look up at a ceiling with 4 shell mosaics of swans and pigeons. Shells also cover the doors, mirrors, windows, and a bird cage. Shells have even been used to create busts of Neptune and Aphrodite.

If you would like to visit the library and share the room with elephant tusks, narwhal tusks, ostrich egg candlesticks, and books about art from all over the world, then make this stop a must on your drive.

Beyond the museum, you pass more farms, rolling bluegrass, limestone fences, and lots of black wooden fences. At 5.8 miles, on the right is a replica of the New Union Christian Church. The original building, built in 1834, was destroyed by fire in the 1970s. Across the road on the left is a gray-weathered barn. At 6.1 miles, the Pike crosses South Elkhorn Creek, and at 7.2 miles, you will see a nice example of one of the many old limestone fences as you pass the turnoff to Pisgah (see Drive 26). At about 8 miles, you will be in a light canopy of trees. There is no undergrowth, however, so you have beautiful views of the horse farms between the trees. At 9.8 miles, there is an old country store on the right. At 10.1 miles, you will cross U.S. 62 at Nugent's Crossroads by the Offutt-Cole Tavern (see Drive 27).

For the next 5 miles, you will continue to see the beautiful rolling bluegrass, horse farms, tree canopies, and more of those great old limestone fences. You may even see some cattle grazing here and there. The Scenic Byway ends at 15.5 miles, but we take you along KY 1681 for another 1.5 miles to the junction with U.S. 60. Here you are just a mile or so from Frankfort. If you haven't yet taken Drive 16 to Rabbit Hash, now is your chance. Or you may want to go back across Old Frankfort Pike, see what you might have missed on the way over and, if you didn't do it on the way, take the Pisgah Pike (Drive 26).

If driving through Thoroughbred country has piqued your interest in racing, you might want to drive over to Keeneland, one of the most beautiful tracks in the country. Keeneland's slogan is "Racing the way it was meant

One of the beautiful horse farms in the Lexington Bluegrass area.

to be." It is a place that would be worth a visit just to see the landscaping even if there were no horses there. Horses are saddled in an area planted with tall trees. There are dogwood, linden, white pine, crab apple, pin oak, American hornbeam, and a giant sycamore. In the spring, the blooms are almost as beautiful as in the fall with the reds and golds of the turning leaves. In the infield of the track there are even Japanese yew trimmed to spell out "Keeneland."

There are two short race meetings run each year, one in April and one in October, each lasting about three weeks. The spring meeting features a stakes race each day, with the highlight being the Blue Grass Stakes, which is a prep race for the Kentucky Derby. The fall meeting has as its showcase the Spinster Stakes. Keeneland attracts both the best horses and the best jockeys and trainers in the country.

Even the Queen of England has been here. Queen Elizabeth II has visited only one racetrack in the United States, and Keeneland was the one. On October 11, 1984, she was on hand for the running of the Queen Elizabeth II Challenge Cup. She went to the walking ring and shook hands with all of the jockeys who rode in the race.

26

Pisgah Pike

The Best of the Bluegrass

(See map on page 150)

General description: This 3-mile drive is a very short, but really beautiful drive through some of the best of the Bluegrass.
Special attractions: Pisgah church.
Location: North-central .
Drive route numbers: Pisgah Pike (Kentucky Highway 1967).
Travel season: All year.
Camping: Campgrounds in Frankfort and Lexington.
Services: There are many motels in Frankfort and Lexington, and bed and breakfast establishments in Lexington, Frankfort, and Versailles. Restaurants and/or fast food in both Frankfort and Lexington.
Nearby attractions: Both Lexington and Frankfort, as well as the towns between, are a tourist's and history buff's paradise. Check the web sites in the appendix or the section on where to write for more information to obtain a Kentucky Vacation Guide from the Kentucky Department of Tourism.

The drive

This drive begins at the junction of Old Frankfort Pike (KY 1681) and Pisgah Pike (KY 1967). This is about 7 miles from Lexington on Drive 25. Pisgah Pike runs approximately through the center of the Pisgah Rural Historic District, an area of historic homes, churches, and horse farms bounded roughly by Old Frankfort Pike, Big Sink Road, Payne's Mill Road, and U.S. 60. The rolling meadows and woodlands must have had a powerful effect on early settlers, since they named their community Pisgah after the biblical Mount Pisgah from which Moses first glimpsed the Promised Land. As you drive through, you may well understand their feelings. After all, not a great deal has changed in over 200 years. There is blacktop on the pike, but it is still a narrow country lane. Many of the stately old homes are not much different to the eye, and the land has endured.

It is the hope of the Pisgah Community Historic Association that not much will change for the next 200 years. Toward that end, the association

Old truss bridge in the Pisgah historic area.

worked to get national recognition for the area, and, due largely to their efforts, in 1988, the Pisgah Rural Historic District was placed on the National Register of Historic Places. The growth of this part of Kentucky has brought about pressure to use land like this for development, and the association has had some battles to keep the rural atmosphere. There is no doubt that we need places for people to live and work, and that progress will march on, but in the midst of "progress" we need some islands of tranquillity that connect us to the past. Pisgah surely qualifies as such an island.

One of the more interesting sights along the way is the canopy of trees formed by the 125-year-old Osage orange trees. The Osage orange grows to 50 feet or more and reaches a trunk diameter from 1 to 4 feet. It is native to Arkansas and the Red River Valleys that were home to the Osage Indians. The bark is brown to orange brown and gets very scaly and fissured. The branches are stiff and thorny and interlaced. This last feature was the reason why they were planted along here. The nature of the interlaced, thorny branches made a perfect living barbed wire fence. There may have been some idea of planting a "cheap" fence, since lumber was expensive, but the labor involved in keeping the trees trimmed down to fence height was excessive. Consequently, many of the trees got out of hand and farmers cut them down and put in fences.

There is not much left of the old limestone fences along Pisgah Pike, but if you keep your eyes peeled, you will spot a couple of really nice examples.

At the end of the drive, you come to the Pisgah Presbyterian Church, built first in 1784 as a log structure and rebuilt in stone in 1812. The building was remodeled in 1868. Next to the church is the Pisgah Cemetery. The cemetery was in use shortly after the log church was built more than 200 years ago, and remains an active cemetery today. Some of the inscriptions can no longer be read, so it is impossible to determine just to whom the first grave belongs. There were about 70 persons buried here prior to 1850. Pioneer families who faced Indian battles, war, and other hardships of the frontier, lie in the older section of the cemetery. In the early days, the cemetery was just a burial ground. There were no records kept for the first 100 years, at least none have ever been found. When someone died, the family picked a spot, dug the grave, and buried the person. In 1966, it was decided that no more graves would be located in the old section. The reason for this was that many unmarked graves were being discovered by those digging new ones. In addition, the more modern equipment used in grave preparation sometimes damaged the old, fragile markers.

Perhaps the most famous gravesite in Pisgah Cemetery is not one of a pioneer settler or a Revolutionary War veteran, but one of a far more contemporary figure: Albert Benjamin Chandler. "Happy" Chandler, two-term governor of Kentucky, United States Senator, and Commissioner of Baseball was laid to rest here in 1991.

27

Midway to Versailles
Bluegrass Horse Country

(See map on page 150)

General description: This 5.8-mile ramble is another short drive along one of Kentucky's Scenic Byways. It follows the section of U.S. 62 from the old railroad town of Midway past more of the magnificent horse farms to the historic city of Versailles. By the way, even though the city got its name from the French city where Revolutionary War hero Lafayette attended school, in Kentucky the name is pronounced "Ver-SALES" and not "Ver-SIGH."

Special attractions: Offutt-Cole Tavern, old limestone fences, beautiful horse farms, Bluegrass Scenic Railroad.

Location: North-central.

Drive route numbers: U.S. 62.

Travel season: All year.

Camping: Campgrounds in Frankfort and Lexington.

Services: There are many motels in Frankfort and Lexington, and bed and breakfast establishments in Lexington, Frankfort, and Versailles. Restaurants and fast food in both Frankfort and Lexington.

Nearby attractions: Both Lexington and Frankfort, as well as the towns between, are a tourist's and history buff's paradise. Check the web sites in the appendix or the section on where to write for more information to obtain a Kentucky Vacation Guide from the Kentucky Department of Tourism.

The drive

The drive begins in Midway, the first town in Kentucky built by a railroad company. Streets were named for members of the board of directors of the Louisville and Nashville Railroad. Today, the tracks run down the middle of the main street, which is lined with shops selling antiques, boutiques with hand made Kentucky crafts, and restaurants. Midway is also the home of Midway College, the only women's college in Kentucky.

Just east of town is the Weisenberger Mill, the oldest continuously operating mill in the state. The mill has been in the same family since August Weisenberger bought it in 1865. Six generations of Weisenbergers have operated it in the same location since that time. In the early years, the primary products were soft wheat flour and white cornmeal. Today, there are over 70 products in their inventory, including a cookbook containing old family recipes as well as those from customers over the years.

The inventory of so many products signals that even though the Weisenbergers have been milling here since 1865, they are very much in the twenty-first century. Not long ago, they had a generator added to the turbines in the mill, and now produce much of their own electricity. In one sense, it can be said that even their computers are run by the water power from South Elkhorn Creek. Speaking of computers, the Weisenbergers have a website so that should you wish to, you can order from them online, or ask them questions via e-mail (see the appendix for more information). To reach the mill from Midway, go southeast on U.S. 421 to Weisenberger Road. Turn right and you will see the mill on the left.

Leave Midway on U.S. 62 and head toward Versailles. In a little more than 1.5 miles, you will come to a four-way stop at the junction of KY 1681, the Old Frankfort Pike (see Drive 25). This was known as Nugents Crossroads, a settlement that grew up around the Offutt-Cole Tavern. The tavern was originally a log structure that served as a stage stop in the early nineteenth century on the Frankfort Pike.

For the balance of the drive, you will travel past more of the splendid horse farms, many with long, tree-lined drives to the homes. There are canopies of trees, rolling bluegrass fields, scattered wooded areas, and many of the great old limestone fences.

All of the drives in the Bluegrass area pass by sections of the old limestone fences that once criss crossed the countryside. There are a number of reasons why so few are left. The turnpike system, which began in 1840, was one of the big destroyers of the fences. Under Kentucky law, property owners who lived along the route of the new roads were required to contribute either labor or materials to the building of the road. Many farmers opted to remove their fences and crush them into gravel for the roads. The portable rock crushers they used were called "fence eaters." The biggest "fence eater" of all, though, is "progress." In much of the Bluegrass, the only things left to mark the places where so many labored to build fences that would last are interstates, shopping malls, subdivisions, and fast food businesses.

The walls hold a fascination beyond just their beauty. They came into being in a large part due to a serious problem thousands of miles and a whole ocean away. From 1846 to 1850, a blight on the potato crop in Ireland left fields covered with a black rot. The price of food soared and farmers watched the food stores in their cellars rotting. Unable to pay their bills, hundreds of thousands of peasants were evicted from their homes and forced into disease-infested workhouses. Estimates of the deaths from the famine range to One-million. With no hope at home, thousands upon thousands of

Old limestone fence between Midway and Versailles.

Irish fled to America, and many of those immigrants were stone masons. A number of these craftsmen found their way to Kentucky where lots of stone was just waiting.

At 5.8 miles, you will come to the junction of U.S. 62 and U.S. 60. Go left for a half-mile or so to Versailles, where there is much to do and see if you have the time. If you like trains as well as bluegrass, you can take a 90-minute ride on the Bluegrass Scenic Railroad through rural Woodford County. There is an optional side trip to Young's High Bridge, an 1888 railroad trestle which reaches 1,658 feet across and 280 feet above the Kentucky River. When you finish the ride, be sure to visit the Bluegrass Railroad Museum. Among the items you can see are a 1960s caboose and a restored steam engine. There is also the Nostalgia Station Toy and Train Museum (see the appendix for where to get more information on many more things to see and do in the Versailles area).

28

Ironworks Pike

Horses, More Horses, and the Kentucky Horse Park

General description: Our 33.1-mile drive follows KY 1973 from White Sulfur past beautiful horse farms, down country road shaded by canopies of trees, past some spots where towns once existed, by the big Kentucky Horse Park, and ends at Athens, southeast of Lexington. KY 1973 begins as Ironworks Pike, but changes names two times along the way. After it crosses U.S. 27/68, it becomes Muir Station Road, and after passing Fenwick, goes by the name of Cleveland Road. Don't be confused. Just follow the KY 1973 signs.

Special attractions: Horse farms, Kentucky Horse Park, The Boone's Creek Baptist Church.

Location: North-central.

Drive route numbers: KY 1973.

Travel season: All year.

Camping: Campgrounds in Lexington and at the Kentucky Horse Park.

Services: There are many motels and bed and breakfast establishments in the Lexington area. Restaurants and/or fast food in Lexington.

Nearby attractions: Lexington (check the web sites in the appendix or the section on where to write for more information to obtain a Kentucky Vacation Guide from the Kentucky Department of Tourism), Boone Station State Historic Site, Double Stink Hog Farm.

The drive

Along KY 1973 you will drive past stands of dogwood, redbud, ash, oak, and maple, and under canopies of locust and Osage orange. You will also see some of the best of the rolling bluegrass country. The crown jewel of the drive, though, is the Kentucky Horse Park. Located right in the heart of the Bluegrass area, this 1,032-acre working horse farm surrounded by 32 miles of white fence, offers visitors a look at two museums, two theaters, and more than 40 different breeds of horses. At the visitor center, you can pick up material about the park's various attractions and special events. If you take the Walking Farm Tour, you will see a farrier practicing the art of horse-shoeing and see how leather harnesses and saddles are made. From March 16 through October, a Parade of Breeds is presented twice daily. Here you will see 24 of the park's 40 breeds put through their paces by authentically

Drive 28: Ironworks Pike

Horses, More Horses, and the Kentucky Horse Park

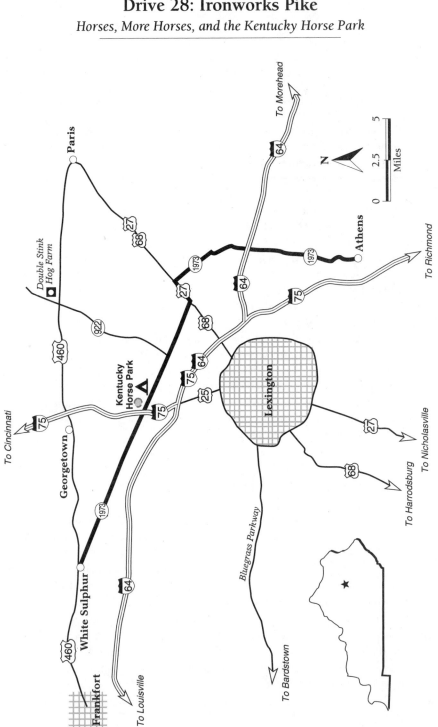

costumed riders. After the show, you can meet and pet the horses and talk with the riders. You can also visit the Draft Barn, where you will see the Belgians, Clydesdales, Percherons, English Sires, Halflingers, and Suffolk Punch. These are the horses that pull the park's horse-drawn trolleys. There are also trail rides around the park and through the surrounding country-side and pony rides for the kids.

You can also visit the International Museum of the Horse, where you will learn about the 58,000,000-year history of the magnificent beasts. There is a collection of nineteenth-century horse-drawn carriages and racing vehicles, a display of 560 gold, silver, and crystal trophies, 35 paintings from the world-famous Calumet Farm, and changing exhibits of equine art. The complete text along with hundreds of photographs can be viewed on the Museum's website (see the appendix for the website address).

It isn't necessary to spend all of your time with the horses. You can take advantage of the campground at the park. Its 260 sites, each with a paved pad, electric and water hookups, and fire rings will make your stay enjoyable. There is also a primitive tenting area. No matter where you camp, you can enjoy the lighted tennis courts and the junior Olympic pool.

To begin the drive, set your odometer at zero at the junction of U.S. 460 and KY 1973 at White Sulfur. Head east on KY 1973 and in just 0.7 mile, you will see the first of many big horse farms. In another 0.1 mile on the left is the Midway Sportsman's Club. In the next few miles, you will enjoy tree canopies, rolling bluegrass fields, a gray-weathered barn, and the historic marker for the Patriot Stage Stop. At 3.5 miles, the "Red Hen Nursery and Garden Center" beckons passersby on the left. The canopies of trees along the route have no undergrowth, so the view between the trunks is beautiful. At 6.1 miles, there is a stop sign at the intersection with U.S. 62. Continue across and stay on KY 1973. For the next 3 miles there are more horse farms with beautiful barns and some grand old limestone fences. At 9.3 miles, you will come to a junction with U.S. 25. KY 1973 goes right and follows U.S. 25 for 0.3 mile, then goes left at a junction with a caution light and turn pocket.

KY 1973 crosses over I-75, becomes a four-lane divided highway and, in one more mile, comes to the entrance to the Kentucky Horse Park. From the entrance to the horse park, the road becomes two-lane blacktop again. For about 1.5 miles, you will be treated to more rolling bluegrass and some pretty ponds on both sides of the road. At 12.8 miles, you will come to a stop at the intersection with KY 922.

If you would like a side trip to the Double Stink Hog Farm, now is your chance. Go left on KY 922 for 3 or 4 miles to the intersection with U.S. 460. Cross U.S. 460 and drive about 0.25 mile to the entrance on the right. Unfortunately for those of you who were looking forward to it, the farm does not have any hogs, and it doesn't even single stink. A few years back, though, it really was a hog farm, usually with more than 1,000 of them on hand at any given time. The name is said to have come from one of the owner's sons who, after cleaning hog pens all day, is reported to have said "This place stinks, we ought to call it Double Stink Hog Farm." Well, the hogs have been gone for several years, now, but the name is the only thing that lingers on. Today, the farm concentrates on selling flowers, nursery stock, sweet corn, vine-ripened tomatoes, jams, jelly and honey, and, most of all, pumpkins. If you are lucky enough to be here in the fall, you can attend one of the best festivals in Kentucky. You can pick pumpkins, eat steaks and wash them down with apple cider, take a wagon ride, shop for crafts, look over the antique tractors, or watch the pumpkin carving.

Retrace your route to KY 1973 and turn left; just past the junction there is a very pretty limestone fence. At 15.2 miles, there is a four-way stop at Russell Cave Road. Beyond the stop there is a nice canopy of trees and, within a mile, another limestone wall. At 17.3 miles, there is a stop at the junction with U.S. 27/68. Turn left and follow KY 1973 as it goes along with U.S. 27/68 for about 1.5 miles. Along here, you will see limestone fences on both sides of the road. A sign on the fence to the left says that it was built in 1715, while a sign on the right one says it was built in 1910. At 18.8 miles, KY 1973 goes right. Keep your eyes peeled, since there is no warning that the junction is coming. After the turn, you can admire some more of the old limestone fences with the rolling bluegrass beyond. At 20.1 miles, there is a stop at the intersection with KY 1970. Keep straight ahead on KY 1973. In the next 3.0 miles, the road makes a gentle sweep to the right past rolling fields, big barns, and more black plank fences. The road narrows down to one lane and goes under an old railroad bridge and comes to a stop at KY 57. KY 1973 goes off to the right and, in a mile, crosses over Interstate 64. At 25.3 miles, you will see the David's Fork Baptist Church on the right. This old church dates back to the late 1700s. If you are interested in such things, they have the minutes of their business meetings from 1802-1850 on their computer. You can access them on the Internet and read these fascinating old documents complete with spelling and grammatical errors (see the appendix for the website address).

Less than half a mile from the church, you will come to a stop at the intersection with U.S. 60. Go straight across on KY 1973, but be careful, this can be a busy road. Enjoy the rural scenery for a couple more miles. At 28.3 miles, there is a stop at the intersection with KY 1927. Continue straight ahead on KY 1973 past a small wooded area until, at 30 miles, you will see the "Fox Trot Farms" on your left. Here you can get a break from looking at horses and maybe see some of the Limousin cattle raised here. Although they are relatively new to the United States, having been here only since the

1970s, Limousin have been bred in France as far back as anyone can remember. In fact, cave drawings more than 20,000 years old show cattle strikingly similar to the present-day Limousin. The sturdy, dark golden red cattle are especially desirable today because they produce beef with about 27 to 42 percent less fat than traditional crossbred cattle.

A mile beyond the Fox Trot Farms is the Boone's Creek Baptist Church in Athens. In 1785, Daniel Boone's brother Samuel and his wife Sarah joined with 18 others and formed the Boone's Creek Baptist Church. A short way down Gentry Road is the Boone Station Historic Site. At the site, there is an area surrounded by chain link fence containing a monument and gravestones of several families who were buried here. Daniel Boone established a station here in 1779. It is said that he lived here for several years after surveying and patenting 400 acres on Boofman's Fork of Boone's Creek. In 1783, due to discrepancies in the patents, he lost title to the 400 acres and moved to Marble Creek, about 5 miles west, where he stayed until 1785. He then moved to Limestone (now Maysville) where he opened a tavern (see Drive 15).

See Drive 29 to continue the scenic driving.

29

Grimes Mill Road
Past the Iroquois Hunt Club

General description: A little more than 8 miles may not seem like much of a drive, but there are times when such a short trip is just right for the day. If a trip like this is what you are after, you couldn't find a more beautiful or unique one. Tucked away in a corner of Fayette County, this designated Kentucky Scenic Byway corkscrews its way past views of the distant rolling hills, winds by the old Grimes Mill which is now the home of the 118-year-old Iroquois Hunt Club and curves past the beautiful St. Hubert's Episcopal Church. There are very narrow stretches and extremely sharp turns, which make driving slow, but when you see the road, you will wonder why anyone would want to rush through here. Most of the route is lined with oaks, maples, redbuds, dogwoods, magnolias, and many more. The variety of wildflowers in the spring is so great that folks travel from far around to view them.

Special attractions: The Grimes House, the Iroquois Hunt Club, St. Hubert's Church, spring wildflowers, fall color.

Location: North-central.

Drive route numbers: KY 418, Grimes Mill Road, McCall Mills Road.

Travel season: All year.

Camping: Campgrounds are available in the Lexington area.

Services: Many motels and bed and breakfast establishments in the Lexington area. Food services of all kinds are available in the Lexington area.

Nearby attractions: Kentucky Horse Park (Drive 28), Keeneland.

The drive

The drive begins at the junction of U.S. 25/421 and Grimes Mill Road. If you are taking this drive following Drive 28, just continue on down KY 1973 to its junction with U.S. 25. Go left on U.S. 25 for about 0.4 mile to Grimes Mill Road on your left. Set your odometer at zero here, and continue down Grimes Mill Road. At 0.6 mile, you will cross McCall Mills Road. Beyond the junction, the road curves downhill to the right and passes by an old limestone fence. The winding through the woods continues, until, at 1.5 miles, the road curves to the left past the bright red barn of the Iroquois Hunt Club, one of the oldest hunt clubs in the United States. It was founded in 1880 by General Roger D. Williams and was named for the first American

Drive 29: Grimes Mill Road
Past the Iroquois Hunt Club

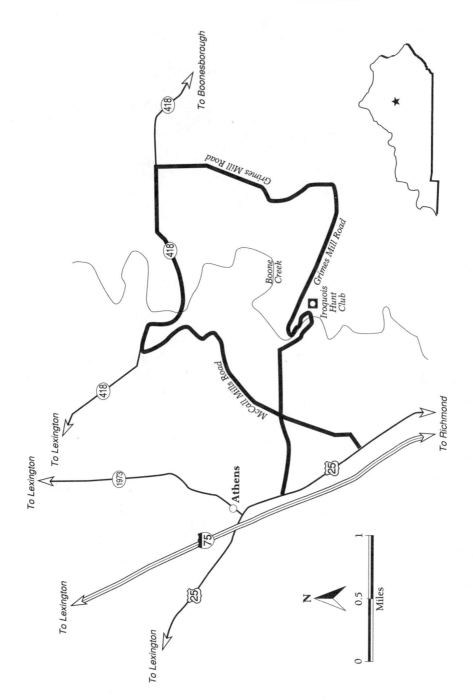

To Boonesborough

Grimes Mill Road

418

418

Boone Creek

Grimes Mill Road

Iroquois Hunt Club

McCall Mills Road

418

To Lexington

To Lexington

1973

To Lexington

Athens

25

To Richmond

75

25

To Lexington

To Lexington

N

Miles

0   0.5   1

Barn at the Iroquois Hunt Club.

horse to win the Epson Derby in England. General Williams led the hunt from 1880 to 1914, at which time, the hunt shut down for a few years. In 1926, the hunt was on again, and by 1929, it was recognized by the Masters of Foxhounds Association of America. The Hunt Club's clubhouse is the building that once housed the old Grimes Mill. Built by Phillip Grimes in 1803, the beautiful old stone grain mill was powered by the waters of Boone Creek. The mill was purchased by the Iroquois Hunt Club in 1928 and converted to their clubhouse.

The formal hunt season begins in November and runs through March. It begins with the hunt blessing by a local church official. This is sometimes referred to as the blessing of the hounds, but, in fact, it is not only the hounds, but the riders, their horses, and the fox that are blessed.

These days, there is not a fox to be blessed, however. Coyotes have reduced the fox population to the point where one is rarely seen anymore. Therefore, the coyotes have become the "fox." In the next 3 miles, in addition to the glorious scenery, you will pass Boone Ridge Lane, Munch's Corner Lane, and Saint Hubert's Episcopal Church.

This pretty stone church, named for the patron saint of hunters and built of Kentucky limestone, measures 25 by 50 feet and seats 135 people. All of the wood used in the building was grown in Kentucky. John Jacob Niles carved the huge oak doors. The carved Eighty-fourth Psalm is bordered with ivy and tobacco leaves. Needlepoint on the kneelers at the altar depicts the hunt. The freestanding bell tower that stands beside the church is made of the same Kentucky limestone as the church. The bell in the belfry, called "Bell Clarence," was a gift from a parishioner. This antique was cast in 1862, and was almost melted down for the war effort during World War II. It was hidden by being buried in a cornfield. Although St. Hubert's appears much older than it is, in this land of seventeenth-century buildings it is the newcomer on the block. The church was completed in 1969.

Beyond St. Hubert's, at 4.7 miles, you will come to a stop sign at the junction of KY 418 (the Athens/Boonesboro Road). Go left, and in just over a mile, you will cross a bridge over Boone Creek, pass the Bluegrass Christian Camp, and climb uphill through the trees. At 6.4 miles, you will be at a junction with McCall Mills Road. Go left, and just past the junction look to your right and see an old, weathered barn. You will keep winding down through the trees and canopies and cross a small creek. At 7.6 miles, you will be out of the trees and passing great bluegrass views. In less than half a mile, you will come to the junction of Grimes Mill Road. If you go right on Grimes Mill, you will end up back on U.S. 25 where you started. If you go straight on McCall Mills Road, you will see a little more scenery and end up on U.S. 25 just a short way from Grimes Mill Road.

30

The Mammoth Cave Area
A Cave Country Tour

General description: This 36-mile drive starts at exit 53 from I-65 in Cave City and follows KY 70 to the Mammoth Cave National Park Visitor Center. After the national park, you will get back on KY 70 through Brownsville and Windyville to Huff. From Huff, you will follow KY 187 to Sunfish, where you will turn onto KY 238 to Bee Spring. From Bee Spring, you will drive along KY 259 back to Brownsville.
Special attractions: Mammoth Cave National Park.
Location: South-central.
Drive route numbers: KY 70,187, 238, 259.
Travel season: All year.
Camping: Campgrounds at Mammoth Cave National Park and Cave City.
Services: Motels at Cave City and Brownsville; hotel, motel, and cottages at Mammoth Cave National Park; coffee shop and restaurant at Mammoth Cave National Park; restaurants and fast food in Cave City and Brownsville.
Nearby attractions: Numerous privately operated caves in the area, Nolin Lake State Park, see the appendix for places to write for complete information.

The drive

This drive winds through some of the prettiest woodlands and rolling hills that Kentucky has to offer, but the big feature of the area is the world famous Mammoth Cave. Mammoth Cave is an exceptional natural feature that provides habitat for threatened and endangered species and is associated with persons and events of historic and archeological significance.

Mammoth Cave has joined such places as the Great Barrier Reef in Australia, the Pyramids of Giza, and Taj Mahal Historic Park as a World Heritage Site. This designation was given in 1981 by the United Nations Educational, Scientific and Cultural Organization (UNESCO). In 1990, Mammoth Cave was designated a Biosphere Reserve by UNESCO.

The object of all of this worldwide attention began more than 350,000,000 years ago at the bottom of a shallow sea. This warm sea produced a large number of shellfish that, as they died, combined with calcium carbonate in the water and formed a layer of limestone more than 500 feet thick. As they emptied into the sea, rivers deposited sand several hundred

Drive 30: The Mammoth Cave Area
A Cave Country Tour

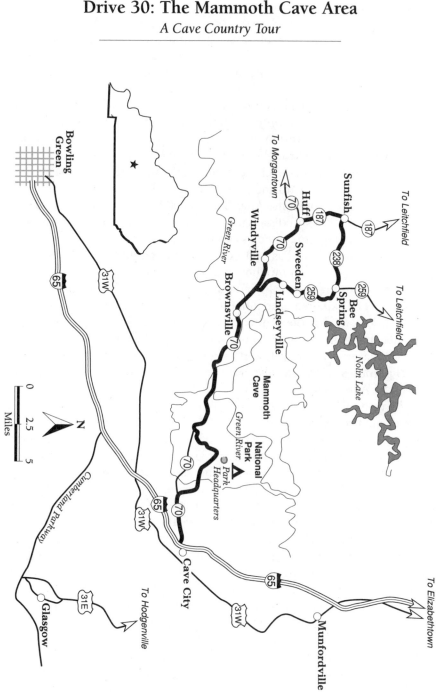

feet deep on top of the limestone. The weight of the sand combined with the weight of the water above created a sandstone cap over the limestone bed. Over the centuries, the level of the sea began to drop and the land began to buckle, warp, and rise. The cracks in the limestone and sandstone caused by this action formed natural channels for flowing water, and a river formed. As the river flowed through the limestone, it dissolved and the river became wider and deeper. The land continued to rise, and the river (the Green River) cut deeper and deeper into the limestone. Because the sandstone cap was more resistant to erosion, it formed a roof of sorts over the river and caverns were formed. Throughout millions of years, the water from the river found more and more cracks and more caverns were created. The river continued to cut downward and created multiple levels of caverns, each one lower than the previous one. After 350,000,000 years, the cave is still not finished. The river is still dissolving limestone and creating more caverns. We can visit but a few of the miles and miles that have been explored so far. In fact, Mammoth Cave has 350 miles of underground caverns that have been explored. No one knows how many more there may be.

Some of the prehistoric Indian tribes used the cave approximately 4,000 years ago. They explored deep into the cave and many surrounding caves as well. It is known that they collected such minerals as selenite, mirabilite, epsomite, and gypsum, but it is not known how they used them. Speculation says that perhaps they used them in some sort of ceremony or for medicinal purposes. They may also have been traded to other groups for food, shells, etc. About the time of Christ, for some unknown reason, Indians stopped using the cave. It was virtually undisturbed until early settlers in Kentucky rediscovered it in the late 1700s. The story goes that a hunter by the name of Houchins chased a wounded bear into the entrance. (How smart is it to chase a wounded bear into a cave?) In any case, the recorded history of the cave goes back to 1799 when a land grant of 200 acres, which included the cave, was awarded to Valentine Simmons (or Simons). Evidence has also been found to show that a British surveyor entered the cave between 1767 and 1769 while on a mission to survey the Green River.

The Mammoth Cave area is as beautiful and diverse above the ground as it is below. Within the boundaries of the park are rivers, bluffs, ridgetops, wetlands, and old-growth forests. All of these provide habitat for a wide variety of wildlife. Hikers on the 73 miles of trails in the park will most often be rewarded with views of deer, wild turkeys, squirrels, chipmunks, and raccoons. Along the rivers are wood ducks, turtles, kingfishers, and great blue herons. The woodlands contain hemlock, yellow birch, magnolia, and holly among other common eastern hardwoods.

To begin the drive, set your odometer at zero at exit 53 off I-65 in Cave City. Drive west on KY 70 toward Mammoth Cave National Park. For the first 3 miles or so, the scenery is pretty much limited to gift shops and other

Mammoth Cave National Park.

tourist attractions. At 3.5 miles, KY 70 goes left. Keep straight ahead on the road to the Park. You will see Big Mike's Rock Shop on the right. Even if you are not rockhounds, you will find something of interest here. In the lower yard there is table after table of chunks of glass slag in all sizes and in all of the colors of the rainbow swirled together.

Just beyond Big Mike's, the scenery begins. At 5 miles, you will pass a sign announcing the boundary of the Park. Just beyond the boundary, there is a very old cemetery next to the road on your left. After a couple of miles of lush woodland scenery, you will come to a stop sign. Going left will take you back to KY 70, while going right will take you to the visitor center and the cave tours.

If you are continuing the drive, turn left, and in just 1.6 miles from the stop sign you will be at the junction with KY 70. Go right on KY 70 toward Brownsville. At 6.9 miles a sign tells you that you are leaving Mammoth Cave National Park. At 10.3 miles, you will enter Brownsville, and in less than a mile, you will be at the junction of KY 259/70. Turn right on KY 259/70. Just north of town, you will cross a long, high bridge over the Green River. At 2.3 miles from the junction, take KY 70 left toward Windyville.

From the junction, the road climbs upward and provides great, long views of the hills and woodlands. At the top of the hill, there are more views of distant hills and woodlands as you enter Windyville. The story goes that a traveling salesman who had experienced the extremely hard winds that sometimes blow across this ridge, asked the local storekeeper the name of the town. When told that it had none, he suggested that they call it Windyville.

Beyond the town, the road continues to meander along the ridge and give you a chance to see more of the peaceful rural views of farms, rolling fields, and lots of trees. At 8.3 miles, go right on KY 187 at Huff, a tiny hamlet with a post office established in 1889. Follow KY 187 through more enjoyable rural scenery for about 4 miles and turn right at the junction with KY 238 at Sunfish, another tiny town with a post office established in 1856. The name comes from nearby Sunfish Creek. At 16.9 miles, you will be at the junction of KY 238 and KY 259 at Bee Spring. Now here is a town that got its name in a straightforward way. It was located near a big spring that attracted lots of bees. In less than a mile, you will pass the Bee Spring post office that was established in 1854. In a little more than 2 miles, you will pass the post office in Sweeden. This strange spelling has never been explained. The town was founded by a land developer, and as part of his promotion, he arranged for several families of Swedish immigrants living in the Chicago area to move here. The post office was established in 1892 as New Sweden. The strange spelling was adopted in 1894.

Just a mile down the road is the Lindseyville post office. When the post office was established in 1935, the name Midway was chosen because it was about midway between Brownsville and Bee Spring. The name Midway was already in use, so Lindseyville was chosen for one of the families in the area. Continue on down KY 259 to Brownsville and you will have completed the drive. You can go on through Brownsville and take KY 259 all the way to I-65 south of Park City, or you can take KY 70 back to Cave City.

31

Bowling Green to Fort Knox
From Corvettes to Gold Bars

General description: On this 94.7-mile drive, you will leave the progressive city of Bowling Green on KY 185 to Caneyville. At Caneyville, you will take KY 79 past Rough River Lake, across the Rough River Dam and on through wide, rolling farmland to Irvington, where you will switch to U.S. 60, then to U.S. 31W, and on to Fort Knox.

Special attractions: Rough River Dam State Resort Park, Fort Knox, Corvette Museum (Bowling Green).

Location: South-central.

Drive route numbers: KY 185, 79; U.S. 60, 31W.

Travel season: All year.

Camping: There are campgrounds in Bowling Green and Rough River Dam State Resort Park.

Services: Motels in Bowling Green, Irvington, and Radcliff. Restaurants and/or fast food available in Bowling Green, Caneyville, Harned, Irvington, Fort Knox, and Radcliff.

Nearby attractions: Nolin Lake State Park, Mammoth Cave National Park.

The drive

The drive begins in Bowling Green. Set your odometer at zero at the junction of KY 185 and KY 234 at the north end of town. Drive north on KY 185. Locally, this is sometimes called the Richardsville Road. In about two blocks, KY 185 goes right at a traffic light. As soon as you leave town, you will be in walls of trees with a nice view of the tree-covered hills ahead. There are lots of oaks, maples, dogwoods, and redbuds along the way. At 2.3 miles, you will cross the Barren River. Beyond the river, the road climbs up through a nice limestone road cut and you will be presented with a great, long view of the tree-covered valley to the right. At 3.7 miles, you will make a 45-degree turn to the left and drop down through some heavily wooded hills. Beyond here, you twist and turn up through some more road cuts. After the road cuts, there is a fine, long view of the valley to your left and of the tree-covered hills on your right. At 6 miles, there is another long limestone road cut. If you are rockhounds, be sure to check out the rubble at the foot of

Drive 31: Bowling Green to Fort Knox
From Corvettes to Gold Bars

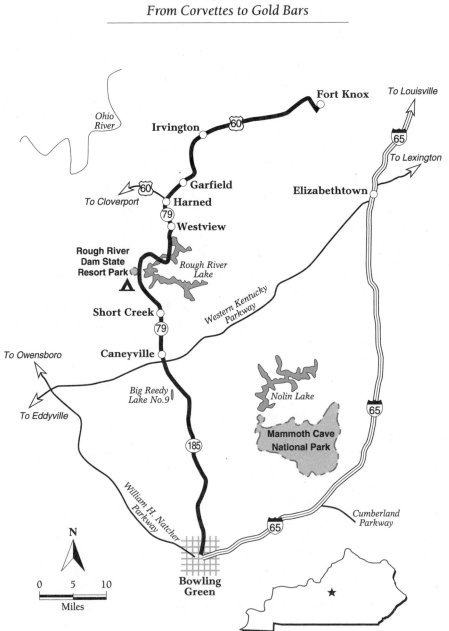

these cuts. You can usually find some shell fossils. Be sure you can park well off the road, though.

For the next 5 miles or so, you will go through twists and turns and ups and downs through wooded areas with trees right up to the sides of the road. At 11.2 miles, there is a gray-weathered barn with foliage growing out of the doors and windows in the middle of a field to your left. At about 15 miles, you will cross the Green River, and at 15.9 miles on your left, there is another old barn tilting precariously. This one may not be here for long. Less than a mile beyond the barn there is a nice view of the distant hills to your left. At 18.4 miles, you arrive at the junction with KY 70. Keep straight ahead on KY 185. At 21 miles you pass through a wide valley between the oak-covered hills, and at 25 miles you will see a lake on your left. Our topographic map tells us that this is Big Reedy Lake Number 9. At 25.8 miles, there are two gray-weathered barns on the right side of the road. For the next few miles, you will climb up through the trees again, then twist and turn down through a canopy of hardwoods. Beyond the canopy, the view widens out and you will be looking at the tops of the hills with lots of fields and farmhouses. There are pretty wooded hills in the distance. At about 32 miles, you cross the Western Kentucky Parkway and enter Caneyville, a bustling little community that is a far cry from the pioneer trading post it was in 1837 when the post office was established. The name comes from nearby Caney Creek, which, in turn, was named for the cane that grows along it.

At Caneyville, KY 185 ends at the junction with KY 79. Keep going north on KY 79. Beyond Caneyville, the hills give way to more farms. The road twists and dips, climbs a little, bends to the left, and passes through Short Creek. In about 6 miles, you will be at the Rough River Dam State Resort Park. At the lodge, you have a choice of one of the 40 rooms, each with a private patio or balcony, or one of the 15 two-bedroom cottages in a wooded area near the lake. The cottages have tableware, cooking utensils, and linens provided. There is also a 66-site campground with hookups, a dump station, and a central service building with showers and rest rooms next to Rough River. If you own an airplane, you can land on the 3,200-foot lighted, paved runway and use the air camping facility. Of course, you can also swim, fish, play golf, tennis, shuffleboard, or volleyball, or rent a boat and enjoy some time on the lake. There is a 1-mile nature trail in the park. Here you can see some of the many hard maples, sugar maples, red and white oaks, red cedars, white flowering dogwoods, redbuds, and tulip poplars that cover the area around the park. There is also a self-guided interpretive trail on federal lands adjacent to the park. The trail is maintained by the U.S. Army Corps of Engineers.

About a mile beyond the park, KY 79 crosses the Rough River Dam, makes a sharp right turn, then curves more to the right and crosses an arm

The view a top Rough River Lake Dam.

of the lake. At 53 miles, the road makes a sharp left turn and crosses another arm of the lake in less than a mile. At 58.6 miles, you pass through Westview. By 62 miles, the hills have flattened out and you will be traveling through gently rolling farmland. At Harned, you will go right on KY 79/U.S. 60. At 66 miles, you will pass through Garfield. By 70 miles, you will be dropping down into a broad valley with lots of gently rolling farmland. At 72 miles, there is a huge farm fenced and cross-fenced with white wood planks. It looks much like the beautiful horse farms in the Bluegrass Area. At 73.5 miles, you enter Irvington. Go right on U.S. 60. In about 4 miles, you will top a small hill through a wooded area and spend the next 17 miles or so on a nice, wide highway with peaceful rural Kentucky views in all directions. At 90.7 miles, you will come to the junction with U.S. 31W. Turn right and go 4 miles to Fort Knox and all that gold.

32

Fort Knox to Owensboro
Along the Ohio River

General description: This 102.7-mile drive begins at Fort Knox and goes north for a few miles along U.S. 31W to KY 1638. It then follows KY 1638 to KY 448 and continues on to Brandenburg. From Brandenburg, the route takes KY 228 north along the Ohio River for a while, then turns west toward Wolf Creek. At the junction with KY 144, it goes west along KY 144 to KY 259. On KY 259, it passes through Mooleyville, then turns south through the Yellowbank Wildlife Management Area. Beyond Yellowbank, the drive goes on to KY 144 to Stephensport and on to the junction of U.S. 60. Here, it proceeds along U.S. 60 past Cloverport, Hawesville, and Lewisport and continues on to Owensboro.

Special attractions: Fort Knox, Yellowbank Wildlife Management Area.

Location: North-central to northwest.

Drive route numbers: U.S. 31W, 60; KY1638, 448, 228, 144.

Travel season: All year.

Camping: Campgrounds in Radcliff, Otter Creek Park, Hawesville, and Owensboro.

Services: Hawesville, Owensboro, Muldraugh, and Radcliff. Restaurants and/or fast food in Fort Knox, Brandenburg, Owensboro, Hawesville, Cloverport, Lewisport, and Maceo.

Nearby attractions: Bridges of the Past, a series of three pre–Civil War stone bridges (West Point), Tioga Falls Trail, Otter Creek Park.

The drive

When most of us hear the phrase Fort Knox, we think of gold, and lots of it. Some of us visualize Scrooge McDuck sitting in the middle of his pile of gold coins and dribbling them over his head. There is much more to Fort Knox than a gold vault, however. The Fort Knox area was a military installation long before anyone had the idea of storing gold there. In the Civil War era, the 6th Michigan Infantry constructed fortifications and bridges north of the present boundaries of the reservation. One of these positions was Fort Duffield at West Point, just on the northern boundary of the present post. At various times during the Civil War, both Union and Confederate troops held positions in the area. Union generals Don Carlos Buell and William Tecumseh Sherman occupied the hills overlooking the Ohio River, and

Confederate hero John Hunt Morgan raided the area and captured several hundred Union troops. He also crossed the Ohio River near Brandenburg as he prepared for his famous raid into Indiana and Ohio.

It was not until 1903 that serious efforts to establish a modern military base were launched. In that year, the army held maneuvers in and around the little village of Stithton. It took World War I to get the government to move, however. Finally, Congress leased 10,000 acres near Stithton, and in January of 1918, established a field artillery training center. The center was named for Major General Henry Knox, the Chief of Artillery for the Continental army in the Revolutionary War, who later became the first secretary of war. On June 25, 1918, Congress appropriated $1.6 million for the purchase of 40,000 acres. Construction of the camp began, but was halted by the end of the war before it was finished. Following the war, when troop strength was reduced, the camp was closed as a permanent facility. It did continue to operate as a training camp for the National Guard and Citizens' Military groups until 1932. In 1925, the camp was given the official title of Camp Henry Knox National Forest. In 1932, the camp was officially changed to Fort Knox, and the 1st Cavalry, the army's oldest mounted unit, was sent there. They arrived without horses, but with combat cars. Thus began a long development of the Army Mechanized Cavalry, now called the Armored Force. At the Patton Museum, you can see exhibits of armored warfare from the early cavalry to Desert Storm.

In December of 1936, the construction of the Gold Vault, officially called the United States Bullion Depository, was completed. Although the site was on the Fort Knox military reservation at one time, it is a separate facility with no ties to the army. The Vault is operated by the Treasury Department, which supplies the guards and other employees. The first shipments of gold began in January 1937 and were completed in June of the same year. Most of the United States's supply of gold is stored at Fort Knox.

Before you leave the Fort Knox area, you may want to try a little hiking through some of Kentucky's hardwood trees and see some very old bridges. The first hike is called Bridges to the Past, and involves a nice, leisurely walk through a forest of catalpas, sassafras, red elms, hickory, dogwoods, oaks, maples, and sumacs to three 150-year-old stone bridges that pre-date the Civil War. There are no electric lines, billboards, or other signs of "civilization" along the way. For the more serious hiker, there is the Tioga Falls Hiking Trail. This self-guided trail makes a 2-mile loop through a part of the Fort Knox military training area. Along this more strenuous hike there are 33 points of interest listed in the trail guide. You will see more of the same species of trees as on the Bridges to the Past trail as well as many species of birds, squirrels, and, perhaps, a deer or 2.

If you have had enough walking and are ready to drive some more, proceed about 5 miles on U.S. 31W past the turnoff to the Gold Depository

Drive 32: Fort Knox to Owensboro

Along the Ohio River

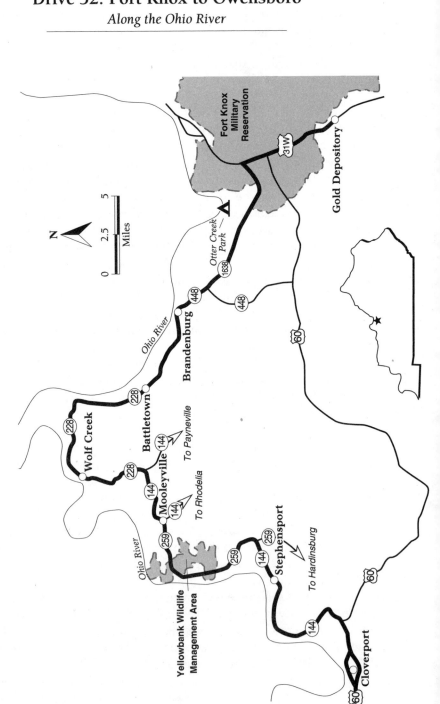

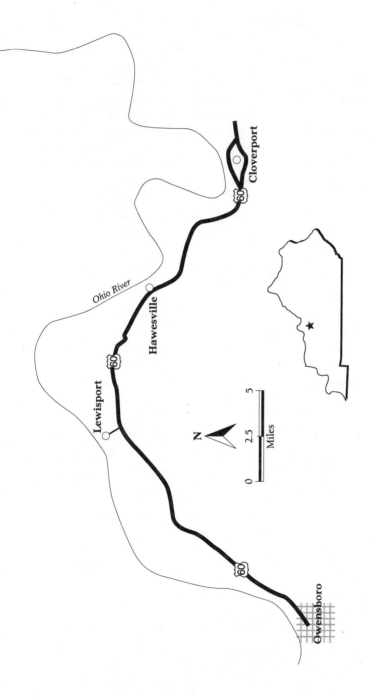

and on to the junction with KY 1638. Set your odometer at zero at the junction, and go left on KY 1638. Within 1 mile, the road drops down through a limestone road cut, crosses Otter Creek, and climbs back up through another road cut. Trees are plentiful on both sides of the road. At 2.7 miles, you will come to the road to Otter Creek Park on the right.

Otter Creek Park is more than 3,000 acres of beautiful woodland, rolling fields, streams, and wildlife operated by the city of Louisville. There is a 24-room lodge, as well as a restaurant, cottages, 165 campsites, horseback riding, swimming, hiking, fishing, and numerous sports activities.

For the next 6 miles or so, you will be treated to beautiful views of rolling fields and dense hardwood woodlands as the road climbs, dips, and turns on its way to Brandenburg. At 9 miles, KY 1638 comes to an end at the junction with KY 448. Turn right on KY 448 and continue for 1.3 miles. At this point, KY 448 makes a left. Stay on KY 448 to Brandenburg. At 12.6 miles, KY 448 goes right again. At 13.9 miles, you will be at the junction with KY 228. Go straight on KY 228. At 14.1 miles, KY 228 makes a 90 degree turn to the left and passes the home where John Hunt Morgan watched his "Raiders" cross the Ohio River on the *McComb* and the *Alice Dean*, two steamboats they had commandeered on their way to skirmishes in Indiana and Ohio. Just past the house, there is a very nice view of the Ohio River below the cliffs.

At 15.8 miles, there is a stop sign at the junction with KY 79. Keep straight ahead on KY 228. By 19 miles, the road begins to twist and wind through walls of trees and past scattered houses and barns. In two more miles, you will climb to the right through another limestone road cut, then drop down into a hollow with trees on both sides. The road continues on, twisting and winding through the woods. At 22.4 miles, you pass the Battletown fire department and post office on your right. Here is another one of those names. Was the town named over a great Revolutionary War battle? Was it a famous Civil War battle? No, it was named after a fistfight between Nathan Hubbard and Jimmy Bennett around 1890.

At 28.4 miles, KY 228 goes left at the Wolf Creek Boat Ramp. Beyond the boat ramp, the trees thin out and there are more fields with just scattered trees for a mile or so, then the road dives back into the trees again. Soon, it drops down and presents a great view of the hills across a valley and a fine view of the Ohio River on the right. For a mile or two, you will pass flat farmland on your right that runs to the bluffs above the Ohio River. At 32.6 miles, you will follow S turns through the old town of Wolf Creek. This was once a river port and manufacturing town, but not much remains to testify to that. The story goes that it was named for the packs of wolves that gathered in the spring to feed on the young buffalo along a trace to the river.

At 37.3 miles, KY 228 ends at a junction with KY 144. Go right on KY 144 past flat farmland running over to the river. In two miles, the road

The gold vault at Fort Knox.

drops down to the left, slides back into the oaks and other hardwoods, twists back and forth, crosses a small creek, and climbs back up through more trees. At 41.5 miles, KY 259 goes right through Mooleyville to the Yellowbank Wildlife Management Area.

Follow KY 259 for 11 beautiful miles through tunnels of oaks and hickories, past old buildings and dense woodlands of more oak and hickory along with dogwood, tulip poplar, beech, and redbud. There are nice views of the Ohio River and a wildlife viewing area. Along the river and the creeks, there are cottonwoods, sycamores, and black willows. There are also miles of old roads for hiking and sightseeing and a self-guided demonstration area where you can see habitat types, prairie grasses, and wetlands. Animals in the area include rabbit, squirrel, raccoon, groundhog, and deer. There are some waterfowl, as well as dove, quail, and turkey. You can fish in ponds or streams, and there is a boat ramp at the creek that will give you access to the Ohio River. There is primitive camping in designated areas. This is a really special area that would make the drive worthwhile even if you saw nothing else.

At 52.5 miles, you will come to an intersection with KY 144. The big Breckenridge Mennonite Church is on the corner. Turn and follow KY 144 toward Stephensport. At 2.5 miles from the intersection, the road leaves the farms behind, twists and turns through the trees, then drops down steeply, crosses the old steel bridge over Sinking Creek, and enters Stephensport. This is another once prosperous port on the Ohio River that was settled prior to 1800. It was built on part of a 94,000-acre Revolutionary War land grant awarded to Richard Stephens.

In about 4 miles, you will come to Addison. This little town had a post office established in 1880 as Holt. At 9.7 miles, you will cross a bridge over a large expanse of water where Town Creek and Bull Creek flow into the Ohio River. At 12 miles, the road climbs back through walls of more typical eastern hardwoods, passes through some more farmland, and comes to the junction with U.S. 60 at 13.2 miles.

Go right on U.S. 60 for about 2 miles to the turnoff to Cloverport, a pretty little river town that has been here since around 1798. You may remember the story of Sacagawea, the Shoshone Indian maiden who guided the Lewis and Clark expedition in the early 1800s. It is said that she and her husband, a French Canadian trader by the name of Toussaint Charbonneau who had purchased her from a roving band of Indians, helped save the expedition by interpreting for various Indian tribes along the way. Charbonneau brought her to the Cloverport area before joining Lewis and Clark in what is now South Dakota. To celebrate this remarkable woman's life, Cloverport has a 4-day Sacagawea Festival every fall.

When you leave Cloverport, get back on U.S. 60 and head for Hawesville, about 10 miles farther along toward Owensboro. Turn right on KY 69 to go into Hawesville, where the *Water Queen*, the showboat with the longest record of service on the inland waterways, was built.

Back on U.S. 60, it is another 10 miles to Lewisport. Go right on KY 657 to get into town. Be sure to drive down to the foot of 4th Street and see the historical markers. Back on U.S. 60 once more, you have only 17 more pleasant miles of nice wide highway through some pretty western Kentucky scenery to Owensboro.

33

Owensboro/Russellville Loop

Scenic Driving in the West

General description: This 150.9-mile drive begins in the Ohio River city of Owensboro and heads south on U.S. 231, where it passes through Masonville, Hartford, Beaver Dam, Cromwell, Aberdeen, and Morgantown. Just beyond Morgantown, the drive leaves U.S. 231 and picks up KY 79, which it follows through wooded, rolling hills and past farms and homes to Russellville. At Russellville, the route heads back to the north on U.S. 431.

Special attractions: Lake Malone State Park, Owensboro, Bibb House Museum, Logan County Glade State Nature Preserve.

Location: Northwest.

Drive route numbers: U.S. 231, 431; KY 79.

Travel season: All year.

Camping: Campgrounds in Owensboro and Lake Malone.

Services: Motels in Owensboro, Russellville, Hartford, and Central City. Restaurants and/or fast food in Owensboro, Russellville, Beaver Dam, Central City, Livermore, and Hartford.

Nearby attractions: Mammoth Cave National Park (see Drive 29), Shaker Museum at South Union, Jefferson Davis Monument.

The drive

This drive makes its way through gentle farmland and peaceful western Kentucky towns. Set your odometer at zero at the south end of Owensboro on the overpass where KY 231 and U.S. 60 intersect. Drive south on KY 231 for 3.5 miles to Masonville, which was settled shortly after the War of 1812. The town was laid out by a Judge Triplett and was named either for George Mason who had owned 60,000 acres along Panther Creek and the Green River, or his grandson, George R. Mason. The post office was established in 1856 and closed in 1907. From Masonville until you cross the Fort Hartford Bridge over the Rough River and enter Hartford at 21.8 miles, you will pass serene western Kentucky scenery made up of small farms, pretty homes, and wooded hills.

Hartford may have been established as Hartford Station as early as 1782, although the actual date is uncertain. The name is said by some to have come from a man named Hart who once owned land in the area, but there is no evidence to prove it. Another story, also not verifiable, says that

Drive 33: Owensboro/Russellville Loop

Scenic Driving in the West

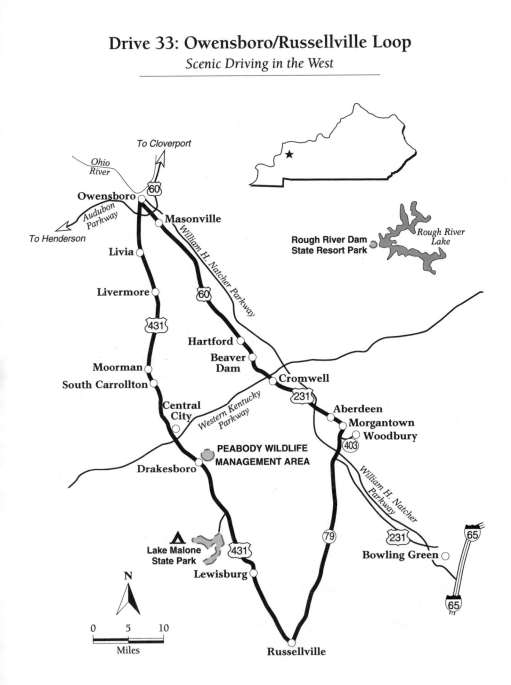

the ford on the Rough River was long ago called Deer Crossing, from which "hart-ford" was derived. Mr. Webster tells us that hart is the name of a male European red deer. The second story gets our vote. We would rather picture a herd of beautiful deer crossing the river than an old geezer sitting on his front porch smoking a corncob pipe.

In just over 2 miles from "Hart-Ford," you will be at Beaver Dam. This town, which seems to go on forever along the road, was settled around 1795 by a German immigrant who, it is told, named the spot for the many beaver dams along a local stream. Now there was a man with the soul of a poet. In 1798, a Baptist church was built, and the town grew up around it. It was not until 1852, however, that the first post office was established.

After leaving Beaver Dam, KY 231 heads back into the gently rolling hills and passes by stands of trees and pleasant western Kentucky farmland, until it enters Cromwell at 32.0 miles. Just south of Cromwell on KY 403 (the Logansport Road) near Logansport is a stone monument marking the place where the first Union soldier in western Kentucky died on October 27, 1861. Allen Granville, from Ohio County, was hiding with two other men in a hollow tree. He looked out to see where the Confederate soldiers who were firing on them were, and was killed by the Confederate fire. He had been in the army for just 24 days.

At 36.8 miles, KY 231 passes over the William H. Natcher Parkway, ducks back into the trees, passes through Aberdeen, crosses a high bridge over the Green River, and enters Morgantown at 42 miles. Morgantown, like so many of the river towns in Kentucky, was once a thriving shipping port.

If you have a little spare time, there is a worthwhile side trip to the little town of Woodbury on the Green River just a couple of miles south on KY 403. At the Green River Museum, you can see photographs, documents, and artifacts from the old riverboats. The museum building is the old headquarters of the district superintendent of the Green and Barren Rivers Navigation System. There is a different historical theme in each of the rooms. In 1833, the Kentucky legislature funded a navigation system for the Green and Barren rivers. Included were locks and dams at Woodbury and Rochester. Today, from the observation point next to the museum, you can see lock #4, which was built, along with dam #4, between 1838 and 1841. They served riverboat traffic until the last packet boat passed through in 1931. Some commercial traffic continued until 1965 when the dam washed out.

Just downhill from the museum is Windswept House, the birthplace of Captain Thomas Hines, who was known during the Civil War as the most dangerous man in the Confederacy. He served with Morgan's Raiders and visited Woodbury several times without being caught by the Union forces, but was finally captured along with Morgan and taken to Ohio. He escaped and joined the Copperheads, a group that worked to get northern states to join the secession. There was a $100,000 bounty on Hines's head, so he sought refuge in Canada, where he remained until 1867 studying law.

From Morgantown, take KY 79 south toward Russellville. At 45.5 miles, you will cross back under the William H. Natcher Parkway. (William H.

Jefferson Davis Monument east of Hopkinsville.

Natcher was a U.S. congressman who died in August of 1994 after 41 years in Congress.) At 46.7 miles, KY 79 goes right at a Y, and heads back into the rolling hills. In less than a mile, the road veers to the right, climbs through a wooded area, tops the hill, and comes out in an area of pretty homes. For the next 5 or 6 miles, you will enjoy rolling wooded hills with lots of trees. Along much of the tree-studded areas, the foliage is made up of light-colored hardwoods and the darker shades of evergreens. The rest of the way to Russellville consists of more rolling hills, woods, farms, and barns. Although we didn't see the sign, the map shows a little hamlet by the intriguing name of Dimple along the way.

At 71 miles, you will enter Russellville. For its size, Russellville has the largest historic district in Kentucky. It also has the dubious distinction of being the first place where there is a documented instance of a bank robbery by Jesse James. There is a collection of ante-bellum antiques in the Bibb House Museum, which is located in a Georgian mansion built by Major Richard Bibb, a Revolutionary War officer and abolitionist. Near downtown is the Logan County Glade State Nature Preserve, a 41-acre chunk of Kentucky beauty set aside to protect the limestone glades. There is an 810-foot-high knob with prairie grasses, Carolina larkspur, glade violet, and limestone fameflower.

If you can spare a little time and wouldn't mind driving 16 miles west on U.S. 68, you can visit the impressive Jefferson Davis Monument. The man who would become the president of the Confederate States of America was born on June 3, 1808, the youngest of five sons and five daughters of Jane Cook Davis and Samuel Emory Davis and was named for Thomas Jefferson. He attended Transylvania University in Lexington and the U.S. Military Academy at West Point. He was a congressman, a senator from Mississippi, and secretary of war under President Franklin Pierce. He was a supporter of slavery, but did not believe that secession was the way to maintain the southern beliefs. In fact, when Mississippi seceded, he resigned from the senate. As president of the Confederacy, he was never able to raise the money needed to fight the Civil War, and he could not win the support of foreign nations. His personality and faith in the southern cause helped to build enthusiasm for the war among the young men of the south, and he encouraged the industrial development of the Confederate states. At the close of the war, he was imprisoned for two years at Fort Monroe, Virginia. In 1866, Davis was indicted for treason, but a $100,000 bond was paid for his release by a group of northerners led by newspaper publisher Horace Greeley.

The monument, to be built at his birthplace, was commissioned in 1907, and a contract was awarded to C. G. Gregg of Louisville for $75,000. A quarry was dug at the end of the park to provide stone to be crushed for use in the cement. Construction was halted in 1918 because of the need for materials in World War I. At the time the building was stopped, the monument was 175 feet tall. The monument was finally completed in 1924, but the cost had risen to $220,000. The monument had risen, too. Its final height is 351 feet, and although not as tall as the Washington Monument at over

555 feet, it is nonetheless a very impressive pile of concrete. The walls at the base are 7 feet thick, tapering to 2 feet at the top. There is an elevator to an observation room at the top.

When you leave Russellville, go north on KY 431. At about 9.4 miles from the north end of town, you will come to Lewisburg, a small town named for Eugene C. Lewis, the chief engineer for the Owensborough and Nashville Railroad who had been the surveyor when construction began on the railroad in 1872.

Beyond Lewisburg, the road winds past wide fields and gently rolling hills with lots of trees to shade the view on both sides of the road. At 17.5 miles, you will come to the turnoff to Lake Malone on the left. It is about 12 miles to the lake, but this is a really pretty lake and well worth the trip. Lake Malone State Park is 338 acres of oaks, white pines, dogwoods, elms, redbuds, holly, mountain laurel, and wildflowers. This is a jewel of a lake, and the surrounding trees and wildflowers make spring and fall seasons of beauty. There is a boat dock with rental boats for your fishing trip, fishing supplies, and sandwiches to eat in case you don't catch any fish. The 788-acre lake is stocked with catfish, largemouth bass, crappie, bluegill, and sunfish. There are 100 primitive campsites and 20 campsites with utility hookups for your RV. A central service building has showers, rest rooms, and a laundry. All campsites have grills and picnic tables. On a hot summer day, you can have a swim at the beach.

When you get back to KY 431, turn left toward Owensboro. For about 10.5 miles, you will be treated to more nice rural scenery. When you reach the little town of Drakesboro, you will be at the edge of part of the big Peabody Wildlife Management Area. There are a number of access points to the area along the nearby roads. There are waterfowl, deer, quail, and turkey; and plenty of good fishing abounds. There are also high ridges, deep pits, and other rough terrain, since much of this wildlife management area consists of land reclaimed from old coal mines. Consequently, there are excavated ridges and water-filled pits. If you decide to visit the area, be careful! You must purchase a use permit and sign a liability waiver (see the appendix for more information).

Continue north on KY 431, and at 20.6 miles, you will come to a T intersection. Go right on KY 431 and enter South Carrollton. In a few miles, you will drive through Moorman and out into more farmland. There are nice, long views of the distant hills beyond the flat fields to the right. You will continue through this flat farmland for about 10 more miles until you cross a bright turquoise-colored bridge over the Green River at Livermore. At 38.1 miles, you enter Livia, and at 38.3 miles, a sign says "Come Again." From here on, the farms and scenery give way more and more to the signs of civilization, and by 48.6 miles you will have left the scenery behind and be back in Owensboro.

34

Dawson Springs to Marion
A Rural Drive in Western Kentucky

General description: This 39.9-mile drive begins in Dawson Springs and follows U.S. 62 to Princeton, a campground on the Cherokee Trail of Tears. From Princeton, it passes through more western Kentucky scenery past little towns like Farmersville, Creswell, and Shady Grove along KY 139. Just beyond Shady Grove, the drive switches to KY 120 and continues on to Marion.

Special attractions: Dawson Springs Museum and Art Center, The Adsmore House (Princeton), Clement Mineral Collection.

Location: West.

Drive route numbers: U.S. 62; KY 139, 120.

Travel season: All year.

Camping: Campground at Pennyrile Forest State Resort Park.

Services: There are motels at Dawson Springs, Princeton, and Marion. A lodge and cottages are available at Pennyrile Forest State Resort Park. Restaurants and/or fast food in Dawson Springs, Princeton, Marion, and Pennyrile Forest State Resort Park.

Nearby attractions: Pennyrile Forest State Resort Park.

The drive

Today, Dawson Springs is an industrial and commercial city on the Tradewater River, but it was much different in the late 1800s and early 1900s, when Dawson Springs was one of the premier health resorts in all of the South. Washington I. Hamby discovered the mineral waters that led to the development of the resort, while digging wells in 1881 and 1893. In its heyday, thousands of people traveled great distances to stay in one of the 38 hotels and boarding houses, and to take advantage of the baths and mineral water. Water was bottled in Dawson Springs and sold all over the United States. By the late 1920s and early 1930s, however, the demand for the water and the resort had faded and other sources of income had to be found to support the community. By the 1950s, coal had taken over, and Dawson Springs was known as the strip mining capital of western Kentucky.

Romance didn't pass Dawson Springs by, either. Out along the Tradewater River, there is a famous spot called Lover's Leap. Long before anyone thought about either mineral water or coal, a legend was born there that

Drive 34: Dawson Springs to Marion
A Rural Drive in Western Kentucky

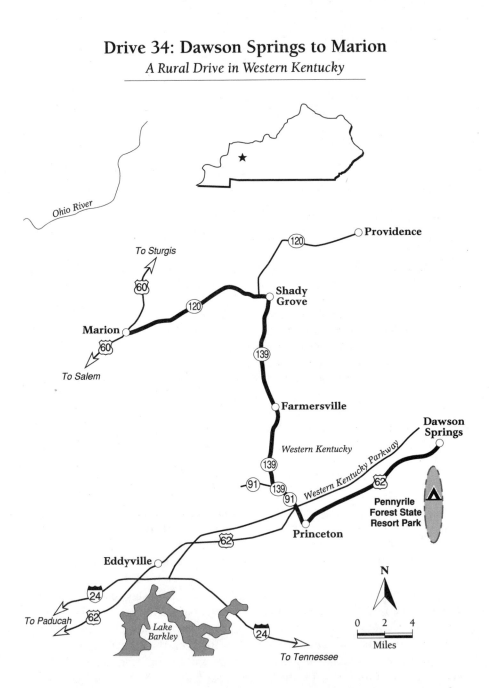

explains the name. The story goes that a roving band of Indians captured a young girl, but because she was so pretty, they spared her the fate that befell most such captives and, instead, decided that she would one day become the wife of the chief.

Years passed, and she became a beautiful young woman. She had forgotten her past and lived the life of the Indians who had captured her, with one exception. She had fallen in love with a young brave whom she had known since her capture, and she disliked the chief for whom she was intended. Of course, if the chief found out about her love for the brave, he would be in grave trouble, so they were forced to meet in secret.

Finally, the day came when she was called to the chief's tepee. She knew that her plans for the future would be destroyed, so she left the camp and found her way to the top of a sheer cliff overlooking the river. She had decided that death was preferable to being the chief's wife, so she began to chant her love song. As she began, her brave came around a bend in the river in his canoe. He heard the chant and, knowing what it meant, paddled furiously toward the foot of the cliff. She leaped into the water far below and was pulled into the canoe. The two lovers paddled down the river to the Ohio and were not seen again by their people. Ever since that time, the cliff has been called Lover's Leap.

If you plan to stay in the Dawson Springs area for a few days, or if you would just like to visit a beautiful western Kentucky forest, you might want to look at Pennyrile Forest State Resort Park. The park is located just south of town in the midst of a lush, secluded forest of oak, cedar, and hickory with some birches along the lake. There is a rustic wood and stone lodge with 24 rooms sitting high on a cliff overlooking Pennyrile Lake. If you would like a little more seclusion than the lodge offers, you can try one of the 13 one- or two-bedroom cottages with either wooded or lake views. You could even choose one with a private boat and fishing dock, a fireplace and screened porch. Tableware, cooking utensils, and linens are provided at the cottages. If you brought your own shelter in the form of a tent or an RV, try the 68-site campground with hookups and a central building with showers, rest rooms, and a laundry. The dining room serves Kentucky breakfasts, lunches, and dinners for you and 199 others.

Now to the drive. Start on U.S. 62 and head west toward Princeton. The 12 miles between Dawson Springs and Princeton will provide you with views of beautiful western Kentucky scenery. U.S. 62 will twist back and forth and dip and roll as it passes through countryside that alternates between walls of trees and rolling farmland. It is a very pleasant drive, and it takes you to a very pleasant place: Princeton. The town had its beginning back in 1805, when a Virginia-born settler by the name of William Prince arrived with a land grant of 1,700 acres, which had been awarded to him for Revolutionary War service. He built a home and a sawmill near the Big Spring Cave opening, which is now in the downtown section of Princeton. The Big Spring is actually the spot where an underground river, which flows under the town and provides its water supply, comes to the surface. The area was originally called Eddy Grove for a swirling spring at the head of

Eddy Creek, but when Caldwell County was created in 1809, the town took the name of Prince after the man who donated the land for the county seat. First called Princetown by order of the court that created it, the name was changed to Princeton, probably because that's what everybody called it. No doubt due to the abundance of good agricultural land, plenty of water, and lots of timber, the town grew rapidly.

To continue the drive, begin where KY 139/91 crosses over the Western Kentucky Parkway. At 1.5 miles from the parkway, KY 91 goes straight and KY 139 makes a sharp right turn. Go right on KY 139. For a while, there are farms and houses intermixed, but as you leave the town behind and the road winds upward into the hills, the houses give way to farms, walls of trees, and, finally, even the farms become more scarce. At 4 miles, you pass through a small farming community with nice views of the fields and, if you hit it at the right season, big rolls of hay. In another mile, you will come over the top of a hill and be treated to views of rolling farmlands and fields on the right stretching a long way to the trees. At 6.2 miles, you enter Farmersville, a crossroads hamlet that was founded around 1848 by Dr. William W. Throckmorton. He named the town for Frederick Farmer who had settled there around 1810. At 10.8 miles, you will begin to twist back and forth as the road snakes its way uphill past dense stands of hardwoods on both sides, and at 15.5 miles, you enter Shady Grove, a beautiful little tree-shaded hamlet.

In the middle of Shady Grove, KY 139 makes a sharp left turn and continues on out of town and through the rolling fields. Just west of Shady Grove, KY 139 ends at the junction with KY 120. Go straight ahead on KY 120. Beyond the junction, you will drop downhill rapidly, swing to the right, and climb back up into the trees. At 20 miles, you will be passing rolling fields with a few farm buildings and scattered trees. From here until you reach Marion, the road will take you through the beauty of western Kentucky as it climbs and dips past farmland and woodlands. At 27.9 miles, you will arrive at the junction of KY 120 and U.S. 60 in Marion.

While in Marion, rock and mineral enthusiasts may enjoy a trip to the Clement Mineral Collection at 205 North Walker Street where they can see some really spectacular examples of fluorite. Fluorite is a finer grade of fluorspar that was mined here for many years. It was discovered back in 1815, when a company headed by Andrew Jackson began to mine silver-bearing galena. Unfortunately for Jackson and his company, the galena in the area did not contain enough silver to make mining profitable, so he disposed of his holdings in the thousands of acres to which he had acquired title. The fluorspar was known in the area, but there was no demand for it until World War I came along. Fluorspar is used as a flux in steel making, and the war effort needed lots of steel. There were lots of mines around the area, and a little local inquiry might find someone who would let you poke around on the tailings.

35

The Land Between the Lakes
The Best of the Western Water Lands

General description: Our main drive follows KY 453 (The Trace) about 35 miles from I-24 to the Tennessee border, but The Trace continues for roughly 30 more miles into Tennessee. Although our drive along the Trace is fairly short, there are many more miles of roads to the lakes for boat launching, camping, fishing, and picnicking that make very nice scenic side trips on their own. All of the drives will be in heavily wooded areas, but the side roads are deep in the woods, while KY 453 is more wide open. We mention the Homeplace and the Great Western Iron Furnace, because they are so interesting and are just over the Tennessee line.

Special attractions: Land Between the Lakes National Recreation Area, Golden Pond Visitor Center and Planetarium, The Nature Station, the Homeplace-1850, Great Western Iron Furnace.

Location: Southwest.

Drive route numbers: KY 453, side roads.

Travel season: All year.

Camping: There are campgrounds in abundance in the whole area. Some of the areas are Aurora, Benton, Murray, Calvert City, Gilbertsville, and Hardin.

Services: Motels and restaurants in Eddyville, Calvert City, Gilbertsville, Hardin, and Benton. In addition, cottages and condos are available at many locations in the Kentucky Lake and Lake Barkley areas.

Nearby attractions: Kentucky Dam Village State Resort Park. Other attractions in the Land between the Lakes area are numerous (see appendices for addresses and web sites for more information).

The drive

When the first settlers came to this heavily wooded peninsula between the Tennessee and Cumberland rivers, they called it the Land between the Rivers. There are very few records of these hardy souls who penetrated so far into the wilderness, often with nothing more than they could carry on their backs, but it seems clear that there were white men living in the area by 1750.

Land Between the Lakes is a 170,000-acre peninsula, about 40 miles long and 8 to 12 miles wide, tucked between Kentucky Lake on the west

Drive 35: The Land between the Lakes

The Best of the Western Water Lands

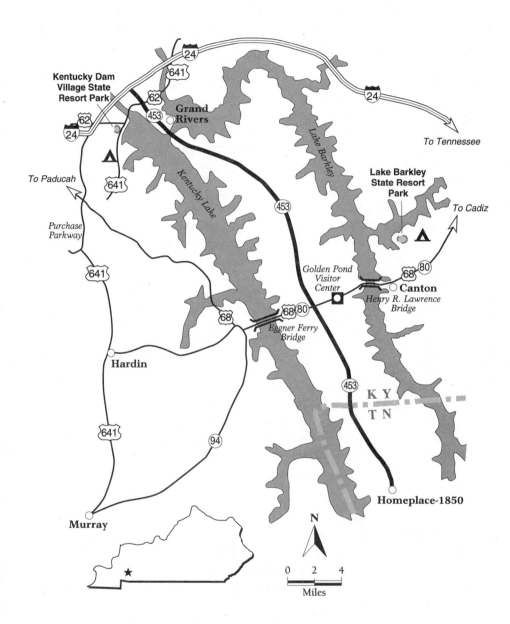

Kentucky Dam Village State Resort Park

Grand Rivers

Lake Barkley

To Tennessee

Lake Barkley State Resort Park

To Cadiz

Purchase Parkway

Kentucky Lake

Golden Pond Visitor Center

Canton

Henry R. Lawrence Bridge

Eggner Ferry Bridge

Hardin

K Y
T N

Homeplace-1850

Murray

N

0   2   4
Miles

and Lake Barkley on the east. Within its confines, you will find tent and RV camping, swimming, hiking, fishing, and boating. There are more than 300 miles of undeveloped shoreline to explore and lots of roads, both paved and gravel, for those who would rather ride than walk. Walking is the best way to enjoy the area, but if you arrive in tick season, be sure to have a few gallons of insect repellent along.

Ticks notwithstanding, this is a remarkably beautiful spot, but it did not come into being without controversy. In 1941, the people who lived in the land between the rivers learned of the plans by the Tennessee Valley Authority (TVA) to buy up the land along the Tennessee River. The agency announced that it was going to acquire approximately 158,000 acres to form Kentucky Lake. In 1942, however, it impounded 234,000 acres. It announced that the towns of Birmingham and Newburg would be obliterated and that numerous villages and other small communities would also be flooded. About 3,500 families, many who had lived there for generations, would have to be moved out to make way for the lake. The TVA promised that the result of the lake and its electrical generating capacity would bring tourism and industry to the region. These promises put dollar signs in the eyes of those who would not be displaced, but meant nothing to those who would. Bitter court fights and condemnation proceedings followed, and a general hatred and distrust of TVA and the government in general prevailed.

Once the government gets started, it is almost impossible to stop, though, and in 1938, construction on Kentucky Dam began. Six years, 1,365,000 cubic yards of concrete, 5,582,000 cubic yards of earth and rock fill, and $118,000,000 later, the lake began to fill. In the late 1950s, the scene was repeated on the Cumberland River with the building of Barkley Dam and the creation of Lake Barkley. More families were displaced, more farms became the bottom of a lake, and more people hated the TVA. In 1963, President Kennedy directed the TVA to create a recreation area in Kentucky and Tennessee that would attract a large number of tourists and stimulate the regional economy. Once again, that was fine planning, unless it was your farm that was under water. Both court and political battles went on for years, but the TVA won and today we have a beautiful park between the lakes, although individuals and groups continue to battle the TVA over its policies and broken promises.

Set your odometer at zero at the junction of Interstate 24 and KY 453 and head south on KY 453. In a little more than a mile, you will come to the junction with U.S. 62. If you turn right here, you will cross Kentucky Dam and come to the Kentucky Dam Village State Resort Park. Each of the 72 rooms in the Village Inn Lodge offers a private patio or balcony. The Village Green Inn by the golf course has 14 rooms and may be rented as an entire unit. There are also 72 cottages with either 1-, 2-, or 3-bedroom designs with 1 or 2 baths. Tableware, cooking utensils, and linen are provided. For campers, there are 221 paved campsites with hookups, a grocery store, two dump stations, and four central service buildings with showers and rest rooms. If you should happen to fly in, there is an Air Camp where you can camp by your airplane. There is a 4,000-foot paved and lighted runway 1.5 miles from the lodge. If you really came in style, there is jet fuel available there, too. As you would expect, all of the attractions of the other state resort parks are also available. Best of all, the rates in this truly first-class establishment are comparable to those of a good motel.

Continue on down KY 453. (This is also called The Trace.) At a little more than 3 miles, you pass the turn to Grand Rivers. At 4.5 miles, you will come to the turn to the Kentucky Lake Loop Drive, a 3-mile, one-way loop that will give you some fine views of Kentucky Lake and the canal connecting the two lakes.

From this point on, there are areas of dense woodlands between the road and Kentucky Lake and Lake Barkley. Look for oaks, hickories, chestnuts, cedars, white pines, short leaf pines, loblolly pines, Virginia pines, dogwoods, and redbuds. In the spring, there are varieties of wildflowers.

At 7.2 miles, there is a small, old cemetery on the right. Before the lakes were created, there were more than 200 cemeteries on the land that is now Land between the Lakes. Relatives still maintain them. About 4.4 miles from the cemetery is an intersection of The Trace and roads going to each of the lakes. Both are paved and pass through heavy stands of both hardwoods and conifers. Both trips are beautiful, but the one to Lake Barkley is about twice as long as the one to Kentucky Lake.

From Grand Rivers to the Tennessee border there are more campgrounds, hiking trails, and wildlife viewing areas than we could possibly cover here. The Land between the Lakes is home to more than 54 different kinds of mammals and 230 species of birds, many of them endangered. There are trails and old roads to hike ranging from very short and easy to the 65-mile north-south trail which runs the entire length of the Land Between the Lakes (see the appendix to find out where to write for maps, guides, etc.).

At 12.6 miles, you will reach the visitor center at Golden Pond where The Trace passes under U.S. 68/KY 80. If you continue on down The Trace for another 12 to 15 miles into Tennessee, you will reach the Homeplace-1850, a living history farm that reflects the life of a rural family in the middle of the 19th century. There you will see some rare and endangered species of livestock that were common at the time, and gardens are even planted with heirloom seeds. Historic interpreters, dressed in period clothing, will demonstrate skills such as plowing, farming tobacco, spinning, or gardening.

Back at Golden Pond, you can visit the planetarium and observatory. In the 88-seat planetarium, you can watch shows that explore such astronomical phenomena as black holes, white dwarves, and the possibility of life on Mars. There is also a nice gift shop with lots of books about the area.

Oaks, hickories, chestnuts, cedars, white pines, short leaf pines, loblolly pines, Virginia pines, dogwoods, and redbuds border Lake Barkley.

If you drive east on U.S. 68/KY 80, you will cross the beautiful Henry R. Lawrence Memorial Bridge on your way to Lake Barkley State Resort Park. If you would like to see another beautiful resort park, continue east on U.S. 68 for a couple of miles to KY 1489 and follow the signs to Lake Barkley State Resort Park on the shore of Lake Barkley. Most of the 120 rooms at the Barkley Lodge have a lake view from their private balconies. There are even 4 suites available. The Little River Lodge has 10 rooms, which can be rented as a unit. This park, too, has a paved and lighted airstrip with jet fuel just 3 miles from the lodge. For campers, there is a 78-site campground with all of the usual amenities. Fishing, golfing, hiking, swimming, and tennis opportunities are available and there is even a lighted trap range. This park abounds in natural beauty, too. Among many others, there are dogwood, redbud, magnolia, and even Japanese cherry trees to greet you in the spring with a profusion of blossoms.

If you travel west on U.S. 68 from Golden Pond, you will cross another pretty bridge, the Eggner Ferry Bridge. If you turn left on KY 94 just after you leave the bridge, you can drive 16 miles to Murray, where you can visit the National Scouting Museum, the Wrather West Kentucky Museum, and the Nathan B. Stubblefield Monument on the campus of Murray State University. Who was Nathan B. Stubblefield? Well here in Murray, Kentucky, in the town square, on January 1, 1902, this poor farmer, with no formal education, demonstrated his amazing invention—the wireless telephone. His bulky transmitter broadcast his voice to 5 different listening stations around town. At the time Guglielmo Marconi, generally considered to be the father of radio, had only been able to transmit beeps. Stubblefield had broadcast the human voice.

Nathan Beverly Stubblefield, the third of 4 sons of William Jefferson and Victoria Frances Stubblefield, was born on December 27, 1860, on a farm just outside of Murray. He was obsessed with electricity from an early age, but did poorly in school. By the age of 15, he had dropped out of school and spent all of his time reading everything he could find about science. He married in 1881 and began farming a tract of land owned by his stepmother in order to support his family. He wasn't much of a farmer, and he used what little money he did accumulate to buy materials for his experiments. He had some modest success in patenting a lamp lighter and electric battery. He had always been a strange person, but his patent success made him even more so. He distrusted everyone, and thought that his neighbors were spying on him trying to find ways to steal his secrets. Although he was peculiar, he did produce. In 1888 he was granted a patent for an improved telephone and set up the first telephone system in Murray. All went well, until the Bell System came along and put him out of business.

His first love was the wireless telephone, though, and he kept working on it until his demonstration in 1902 brought him to national prominence. He had an arrangement with the Wireless Telephone Company of America to travel about the country demonstrating his invention. At first everything went fine, but after a problem in New York with a failed demonstration, he learned that the company was a fake and that he was just being utilized to free people from their money. Completely disillusioned, he headed back home to Murray, where he continued to conduct his experiments. Up to that point, his demonstrations had been with so-called ground induction, where the earth carried the signal. The latest experimenters were using magnetic induction. He began to work with this method, but his financial condition was getting worse. He was so obsessed with his experiments that he became estranged from his family. One by one his children left, and when his last daughter married and moved away, his wife left, too. He did odd jobs for a while after he lost the home he had lived in so long, and retreated to a rude shack on a friend's property. On March 28, 1928, the first man ever to broadcast the human voice was found dead of starvation on the floor of his shack. He was 68 years old.

After visiting the Stubblefield monument, if you haven't visited the Homeplace-1850, and would like to, drive back up KY 94 and to The Trace and head south into Tennessee. If you want to get a head start on the Great River Road drive, go north from Murray on U.S. 641 to the Purchase Parkway. Follow the parkway north to I-24, and go left to Paducah.

36

The Great River Road
Old Towns along the Ohio and Mississippi

General description: We called this 63-mile drive the Great River Road, even though only part of it is along that byway. The Great River Road is a network of federal, state, and local roads created in 1938 to follow, as closely as possible, the Mississippi River from its beginning in Minnesota to the Gulf of Mexico. The portion in Kentucky is very short in comparison to the total length, but it runs through some of the most peaceful and least-industrialized country on the whole road. We started in Paducah and followed KY 305 and KY 358 to Monkey's Eyebrow. From there, we took KY 473 and KY 1105 to Barlow and U.S. 60 to Wickliffe at the confluence of the Mississippi and the Ohio rivers. From there, KY 123 and KY 239 took us to Cayce, the boyhood home of Casey Jones. From Cayce, it was only 9 miles to Hickman, one of Mark Twain's favorite towns along the Mississippi.

Special attractions: Barlow House Museum (Barlow), Columbus-Belmont State Park, Hickman, Monkey's Eyebrow.

Location: Southwest.

Drive route numbers: U.S. 60, 51/62; KY 305, 358, 473, 1105, 123, 239, 94.

Travel season: All year.

Camping: Campgrounds at Paducah and Columbus-Belmont State Park.

Services: Motels in Paducah, Wickliffe, and Cayce. Restaurants and/or fast food in Paducah, Barlow, Wickliffe, Bardwell, Columbus, Cayce, and Hickman.

Nearby attractions: The Ballard Wildlife Management Area, Metropolis Lake State Nature Preserve.

 # The drive

The drive begins in Paducah, one of western Kentucky's major cities. It is believed that the first house here was built around 1821 by James and William Pore. The town was founded in 1827 by William Clark, the brother of George Rogers Clark, who along with Meriwether Lewis led the famed Lewis and Clark Expedition. It was Clark who gave the town the name Paducah, supposedly after his Chickasaw Indian friend Chief Paduke. This is disputed by some, who say that there never was a Chief Paduke, and that the Chickasaw language contains no such word. Whatever the origin of the

Drive 36: The Great River Road
Old Towns along the Ohio and Mississippi

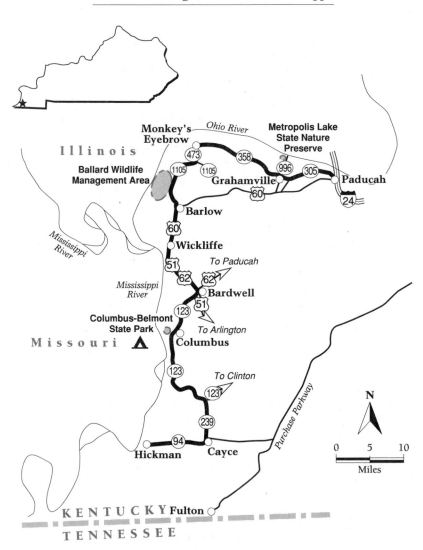

name, it was Paducah in 1827, and it is Paducah today.

There is much to see and do in Paducah, but if you don't get a chance to see anything else, be sure to see the murals on the flood wall before you leave. When you are ready to go, set your odometer at zero at the junction of I-24 and KY 305. This is exit 3 on the interstate. Go west on KY 358. At 2.1 miles, go right on KY 358. In less than 0.5 mile, you will cross a bridge over a creek, and at 5 miles, you will enter Grahamville. Zelotes Clinton

Graham opened a store here in 1877. At 5.4 miles, go right on KY 358 at the stop sign. In only 0.2 mile, you will have to make a decision. The main drive goes left on KY 358, but if you keep ahead on KY 996, you will come to Metropolis Lake State Nature Preserve. The preserve contains a 50-acre lake that is one of the few remaining natural lakes in the Ohio River floodplain. It is ringed with bald cypress and swamp tupelo. There is a moderate 0.75-mile interpretive hike over some uneven terrain.

Back at the junction, if you go left on KY 358, you will pass through a pretty area of rolling hills and farmland. At 13.1 miles, there is a 90-degree turn to the left, and at 15.4 miles you will come to a stop sign. A street sign here says Monkey's Eyebrow Road. Go straight ahead down this road a short distance to the Monkey's Eyebrow City Limits sign.

We have to confess that, even though this is a very pretty drive, the real reason we came this way was to see Monkey's Eyebrow. Who could resist a name like that? The reason for the name is obscure, but there are plenty of stories. The most prevalent one says that there were some bushes on a hill behind the store that someone with a vivid imagination thought looked like a monkey's eyebrows. Needless to say, we saw no monkey's eyebrows, but it is a pretty little spot and we are glad we went. Continue on just a short way to the junction with KY 473. At 1.7 miles from the Monkey's Eyebrow sign, you will pass the entrance to the Ballard Wildlife Management Area and viewing area.

This 8,373-acre area in the Ohio River floodplain is home to a variety of wildlife, including bobcats, otters, deer, squirrels, and bald eagles. There are 25 miles of roads in the area to view the wildlife and the stands of oak and hickory. The lakes and wetlands contain many cypresses. There is even a small wooden viewing platform on the east end of the area. Although there are no established hiking trails, you are welcome to hike in the wooded areas and along the wetlands.

Beyond the wildlife management area, there are a few trees, but peaceful rolling farmland predominates. At 4 miles, there is a stop sign at the junction with KY 1105. Go right past Oscar, and in about 4 miles there is a unique barn on the right with diagonal wooden siding. In another 4 miles or so, you will pass through the middle of the old Barlow cemetery. Just past the cemetery is the junction with U.S. 60 in Barlow. Go left on U.S. 60. The terrain alternates between woodlands and rolling farmland until you reach Wickliffe.

U.S. 60 winds through this old river town, which sits just below the confluence of the Mississippi and Ohio rivers. Wickliffe was a part of the golden age of steamboating that Mark Twain wrote about. It was also a landing for the ferry boats that served the tri-state area. The ferries are all gone now—replaced with a bridge just a few miles north on U.S. 60/62/51. Here, you can cross the Ohio River into Illinois, then make a sharp left turn and cross another bridge over the Mississippi River into Missouri, all in the space of a few miles. The Wickliffe Mounds Research Center is north of town. The ancient mounds are the only reminder of a civilization that lived in this area between A.D.1100 and 1350.

At the junction with U.S. 62/51 at the edge of town, U.S. 60 goes right to the mounds and the bridge. Keep straight ahead on U.S. 62/51 toward Bardwell, an old town that grew up around a railroad station on the Mississippi Central Line. The origin of the name of the town is not clear. One tale says that it was named for the superintendent of construction on the railroad. Another story says that it is a corruption of "bored well," a nearby well dug to supply water for the railroad station. Still another tale is that it stands for "boarded well," a means of lining a well with boards to keep it from collapsing while it is being dug.

From Bardwell, go right on KY 123 and enjoy the farmland and trees. This is a tranquil country. Make a gentle right turn followed by a gentle left turn through Berkley and continue on through the pastoral scenes to Columbus, the oldest town in the Jackson Purchase. It was settled in 1804 on the Mississippi floodplain and called Iron Banks for the rusty colored cliffs. A post office was established in 1820 and was named Columbus for Christopher Columbus, an Italian sailor who had 3 vessels under Spanish registry. After the horrible floods of 1927, the town was relocated to the 150-foot bluff 0.5 mile east. Today, nothing remains of the original town.

While in Columbus, don't miss the Columbus-Belmont State Park. It is a beautiful tree-shaded spot with cottonwoods, maples, oaks, elms, dogwoods, and redbuds all situated on a bluff above the Mississippi River. A 38-site campground with utility hookups, rest rooms, showers and laundry facilities, and 2.5 miles of self-guided trails make this an ideal stop over. There is also a museum where you can see some Civil War artifacts and view a video about the Battle of Belmont.

This area played an important role in the Civil War, as Columbus was a strategic point for controlling the Mississippi River. Consequently, the Confederates stationed a force of 19,000 men here at a place called Fort De Russey. A floating battery of gunboats was positioned on the river, and even river steamers were converted to warships. Heavy guns were installed on the bluff, and a second battery was set up at Belmont, on the Missouri side. Columbus was known as "The Gibraltar of the West." As a final measure, a huge chain was stretched across the river to stop any Union boats. In November of 1861, Ulysses S. Grant, engaging in his first active duty of the war, attacked the camp at Belmont. There was a skirmish, and the Confederates retreated. Grant then tried to attack Columbus, but was badly overpowered, so he moved back up river after burning Belmont. The Union Army, realizing that a direct attack on Columbus was futile, took smaller camps around Columbus one by one. When they outflanked the Confederates, they withdrew and the Union troops occupied Columbus and

At the Columbus-Belmont State Park you can see a massive chain and anchor, which were used to block Union gunboats during the Civil War.

reopened the river. A cannon, one of the 6-ton anchors, and a piece of the great chain are on display under the big cottonwoods in the park.

When you leave, go back to the park entrance and turn right on KY 123. In just 0.2 mile, KY 123 goes right and becomes both a Kentucky Scenic Byway and a part of the Great River Road. Follow the scenic byway signs to Oakton. About halfway there, you will make a 90-degree turn to the left, cross a floodplain, and pass through a beautiful tree canopy. Just beyond Oakton, KY 123 makes a 90-degree turn to the right, followed in a short distance by an equally sharp turn to the left, before coming to the junction with KY 239. Go right right on KY 239 for about 3 miles to Cayce.

No, the town was not named for Edgar Cayce, the famed mystic. He was born in Kentucky, but on a farm near Hopkinsville, not here. Nor was it named for Casey Jones, the legendary brave engineer. Rather, as we shall see, Casey Jones got his name from Cayce. In fact, the town was named for James Hardie Cayce, the first postmaster of what was then called Cacey's Station. The misspelling was corrected in 1874, and the "Station" dropped in 1880.

But back to Casey Jones. John Luther Jones was not born in Cayce, nor was he born in Kentucky. He did move to Cayce with his family when he was just a boy. At 15 years of age, he went to work for the railroad as an apprentice telegraph operator and worked his way up to engineer. Early in 1900, he was promoted to engineer of the Illinois Central Railroad's crack train, the "Cannonball," which ran from Memphis, Tennessee, to Canton, Mississippi. On April 29, 1900, he and his fireman, Sim Webb, had just pulled into Memphis and were ready to go home when the engineer of the outgoing train took ill. Casey and Sim volunteered to make the run to Canton. At eleven o'clock on that rainy Sunday morning, they climbed aboard old Number 382 and pulled out. At four o'clock on the morning of April 30, 1900, just outside Vaughn, Mississippi, his train hit the back of a freight train that was partially blocking the tracks. Accounts vary as to just why the accident happened, but it is generally accepted that Jones was going too fast. The official accident report puts the blame on Casey, but his fireman said there was no warning and no flagman. No one will ever know the truth, but we do know that Casey was the only one killed. Wallace Saunders, an engine wiper in the Canton roundhouse, had idolized Casey, and it was he who started the *Ballad of Casey Jones* that elevated the young engineer's name to national recognition. Oh yes, he was called "Cayce" because of the town where he had grown up. And he went by "Cayce" all his life. It wasn't until the ballad became popular that people started spelling the name Casey.

At Cayce, go west on KY 94 toward Hickman. From Cayce to Hickman is 9 miles of western Kentucky farmland. About 3 miles out of Cayce, you will pass the R. N. Henson Broommaker's Museum with the largest collection of broom-making equipment in the country. Generations of Hensons have made brooms in this shop, and they have a collection that includes the original Leather Kentucky Cabin Broom. In Hickman, the town that Mark Twain called "the most beautiful town on the Mississippi," you can ride the Hickman-Dorena Ferry to Dorena, Missouri, or visit the Warren Thomas Museum, where the history of the local African-American community is preserved.

Although there isn't much to make you think it, one of the most cataclysmic events in the history of America happened just a few miles from Hickman. In 1811 and 1812, three earthquakes occurred near New Madrid, Missouri, that rank among the greatest earthquakes in known history. They affected the topography more than any other earthquakes on the North American continent, and, although no measuring equipment was available in those days, they must have been the equivalent of an 8.0 on the Richter scale. Felt over most of the United States, more than 150,000 acres of forest were destroyed by the quake, vast areas of land sank into the ground, new lakes were formed, houses were tumbled, the course of the Mississippi River was changed, and, for a time, the Mississippi even ran backwards in the area. If you look at a map of Kentucky, you will see a little bump way down in the southwest corner where the Mississippi makes a loop. This is a spot where the river's course was changed. It changed so much, in fact, that today it is necessary to drive into Tennessee in order to get to that little piece of Kentucky.

Appendix A
Sources of More Information

Drive 1

Ashland Area Convention and Visitors
  Bureau
PO Box 987, 728 Greenup Avenue
Ashland, KY 41105

Paintsville Tourism Commission
PO Box 809
304 Main Street
Paintsville, KY 41240

Paintsville Lake State Park
PO Box 726
Paintsville, KY 41240

Pike County Tourism Commission
PO Box 1497
Pikeville, KY 41502

Prestonsburg Tourism Commission
One Hal Rogers Drive, KY 114
Prestonsburg, KY 41653

Greenbo Lake State Resort Park
HC 60, Box 562
Greenup, KY 41144-9517

Jenny Wiley State Resort Park
39 Jenny Wiley Road
Prestonsburg, KY 41653-9799

Yatesville Lake State Park
PO Box 767
Louisa, KY 41230

Breaks Interstate Park
PO Box 100
Breaks, VA 24607

Drive 2

Grayson Tourism and Convention
  Commission
PO Box 296
Grayson, KY 41143

Carter Caves State Resort Park
Route 5, Box 1120
Olive Hill, KY 41164-9032

Greenbo Lake State Resort Park
HC 60, Box 562
Greenup, KY 41144-9517

Grayson Lake State Park
Route 3, Box 800
Olive Hill, KY 41164-9213

Drive 3

Grayson Tourism and Convention Center
PO Box 296
Grayson, KY 41143

Paintsville Tourism Commission
PO Box 809
304 Main Street
Paintsville, KY 41420

Paintsville Lake State Park
PO Box 726
Paintsville, KY 41240

Carter Caves State Resort Park
Route 5, Box 1120
Olive Hill, KY 41164-9032

Grayson Lake State Park
Route 3, Box 800
Olive Hill, KY 41164-9213

Drive 4

Morehead Tourism Commission
150 East First Street
Morehead, KY 40351

Yatesville Lake State Park
PO Box 767
Louisa, KY 41230

Cave Run Lake
Park Manager, U.S. Army Corps of
    Engineers
150 KY 826
Morehead, KY 40351-9211
or
District Ranger
U.S. Forest Service
PO Box 910
2375 KY 801
Morehead, KY 40351

Drive 5

Harlan Tourist and Convention
    Commission
PO Box 489
Harlan, KY 40831

Hazard-Perry County Tourist Commission
601 Main Street #3
Hazard, KY 41701

Letcher County Tourist Commission
306 Madison Avenue
Whitesburg, KY 41858

Carr Creek State Park
PO Box 249
Sassafras, KY 41759

Buckhorn Lake State Resort Park
HC 36, Box 1000
Buckhorn, KY 41721-9602

Kingdom Come State Park
Box M
Cumberland, KY 40823-0420

Pine Mountain State Resort Park
1050 State Park Road
Pineville, KY 40977-0610

Bell County Tourism Commission
PO Box 788
Middlesboro, KY 40965

Cumberland–Benham–Lynch Tourist
    Commission
PO Box J
104 Freeman Street
Cumberland, KY 40823

Cumberland Gap National Historical Park
PO Box 1848
Middlesboro, KY 40965

Superintendent, Lilley Cornett Woods
HC 63, Box 2710
Skyline, KY 41851
or
Director, Division of Natural Areas
McCreary 224
Eastern Kentucky University
Richmond, KY 40475

Drive 6

Harlan Tourist and Convention
    Commission
PO Box 489
Harlan, KY 40831

Leslie County Tourism Commission
PO Box 948
Hyden, KY 41749

Buckhorn Lake State Resort Park
HC 36, Box 1000
Buckhorn, KY 41721-9602

Pine Mountain State Resort Park
1050 State Park Road
Pineville, KY 40977-0610

Cumberland Gap National Historical Park
PO Box 1848
Middlesboro, KY 40965

Bell County Tourism Commission
PO Box 788
Middlesboro, KY40965

Letcher County Tourist Commission
306 Madison Street
Whitesburg, KY 41858

Drive 7

Powell County Tourism Commission
PO Box 1028
Stanton, KY 40380

Natural Bridge State Resort Park
2135 Natural Bridge Road
Slade, KY 40376-9999

Drive 8

Daniel Boone National Forest (Zilpo
   Road Scenic Byway)
1700 Bypass Road
Winchester, KY 40391

Cave Run Lake
Park Manager
U.S. Corps of Engineers
150 KY 826
Morehead, KY 40351-9211
or
District Ranger
U.S. Forest Service
PO Box 910
2375 KY 801
Morehead, KY 40351

Morehead Tourism Commission
150 East First Street
Morehead, KY 40351

Drive 9

Richmond Tourism Commission
354 Lancaster Avenue
Richmond, KY 40475

Berea Recreation Tourism and Convention
   Commission
PO Box 556
201 North Broadway
Berea, KY 40403

Daniel Boone National Forest
1700 Bypass Road
Winchester, KY 40391

Drive 10

London-Laurel County Tourism
   Commission
104 West Daniel Boone Parkway
I-75 Exit 41
London, KY 40741

Williamsburg Tourist and Convention
   Commission
PO Box 2
Williamsburg, KY 40769

Cumberland College
Reservations/Information
Cumberland Inn
Williamsburg, KY 40769

Dr. Thomas Walker State Historic Site
HC 83, Box 868
Barboursville, KY 40906-9603

Big South Fork National River and
   Recreation Area
Park Headquarters
4564 Leatherwood Road
Oneida, TN 37841

Levi Jackson Wilderness Road State Park
996 Levi Jackson Mill Road
London, KY 40744-8944

Drive 11

Winchester-Clark County Tourism
   Commission
2 South Maple, Suite A
Winchester, KY 40391

Mount Vernon–Rockcastle County
Tourism Commission
PO Box 1261
Mount Vernon, KY 40456

Fort Boonesboro State Park
4375 Boonesboro Road
Richmond, KY 40475-9316

Drive 12

Daniel Boone National Forest
1700 Bypass Road
Winchester, KY 40391

Richmond Tourism Commission
345 Lancaster Avenue
Richmond, KY 40475

Hummel Planetarium and Space Theater
Eastern Kentucky University
Richmond, KY 40475

Battle of Richmond Driving Tour
Visitor Center
345 Lancaster Avenue
Richmond, KY 40475

Bybee Pottery
PO Box 555
610 Waco Loop
Waco, KY 40385

The Kentucky Explorer Magazine
PO Box 227 - 1248 Highway 15N
Jackson, KY 42339

White Hall State Historic Site
500 White Hall Shrine Road
Richmond, KY 40475-9159

Drive 13

Georgetown–Scott County Tourist
Commission
401 Outlet Center Drive240
Georgetown, KY 40324

Maysville-Mason County Tourist
Commission
216 Bridge Street
Maysville, KY 41056

Paris–Bourbon County Tourist
Commission
2011 Averson Drive
Paris, KY 40361

Duncan Tavern
323 High Street
Paris, KY 40361

Blue Licks Battlefield State Park
PO Box 66
Mt. Olivet, KY 41064-0066

Kincaid Lake State Park
Route #1, Box33
Falmouth, KY 41040

Toyota Motor Manufacturing Kentucky
1001 Cherry Blossom Way
Georgetown, KY 40324

Drive 14

Maysville–Mason County Tourist
Commission
216 Bridge Street
Maysville, KY 41056

Kentucky Covered Bridge Association
62 Miami Parkway
Ft. Thomas, KY 41075-1137

Drive 15

Maysville-Mason County Tourist
Commission
216 Bridge Street
Maysville, KY 41056

Kincaid Lake State Park
Route #1, Box 33
Falmouth, KY 41040

Kentucky Covered Bridge Association
62 Miami Parkway
Ft. Thomas, KY 41075-1137

Drive 16

Frankfort–Franklin County Tourism and
Convention Commission
100 Capitol Ave.
Frankfort, KY 40601

Carrollton–Carroll County Tourism
Commission
PO Box 293
Old Stone Jail, Court Street
Carrollton, KY 41008

Big Bone Lick State Park
3380 Beaver Road
Union, KY 41091-9627

General Butler State Resort Park
PO Box 325
Carrollton, KY 41008-0325

Drive 17

Somerset-Pulaski County Tourist
Commission
PO Box 622
522 Ogden
Somerset, KY 42502

Levi Jackson Wilderness Road State Park
996 Levi Jackson Mill Road
London, KY 40744-8944

General Burnside Island State Park
PO Box 488
Burnside, KY 42519-0488

Drive 18

Russell County Tourist Commission
PO Box 64
U.S. 127 South
Russell Springs, KY 42642

Somerset-Pulaski County Tourist
Commission
PO Box 622
522 Ogden
Somerset, KY 42502

Lake Cumberland State Resort Park
5465 State Park Road
Jamestown, KY 42629-7801

General Burnside Island State Park
PO Box 488
Burnside, KY 42519-0488

Drive 19

Columbia-Adair County Tourist
Commission
1115 Jamestown Street #3
Columbia, KY 42728

Russell County Tourist Commission
PO Box 64
U.S. 127 South
Russell Springs, KY 42642

Danville-Boyle County Convention and
Visitors Bureau
McClure-Barbee House
304 South Fourth #201
Danville, KY 40422

Somerset–Pulaski County Tourist
Commission
PO Box 622
522 Ogden
Somerset, KY 42502

Perryville Battlefield State Historic Site
PO Box 296
Perryville, KY 40468-9999

William Whitley House State Historic Site
625 William Whitley Road
Stanford, KY 40484-9770

Drive 20

Corbin Tourist and Convention
  Commission
101 North Depot Street
Corbin, KY 40701

Cumberland Falls State Resort Park
7351 Kentucky 90
Corbin, KY 40701-8814

Daniel Boone National Forest
1700 Bypass Road
Winchester, KY 40391

Drive 21

Lexington Convention and Visitors
  Bureau
301 East Vine
Lexington, KY 40507

Bardstown–Nelson County Tourist and
  Convention Commission
107 East Stephen Foster
Bardstown, KY 40004

Abraham Lincoln Birthplace National
  Historic Site
2995 Lincoln Farm Road
Hodgenville, KY 42748

The Kentucky Railway Museum
136 South Main Street
New Haven, KY 40051-0240

My Old Kentucky Home State Park
PO Box 323
Bardstown, KY 40004-0323

Waveland State Historic Site
225 Higbee Mill Road
Lexington, KY 40514-1601

Drive 22

Campbellsville-Taylor County Tourist
  Commission
PO Box 4021
Broadway and Court
Campbellsville, KY 42719

Danville–Boyle County Convention and
  Visitors Bureau
McClure-Barbee House
304 South Fourth #201
Danville, KY 40422

Lebanon–Marion County Chamber of
  Commerce
21 Court Street
Lebanon, KY 40033

Perryville Battlefield State Historic Site
PO Box 296
Perryville, KY 40468-9999

Green River Lake State Park
179 Park Office Road
Campbellsville, KY 42718-9351

Harrodsburg–Mercer County Tourist
  Commission
PO Box 283
103 South Main
Harrodsburg, KY 40330

Lexington Convention and Visitors
  Bureau
301 East Vine
Lexington, KY 40507

Waveland State Historic Site
225 Higbee Mill Road
Lexington, KY 40514-1601

Old Fort Harrod State Park
PO Box 150
Harrodsburg, KY 40330-0156

Shaker Village of Pleasant Hill
3501 Lexington Road
Harrodsburg, KY 40330

Drive 23

Barren River Lake State Resort Park
1149 State Park Road
Lucas, KY 42156-9709

Dale Hollow Lake State Park
6371 State Park Road
Bow, KY 42717-9728

Drive 24

Williamsburg Tourist and Convention
    Commission
PO Box 2
Williamsburg, KY 40769

Dale Hollow Lake State Park
6371 State Park Road
Bow, KY 42717-9728

McCreary County Tourist Commission
PO Box 72
Whitley City, KY 42653

Big South Fork Scenic Railway
PO Box 368
Stearns, KY 42647

Big South Fork National River and
    Recreation Area
Park Headquarters
4564 Leatherwood Road
Oneida, TN 37841

Drive 25,26,27,28,29

Frankfort-Franklin County Tourism and
    Convention Commission
100 Capitol Ave.
Frankfort, KY 40601

Lexington Convention and Visitors
    Bureau
301 East Vine
Lexington, KY 40507

Woodford County Tourism Commission
110 North Main
Versailles, KY 40383

Kentucky Horse Park and International
    Museum of the Horse
4089 Iron Works Pike
Lexington, KY 40511

Drive 30

Cave City Tourist and Convention
    Commission
PO Box 518
Cave City, KY 42127

Edmonson County Tourist and
    Convention Commission
PO Box 628
Brownsville, KY 42210

Mammoth Cave National Park
Mammoth Cave
KY 42259

Drive 31

Bowling Green–Warren County Tourist
    Commission
352 Three Springs Road
Bowling Green, KY 42104

Radcliff–Fort Knox Tourist Commission
PO Box 845
306 North Wilson
Radcliff, KY 40159

Nolin Lake State Park
Box 340
Bee Spring, KY 42207

Rough River Dam State Resort Park
450 Lodge Roads
Falls of Rough, KY 40119-9701

Leitchfield–Grayson County Tourist
    Commission
10 Court Street
Leitchfield, KY 42755

Drive 32

Radcliff–Fort Knox Tourist Commission
PO Box 845
306 North Wilson
Radcliff, KY 40159

Owensboro–Daviess County Tourist
   Commission
212 East Second
Owensboro, KY 42301

Ben Hawes State Park
400 Booth Field Road
Owensboro, KY 42301

Drive 33

Owensboro–Daviess County Tourist
   Commission
212 East Second
Owensboro, KY 42301

Ben Hawes State Park
400 Booth Field Road
Owensboro, KY 42301

Lake Malone State Park
General Delivery
Dunmore, KY 42339-0093

Kentucky Department of Fish and
   Wildlife Resources
I&E Division #1 Game Farm Road
Frankfort, KY 40601

Drive 34

Pennyrile Forest State Resort Park
20781 Pennyrile Lodge Road
Dawson Springs, KY 42408-9212

Princeton Tourism Commission
206 Jefferson Street
Princeton, KY 42445

Lyon County Tourism Commission
PO Box 1030
Eddyville, KY

Drive 35

Land Between the Lakes (TVA)
100 Van Morgan Drive
Golden Pond, KY 42211

Livingston County Tourism Commission
721 Complex Drive
Grand Rivers, KY 42045

Paducah–McCracken County Convention
   and Business Bureau
128 Broadway
Paducah, KY 42001

Kenlake State Resort Park
542 Kenlake Road
Hardin, KY 42048

Kentucky Dam Lake State Resort Park
PO Box 69
Gilbertsville, KY 42044-0069

Drive 36

Columbus–Belmont State Park
PO Box 8
Columbus, KY 42032-0008

Fulton Tourism Commission
1010 West State Line
Fulton, KY 42041

Paducah–McCracken County Convention
   and Business Bureau
128 Broadway
Paducah, KY 42001

General Information

Kentucky Department of Parks
Capital Plaze Tower
500 Mero Street, 10th Floor
Frankfort, KY 40601-1968

Kentucky Department of Travel
Capital Plaza Tower
500 Mero Street, 22nd Floor
Frankfort, KY 40601-1968

Appendix B
Internet Sites of Interest

The following sites are just a few of the many places on the Internet where information on Kentucky can be found. If you would like more, just type Kentucky into your favorite search engine and prepare yourself for an information overload.

Some of the sites listed here are linked to one another, and others are somewhat repetitive, but all contain a wealth of information for your trip. If you have access to the Internet, give them a try. You won't be disappointed.

http://www.state.ky.us/tour/tour.htm
This is probably the best tourism site on the whole Internet. It is the Official Kentucky Vacation Guide and contains just about anything you could want to know about touring in the state. The site is divided into four sections: the Eastern Highlands, the Bluegrass Heartlands, the Scenic Wonderlands, and the Western Waterlands. In each section, you can find a list of attractions, bed and breakfasts, campgrounds, state parks, recreation sites, and much, much more. There are hyperlinks to all kinds of things from covered bridges to descriptions of Civil War battles. If you never check out another site, don't miss this one.

http://www.state.ky.us/
This is primarily a site for state government information, but it includes good information on tourism, state parks, an interesting look at the Kentucky Information Highway and a very long list of links to other Kentucky sites.

http://www.kytravel.com/ktgcover.htm
This is the Online Kentucky Travel Guide that contains lots of information on points of interest, attractions, crafts, lakes, museums etc.

http://www.louisvillescene.com
This site contains about all you would want to know about Louisville. It also includes a search function.

http://www.weather.com/weather/us/states/Kentucky
This is the weather channel's web site for Kentucky. You can find current weather, 5-day forecasts, and even view the Doppler radar weather maps for most of the major cities. A search function lets you access information for the whole state.

http://www.uky.edu/KentuckyAtlas/kentucky.html
The University of Kentucky has developed this atlas and gazetteer with lots of information about all of Kentucky. Descriptions of cities are short, but contain all essential information.

http://www.onlinekentucky.com
Online Kentucky contains information on tourism, the arts, sports, and more. There is even a procedure for sending a Kentucky postcard online. Another plus is a very interesting section for the kids.

http://www.mammothcave.com
This is just what it sounds like—all you could want to know about the Mammoth Cave area.

http://www.nps.gov/maca/
If you can't find what you want about Mammoth Cave from the above site, try this one. It is the National Park Service's home page for Mammoth Cave.

http://www.lbl.org
The Tennessee Valley Authority maintains this site to provide information about the Land between the Lakes region.

http://www.fws.gov/r4eao/nwrrlf.html
The National Park Service provides this site to dispense information about the Reelfoot National Wildlife Refuge in southwestern Kentucky and northwestern Tennessee.

http://www.nps.gov/
This is the main National Park Service site for general and specific information about the mission of the service.

http://www.state.ky.us/tour/outdoors/covered.htm
Here you will find information about Kentucky's remaining covered bridges.

http://www.state.ky.us/agencies/parks/parkhome-body.htm
On this home page for the state park system you will find general information about the system as well as links to each of the individual parks.

http://www.nps.gov/biso/bheron.htm
Go to this site for the audio portions of the Blue Heron Mining Camp Tour.

http://www.weisenberger.com
Use this home page to find out about Weisenberger Mills in Midway, or to order online. You can also e-mail them at info@weisenberger.com

http://www.imh.org/imh/kyhpl3b.html
Use this to view the text and photographs at the International Museum of the Horse at the Kentucky Horse Park.

http://www.geocities.com/Heartland/Meadows/5400/history.html
This will allow you to read the minutes of the David's Fork Baptist Church from 1801–1850.

http://www.wku.edu/Library/200Years/
Some great historical data on Bowling Green and Warren County can be found here.

http://www.ci.bowling-green.ky.us/
Use this to access Bowling Green's fine website, which contains both historical information and ideas on what to do in the area.

http://www.kentuckyexplorer.com
This is the home page for the *Kentucky Explorer* magazine. It is full of all kinds of historical data about Kentucky.

Index

Page numbers in *italics* refer to photos.
Page numbers in **bold** refer to maps.

About the Authors

In their 44 years of marriage, Bill and Cora Kappele have roamed around the highways, byways, and four-wheel-drive roads of the western United States looking for agates, jaspers, petrified wood, and other semi-precious "rocks" to haul home. Although Bill has written and co-authored books on a wide variety of subjects from English grammar to wire wrapped jewelry, he has devoted most of his time to the rockhounding hobby. He writes the "Shop Talk" column and serves as a contributing editor to Rock and Gem Magazine, and is also the author of Rockhounding Colorado, Rockhounding Utah, and Rockhounding Nevada, published by Falcon.

When their older son, Bill, his wife Beth, granddaughter Katy, and grandson David moved to Kentucky a few years ago, Bill and Cora drove back to visit, and while they took some rockhounding trips, they found a whole new and fascinating world to explore and to write about. This time, they decided to collaborate on the writing and give Cora some long-over-due credit. After several trips, many months of research, and nearly 10,000 miles on rental cars, Scenic Driving Kentucky was born. It was a labor of love, and they can't wait to get back and drive through some more of the Bluegrass State. After all, there is lots more to see. How does Son of Scenic Driving Kentucky sound?

FALCONGUIDES® Leading the Way™

WILDLIFE VIEWING GUIDES

Alaska Wildlife Viewing Guide
Arizona Wildlife Viewing Guide
California Wildlife Viewing Guide
Colorado Wildlife Viewing Guide
Florida Wildlife Viewing Guide
Indiana Wildlife Vewing Guide
Iowa Wildlife Viewing Guide
Kentucky Wildlife Viewing Guide
Massachusetts Wildlife Viewing Guide
Montana Wildlife Viewing Guide
Nebraska Wildlife Viewing Guide
Nevada Wildlife Viewing Guide
New Hampshire Wildlife Viewing Guide
New Jersey Wildlife Viewing Guide
New Mexico Wildlife Viewing Guide
New York Wildlife Viewing Guide
North Carolina Wildlife Viewing Guide
North Dakota Wildlife Viewing Guide
Ohio Wildlife Viewing Guide
Oregon Wildlife Viewing Guide
Puerto Rico and the Virgin Islands WVG
Tennessee Wildlife Viewing Guide
Texas Wildlife Viewing Guide
Utah Wildlife Viewing Guide
Vermont Wildlife Viewing Guide
Virginia Wildlife Viewing Guide
Washington Wildlife Viewing Guide
West Virginia Wildlife Viewing Guide
Wisconsin Wildlife Viewing Guide

HISTORIC TRAIL GUIDES

Traveling California's Gold Rush Country
Traveling the Lewis & Clark Trail
Traveling the Oregon Trail
Traveler's Guide to the Pony Express Trail

SCENIC DRIVING GUIDES

Scenic Driving Alaska and the Yukon
Scenic Driving Arizona
Scenic Driving the Beartooth Highway
Scenic Driving California
Scenic Driving Colorado
Scenic Driving Florida
Scenic Driving Georgia
Scenic Driving Hawaii
Scenic Driving Idaho
Scenic Driving Indiana
Scenic Driving Kentucky
Scenic Driving Michigan
Scenic Driving Minnesota
Scenic Driving Montana
Scenic Driving New England
Scenic Driving New Mexico
Scenic Driving North Carolina
Scenic Driving Oregon
Scenic Driving the Ozarks including the
    Ouchita Mountains
Scenic Driving Pennsylvania
Scenic Driving Texas
Scenic Driving Utah
Scenic Driving Virginia
Scenic Driving Washington
Scenic Driving Wisconsin
Scenic Driving Wyoming
Scenic Driving Yellowstone & Grand Teton
    National Parks
Scenic Byways East & South
Scenic Byways Far West
Scenic Byways Rocky Mountains

Discover the Thrill of Watching Wildlife.

 The Watchable Wildlife® Series

Published in cooperation with Defenders of Wildlife, these high-quality, full color guidebooks feature detailed descriptions, side trips, viewing tips, and easy-to-follow maps. Wildlife viewing guides for the following states are now available with more on the way.

Alaska
Arizona
California
Colorado
Florida
Indiana
Iowa
Kentucky
Massachusetts
Montana

Nebraska
Nevada
New Hampshire
New Jersey
New Mexico
New York
North Carolina
North Dakota
Ohio
Oregon

Puerto Rico &
  Virgin Islands
Tennessee
Texas
Utah
Vermont
Virginia
Washington
West Virginia
Wisconsin

Watch for this sign along roadways. It's the official sign indicating wildlife viewing areas included in the Watchable Wildlife® Series.

FALCON GUIDES ® Leading the way™

FalconGuides® are available for where-to-go hiking, mountain biking, rock climbing, walking, scenic driving, fishing, rockhounding, paddling, birding, wildlife viewing, and camping. We also have FalconGuides on essential outdoor skills and subjects and field identification. The following titles are currently available, but this list grows every year. For a free catalog with a complete list of titles, call FALCON toll-free at 1-800-582-2665.

BIRDING GUIDES

Birding Georgia
Birding Illinois
Birding Minnesota
Birding Montana
Birding Northern California
Birding Texas
Birding Utah

PADDLING GUIDES

Paddling Minnesota
Paddling Montana
Paddling Okefenokee
Paddling Oregon
Paddling Yellowstone & Grand
   Teton National Parks

WALKING

Walking Colorado Springs
Walking Denver
Walking Portland
Walking Seattle
Walking St. Louis
Walking San Francisco
Walking Virginia Beach

CAMPING GUIDES

Camping Arizona
Camping California's
   National Forests
Camping Colorado
Camping Oregon
Camping Southern California
Camping Washington
Recreation Guide to Washington
   National Forests

FIELD GUIDES

Bitterroot: Montana State Flower
Canyon Country Wildflowers
Central Rocky Mountain
   Wildflowers
Chihuahuan Desert Wildflowers
Great Lakes Berry Book
New England Berry Book
Ozark Wildflowers
Pacific Northwest Berry Book
Plants of Arizona
Rare Plants of Colorado
Rocky Mountain Berry Book
Scats & Tracks of the Pacific
   Coast States
Scats & Tracks of the Rocky Mtns.
Sierra Nevada Wildflowers
Southern Rocky Mountain
   Wildflowers
Tallgrass Prairie Wildflowers
Western Trees

ROCKHOUNDING GUIDES

Rockhounding Arizona
Rockhounding California
Rockhounding Colorado
Rockhounding Montana
Rockhounding Nevada
Rockhounding New Mexico
Rockhounding Texas
Rockhounding Utah
Rockhounding Wyoming

HOW-TO GUIDES

Avalanche Aware
Backpacking Tips
Bear Aware
Desert Hiking Tips
Hiking with Dogs
Hiking with Kids
Mountain Lion Alert
Reading Weather
Route Finding
Using GPS
Wild Country Companion
Wilderness First Aid
Wilderness Survival

MORE GUIDEBOOKS

Backcountry Horseman's
   Guide to Washington
Family Fun in Montana
Family Fun in Yellowstone
Exploring Canyonlands & Arches
   National Parks
Exploring Hawaii's Parklands
Exploring Mount Helena
Exploring Southern California
   Beaches
Hiking Hot Springs of the Pacific
   Northwest
Touring Arizona Hot Springs
Touring California & Nevada
   Hot Springs
Touring Colorado Hot Springs
Touring Montana and Wyoming
   Hot Springs
Trail Riding Western Montana
Wilderness Directory
Wild Montana
Wild Utah
Wild Virginia

■ *To order any of these books, check with your local bookseller*
*or call FALCON ® at **1-800-582-2665**.*
Visit us on the world wide web at:
www.Falcon.com

FALCON®

FALCON GUIDES® Leading the Way™

FALCON GUIDES® are available for where-to-go hiking, mountain biking, rock climbing, walking, scenic driving, fishing, rockhounding, paddling, birding, wildlife viewing, and camping. We also have FalconGuides® on essential outdoor skills and subjects and field identification. The following titles are currently available, but this list grows every year. For a free catalog with a complete list of titles, call FALCON® toll-free at 1-800-582-2665.

MOUNTAIN BIKING GUIDES

Mountain Biking Arizona
Mountain Biking Colorado
Mountain Biking Georgia
Mountain Biking Idaho
Mountain Biking New Mexico
Mountain Biking New York
Mountain Biking North Carolina
Mountain Biking Northern New England
Mountain Biking Oregon
Mountain Biking Pennsylvania
Mountain Biking South Carolina
Mountain Biking Southern California
Mountain Biking Southern New England
Mountain Biking Utah
Mountain Biking Washington
Mountain Biking Wisconsin
Mountain Biking Wyoming

LOCAL CYCLING SERIES

Mountain Biking Albuquerque
Mountain Biking Bend
Mountain Biking Boise
Mountain Biking Chequamegon
Mountain Biking Chico
Mountain Biking Colorado Springs
Mountain Biking Denver/Boulder
Mountain Biking Durango
Mountain Biking Flagstaff and Sedona
Mountain Biking Grand Junction & Fruita
Mountain Biking Helena
Mountain Biking Moab
Mountain Biking Phoenix
Mountain Biking Spokane and Coeur d'Alene
Mountain Biking the Twin Cities
Mountain Biking Utah's St. George/Cedar City Area
Mountain Biking the White Mountains (West)

■ *To order any of these books, check with your local bookseller or call FALCON® at **1-800-582-2665**.*
Visit us on the world wide web at:
www.Falcon.com

FALCON®

FALCONGUIDES ®Leading the Way™

BEST EASY DAY HIKES SERIES
Beartooths
Boulder
Canyonlands & Arches
Cape Cod
Colorado Springs
Denver
Glacier & Wateron Lakes
Grand Staircase-Escalante and
    the Glen Canyon Region
Grand Canyon
Grand Teton
Lake Tahoe
Mount Rainier
Mount St. Helens
North Cascades
Northern Sierra
Olympics
Orange County
Phoenix
Salt Lake City
San Diego
Santa Fe
Shenandoah
Yellowstone
Yosemite

12 SHORT HIKES SERIES
Colorado
Aspen
Boulder
Denver Foothills Central
Denver Foothills North
Denver Foothills South
Rocky Mountain National Park-Estes Park
Rocky Mountain National Park-Grand Lake
Steamboat Springs
Summit County
Vail
California
San Diego Coast
San Diego Mountains
San Francisco Bay Area-Coastal
San Francisco Bay Area-East Bay
San Francisco Bay Area-North Bay
San Francisco Bay Area-South Bay
Washington
Mount Rainier National Park-Paradise
Mount Rainier National Park-Sunrise

■ *To order any of these books, check with your local bookseller
or call FALCON ® at **1-800-582-2665**.
Visit us on the world wide web at:
www.Falcon.com*

FALCON®

FALCON GUIDES ® Leading the Way™

■ *To order any of these books, check with your local bookseller
or call FALCON ® at **1-800-582-2665**.
Visit us on the world wide web at:*
www.Falcon.com

FALCON®

FALCONGUIDES ® Leading the Way™

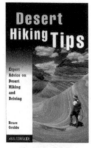

DESERT HIKING TIPS

By Bruce Grubbs

This pocket-sized book explains how to enjoy hiking and exploring the American desert.

HIKING WITH DOGS

by Linda Mullally

This comprehensive hiking guide highlights the benefits of hiking with your dog while helping readers choose, train, condition and care for their canine hiking companions.

ROUTE FINDING

by Gregory Crouch

Explains step-by-step the map reading, land navigation, and route finding techniques crucial to success and safety in the outdoors.

Also Available:
Avalanche Aware, Backpacking Tips, Bear Aware, Hiking With Kids, Mountain Lion Alert, Reading Weather, Using GPS, Wild Country Companion, Wilderness First Aid, Wilderness Survival

*To order these titles check with your local bookseller or call FALCON ® at **1-800-582-2665.**
www.Falcon.com*